Homo Viator

Homo Viator

Introduction to the Metaphysic of Hope

Gabriel Marcel

Translated by Emma Craufurd and Paul Seaton

St. Augustine's Press
South Bend, Indiana
2010

This book was originally published in English in 1952 by Victor
Gollancz, Ltd, London, and Henry Regnery, Chicago, in 1952.

Manufactured in the United States of America

1 2 3 4 5 6   16 15 14 13 12 11 10

Library of Congress Cataloging in Publication Data
Marcel, Gabriel, 1889–1973.
      Homo viator: introduction to the metaphysic of hope /
      Gabriel Marcel ; translated by Emma Craufurd and Paul
      Seaton. – [Updated ed.].
          p. cm.
      ISBN-13: 978-1-58731-361-5 (pbk.: alk. paper)
    - ISBN-10: 1-58731-361-8 (pbk.: alk. paper)
      Philosophy. I. Title.
      B2430.M253H63 2009
      194 – dc22   2009002286

ST. AUGUSTINE'S PRESS
www.staugustine.net

CONTENTS

PREFACE

"Perhaps a stable order can only be established on earth if man always remains acutely conscious that his condition is that of a traveller."

I should like this paradoxical sentence, which concludes the essay on *Value and Immortality*, to serve as Ariadne's thread, guiding the reader through what it might perhaps be a little pretentious to call the labyrinth formed by these essays. Pretentious, but not altogether untrue: it is certainly less easy to find our way in a series of meditations, in their essence dramatic or to be more exact musical, than in a treatise through the whole of which a sequence of thoughts, following one from the other, is logically developed. I should have liked to produce such a treatise, although I see more and more clearly the reasons, some valid and some the reverse, which prevented me from doing so. Now, however, I have reached the melancholy conclusion that I never shall write it. Moreover, I feel rather irritated and annoyed with myself, because I am aware that I shall most certainly not be conforming to all the rules which have been almost universally observed in the philosophic game up to the present day. Under these conditions, am I not obliged to facilitate the reader's task to some extent, by offering him on the threshold of this book, in as clear a form as possible, the essential idea which animates it from end to end?

Nothing could seem more irrational at a first glance than to connect the existence of a stable earthly order with the consciousness of our being travellers, that is to say on a journey. But what journey is meant here? Obviously, if we want to avoid the worst possible confusion, we must begin by eliminating everything in any way connected with evolution from our discussion. It has nothing to do with what we are considering here, and it is to be wondered whether it does not tend to introduce into strictly human affairs an element of disorder and a principle of disproportion and discord. This notion, in fact, can only be made clear if we start from a particular idea of the sub-human order. There is probably no system of ethics or sociology with evolutionary tendencies which does not at bottom involve references to a world radically foreign to the values which give human conduct its peculiar weight and dignity. You will forgive me if I here reproduce the incomparable passage of *La Prisonnière* which will help to guide the reader:

"All that can be said is that everything in our life happens as though we entered upon it with a load of obligations contracted in a previous existence. There is no reason arising from the conditions of our life on this earth for us to consider ourselves obliged to do good, to be tactful, even to be polite, nor for the cultured artist to consider himself obliged to begin again twenty times; the admiration his work will arouse cannot matter much to his body eaten by worms, as for instance the space of yellow wall painted with so much knowledge and taste by an artist for ever unknown and scarcely identified under the name of Ver Meer. All these obligations whose sanction is not of this present life, seem to belong to a different world, founded on kindness, scruples, sacrifice, a world entirely different from this one, a world whence we emerge to be born on this earth, before returning thither, perhaps, to live under the empire of those unknown laws we have obeyed because we bore their teaching within us without knowing who had taught us, those laws which all deep work of our intelligence brings closer to us, and which are only invisible (and scarcely even then!) to fools. So then the idea that Bergotte was not dead for ever was not improbable." We are probably at first tempted to refer back to the Platonic myth which underlies this. There is, however, every reason to think that we should be making a serious mistake if we put the accent here on the word myth. There is, in fact, no reason to insist specially upon Proust's hypothesis of a former existence in the course of which the soul contracts the obligations it has to fulfil afterwards here below, though to start with this hypothesis conflicts with certain theological presuppositions which philosophy as such is in no way obliged to adopt. On the other hand, what is here strongly asserted, and what should certainly be retained, is the transcendent character (in the exact and non-theological sense of the word) of the standards to which the true man, together with the artist, recognises that he must conform his life; but it is also the refusal, implicit at least, to be satisfied with a purely abstract set of rules; it is consequently the rehabilitation of what in the last analysis we must agree to call the Beyond. It is no good for us to wonder how far Proust is contradicting the postulates which all his work takes for granted by introducing such a reference here; the truth is that his work develops between two very different planes: that of Platonism on the one hand, and of an empiricism inspired by nihilism on the other. We might say rather that what is reflected in this work and in its internal contradictions is the dull tragedy of a soul shutting itself out more and more in an exile of which it tends to lose all consciousness as it becomes more cut off. Taking everything into account, it seems to me admirable that the writer who has perhaps gone further than any other in micro-psychological investigation should have been able to recognise, at least at certain great moments, the existence of fixed stars in the heaven of the soul.

The fact can not be disguised, however, that in speaking of the Beyond, or simply of our situation as travellers here below, we are laying ourselves open to a fundamental objection; we shall, in fact, probably be reproached for pursuing the mirage of an imagination that works in spatial terms of which thought becomes only too easily the dupe. What importance should we give to such an accusation? In a certain sense it is well founded. It remains to be seen whether, when we try to think of our life, we can ever free ourselves completely from a spatial or quasi-spatial mode of figuration. It does not seem as though we can. If we consider the past we inevitably look back as it were at a road we have been following; we recall those who bore us company, that is to say who did such and such a part of the journey with us. The idea of a journey, which is not usually considered as having any value or application of a specifically philosophic order, does however offer the inestimable advantage of gathering together determinations which belong both to time and space; and it would be worthwhile to try to find out how it accomplishes such a synthesis. It will no doubt be replied that we have no right to extrapolate, that is to say to produce the curve beyond the region where observation is possible, for this curve may in fact be interrupted or perhaps stop just where a definite equipment can no longer function. But this is precisely where hope comes into its own.

It is not a question here of resting on anything like the postulates of Kant, since these only have to do with pure subjectivity considered as far as this is possible, apart from the conditions of its insertion in concrete experience, experience which involves an element of specificity in a sense infinite. These postulates can not be conceived apart from a moral formalism which seems precisely to miss what is irreducible in the human drama and in the very fact that all human life develops in the manner of a drama. I think it is superfluous to give a summary here of the long analyses which form the core of the present volume and which lead up to the definition at the end of the essay on the Metaphysics of Hope. Perhaps, instead, it might be useful to point out the essential characteristics of the definition itself. First of all it must be noticed that the experiences it summarises can in no way be reduced to the image which an abstract and devitalising method of thought forms of them. "Hope is essentially . . . the availability of a soul which has entered intimately enough into the experience of communion to accomplish in the teeth of will and knowledge, the transcendent act – the act establishing the vital regeneration of which this experience affords both the pledge and the first-fruits."

This means that in the first place hope is only possible on the level of the *us*, or we might say of the *agape*, and that it does not exist on the level of the solitary *ego*, self-hypnotised and concentrating exclusively on individual aims. Thus it also implies that we must not confuse hope and ambition, for they are not of the same spiritual dimension.

In the second place, there is only room for hope when the soul manages to get free from the categories in which consciousness confines itself as soon as it makes a clear line of demarcation between what it knows for a fact on the one hand and what it wishes or desires on the other. Perhaps hope means first of all the act by which this line of demarcation is obliterated or denied. This constitutes what I have elsewhere termed its prophetic character; hope is a knowing which outstrips the unknown – but it is a knowing which excludes all presumption, a knowing accorded, granted, a knowing which may be a grace but is in no degree a conquest.

I spoke of the soul. This word, so long discredited, should here be given its priority once more. We cannot help seeing that there is the closest of connections between the soul and hope. I almost think that hope is for the soul what breathing is for the living organism. Where hope is lacking the soul dries up and withers; it is no more than a function, it is merely fit to serve as an object of study to a psychology that can never register anything but its location or absence. It is precisely the soul that is the traveller; it is of the soul and of the soul alone that we can say with supreme truth that "being" necessarily means "being on the way" *(en route)*. This has without a doubt been strongly felt throughout the ages by the spiritually minded; but alas, an arid scholasticism stifled the intuition. It is for us today to liberate it once more, without, however, falling into what we must surely call the error of Bergsonism. And I mean by this word a theory of the intelligence which does not really understand it, but instead of thinking its character, instead of apprehending its movements from within, tends to stop short at the materialising impression it forms of it.

I think that in starting from this knot of thoughts there should be no difficulty in understanding what appear to me to be the philosophical implications of the *Mystery of the Family* and of the *Creative Vow as Essence of Paternity*. The reader must not be misled by the mode of exposition which may appear somewhat exoteric; the thought I have tried to express in these two studies is really metaphysical in the highest degree. We have reason to assert, as I have said, that family relations, like human things in general, do not of themselves offer any consistency or any guarantee of solidity. It is only when they are referred back to a superhuman order of which here below we are able but to trace the indications, that they take on a truly holy character. Here indeed we have the living renewal which is given or revealed through hope, and which appears consequently to envelop our transitory existence and yet only to be attainable at its termination, that is to say at the end of the journey to which all life is finally reducible. No one could dispute the fact that there is a paradox or anomaly here; but on the other hand it

seems very much as though the attempts made to eliminate this
paradox, and to rationalise this anomaly, are doomed to reach further than what might be superficially intelligible and to end in the
monstrosities which proliferate from any kind of giganticism. I
have used the word giganticism; the religion of technics at any rate
must be included under this head. We have there an indication
which is perhaps only implicit in the present volume, but which the
reader will have no difficulty in developing in his own way from
the fundamental themes running through this collection of essays.

The study of *Rilke, a Witness to the Spiritual*, although it is very
different in tone, was conceived in the same spirit and culminates
in an intuition which coincides fundamentally with those per-
vading the *Mystery of the Family*, and perhaps in particular the
Dangerous Situation of Ethical Values. There is a permanent value in
Orphism which can never be disregarded with impunity. That
value I have tried to bring out at the end of this book, not abstractly but by an appeal which I do not think will go unheeded. How can
the spectacle of widespread ruin of which we who follow after Rilke
are the horrified witnesses, how can such a spectacle fail to awaken
in us the assurance that this mad, unbridled destruction cannot take
place without infinite reserves accumulating, in an irreparable
domain where the reasoning and folly of men have no access,
reserves from which it seems to be given us to draw at the extreme
summit of recollection or of that sorrow which is but its haggard
and wounded sister? "The interconnected consciousness of death
and resurrection which pervades the *Sonnets to Orpheus* like a
breath of air from another world is the principle of a reverence for
souls and things of which the secret has to be rediscovered today."
It is of such a reverence that I want to awaken an echo in this time
of universal sacrilege when some of the most vigorous minds which
have been known in France for the last twenty years really seem to
imagine that blasphemy, conceived moreover rather as statement
than invective, can become the corner-stone of philosophy and pol-
itics. This is a fatal illusion, and it rests not only with faith, but
above all with reflection to strive tirelessly to dispel it.

To Mme. Jeanne Vial

THE EGO AND ITS RELATION TO OTHERS[1]

In our subject today we shall find that the distinction, in any case uncertain, between child psychology and psychology pure and simple has practically no importance. If we forget, as I think we should, the theories and definitions of philosophy in order to learn all we can from direct experiences, we are led to the conclusion that the act which establishes the *ego*, or rather by which the *ego* establishes itself, is always identically the same: it is this act which we must try to grasp without allowing ourselves to be led astray by the fictitious speculations which throughout human history have been accumulating in this field. I think that we should employ current forms of ordinary language which distort our experiences far less than the elaborate expressions in which philosophical language is crystallised. The most elementary example, the closest to earth, is also the most instructive. Take, for instance, the child who brings his mother flowers he has just been gathering in the meadow. "Look," he cries, "I picked these." Mark the triumph in his voice and above all the gesture, simple and rapid enough, perhaps, which accompanies his announcement. The child points himself out for admiration and gratitude: "It was I, I who am with you here, who picked these lovely flowers, don't go thinking it was Nanny or my sister; it was I and *no one else.*" This exclusion is of the greatest importance: it seems that the child wants to attract attention almost materially. He claims enthusiastic praise, and it would be the most calamitous

1   Lecture given to the *Institut Supérieur de Pédagogie* at Lyons, December 13th, 1942.

thing in the world if by mistake it was bestowed on someone who
did not deserve it. Thus the child draws attention to himself, he
offers himself to the other in order to receive a special tribute. I do
not believe it is possible to insist too much upon the presence of the
other, or more exactly others, involved in the statement: "It is I who
. . ." It implies that "There are, on the one hand, those who are
excluded about whom you must be careful not to think, and, on the
other, there is the you to whom the child speaks and whom he
wants as a witness."

The same affirmation on the part of an adult would be less
openly advertised; it would be enveloped in a halo of false modesty
where the complexities of the game of social hypocrisy are discernible. Think of the amateur composer who has just been singing
an unknown melody in some drawing-room. People exclaim:
"What is that? Is it an unpublished song by Fauré?" etc. "No, as a
matter of fact, it is my own . . ." etc. If we leave on one side, as we
should, all the elaborations of social convention, we shall recognise
the fundamental identity of the act. The difference has only to do
with the attitude adopted or simulated regarding the expected tribute.

To go on with our analysis, we observe that this ego here before
us, considered as a centre of magnetism, cannot be reduced to certain parts which can be specified such as "my body, my hands, my
brain"; it is a global presence – a presence which gains glory from
the magnificent bouquet which I myself have picked, which I have
brought you; and I do not know whether you should admire more
the artistic taste of which it is a proof or the generosity which I have
shown in giving it to you, I, who might so easily have kept it for
myself. Thus the beauty of the object is in a fashion reflected upon
me, and if I appeal to you, then, I repeat, I do so as to a qualified
witness whom I invite to wonder at the *whole* we form – the bouquet and I.

But we must not fail to notice that the admiration which I
expect from you, which you give me, can only confirm and height-
en the satisfaction I feel in recognising my own merits. Why should
we not conclude from this that the *ego here present* certainly involves
a reference to someone else, only this other someone is treated as a
foil or amplifier for my own self-satisfaction.

"But," you will object, "self-satisfaction, self-confidence, self-love: all this takes for granted a self already established which it is necessary to define." I think that here we must be careful not to fall into a trap of language. This pre-existent *ego* can only be postulated, and if we try to describe it, we can only do so negatively, by way of exclusion. On the other hand it is very instructive to give a careful account of the act which establishes what I call myself, the act, for instance, by which I attract the attention of others so that they may praise me, maybe, or blame me, but at all events so that they notice me. In every case *I produce* myself, in the etymological sense of the word, that is to say I put myself forward.

Other examples bring us to the same conclusion. Let us keep to the level of a child's experience. A little stranger stretches out his hand to take the ball which I have left on the ground; I jump up; the ball is mine. Here again the relationship with others is at the root of the matter, but it takes the form of an order: *Do not touch.* I have no hesitation in saying that the instantaneous claiming of our own property is one of the most significant of our experiences. Here again I "produce" myself. I warn the other person that he must conform his conduct to the rule I have given him. It can be observed without any great subtlety that the sense of possession was already implicit in the previous examples, only it was possession of a virtue rather than a thing. Here, however, more clearly than just now, the *ego* is seen as a global and indefinable presence. I, here before you, possess the ball, perhaps I might consent to lend it to you for a few moments, but you must quite understand that it is I who am very kindly lending it to you and that, in consequence, I can take it back from you at any minute if I so wish; I the despot, I the autocrat.

I have used the term presence several times; now I will try as far as possible to define what I mean by it. Presence denotes something rather different and more comprehensive than the fact of just being there; to be quite exact one should not actually say that an object is present. We might say that presence is always dependent on an experience which is at the same time irreducible and vague, the sense of existing, of being in the world. Very early in the development of a human being this consciousness of existing, which we surely have no reason to doubt is common also to animals, is linked up with the urge to make ourselves *recognised* by some other person, some witness, helper, rival or adversary who, whatever may be said, is needed to integrate the self, but whose place in the field of consciousness can vary almost indefinitely.

If this analysis as a whole is correct, it is necessary to see what I call my *ego* in no way as an isolated reality, whether it be an element or a principle, but as an *emphasis* which I give, not of course to the whole of my experience, but to that part of it which I want to safeguard in a special manner against some attack or possible infringement. It is in this sense that the impossibility of establishing any precise frontiers of the *ego* has been often and rightly pointed out. This becomes clear as soon as one understands that the *ego* can never be thought of as a portion of space. On the other hand, it cannot be repeated often enough that, after all, the self is *here, now;* or at any rate there are such close affinities between these facts that we really cannot separate them. I own that I cannot in any way conceive how a being for whom there was neither a here nor a now could nevertheless appear as "I." From this it follows paradoxically enough that the emphasis of which I have spoken cannot avoid tending to conceive of itself as an enclosure, that is to say as exactly the thing it is not; and it is only on deeper reflection that it will be possible to detect what is deceptive in this localisation.

I spoke of an enclosure, but it is an enclosure which moves, and what is even more essential, it is vulnerable: *a highly sensitive enclosure.* The incomparable analyses of Meredith in *The Egoist* would fit in very naturally here. Nobody, perhaps, has ever gone so far in the analysis of a susceptibility for which the term self-love is manifestly incomplete. Actually, this susceptibility is rooted in anguish rather than in love. Burdened with myself, plunged in this disturbing world, sometimes threatening me, sometimes my accomplice, I keep an eager look-out for everything emanating from it which might either soothe or ulcerate the wound I bear within me, which is my *ego*. This state is strikingly analogous to that of a man who has an abscess at the root of his tooth and who experiments cautiously with heat and cold, acid and sugar, to get relief. What then is this anguish, this wound? The answer is that it is above all the experience of being torn by a contradiction between the all which I aspire to possess, to annex, or, still more absurd, to monopolise, and the obscure consciousness that after all I am nothing but an empty void;

for, still, I can affirm nothing about myself which would be really myself; nothing, either, which would be permanent; nothing which would be secure against criticism and the passage of time. Hence the craving to be confirmed from outside, by another; this paradox, by virtue of which even the most self-centred among us looks to others and only to others for his final investiture.

This contradiction is constantly appearing here. Nowhere does it show up in greater relief than in the attitude which our everyday language so aptly terms pose. The poseur who seems only to be pre-occupied with others is in reality entirely taken up with himself. Indeed, the person he is with only interests him in so far as he is likely to form a favourable picture of him which in turn he will receive back. The other person reflects him, returns to him this pic-ture which he finds so enchanting. It would be interesting to find out what social climate is most favourable for posing, and what on the other hand are the conditions most likely to discourage it. It might generally be said that in a virile atmosphere posing is unmasked immediately and made fun of. At school or in barracks the poseur has practically no chance of success. A consensus of opinion is almost certain to be formed against him; his companions see through him at once, each one of them accuses him of infring-ing a certain implicit pact, that of the little community to which he belongs. It is not easy to formulate it exactly, but it is a distinct per-ception of the incompatibility between a certain reality in which each one participates and this play-acting which degrades and betrays it. On the other hand, the more artificial, unreal and, in a certain sense, effeminate the environment, the less the incompatibil-ity will be felt. This is because in such circles everything depends upon opinions and appearances, from which it follows that seduc-tion and flattery have the last word.

Now, posing is a form of flattery, a manner of paying court while seeming to obtrude oneself. Beneath it all we invariably find self-love and, I might add, pretension. This last, by its very ambigu-ity, is particularly instructive. To pretend is not only to aspire or to aim high, it is also to simulate, and actually there is simulation in all posing. To realise this we only need to recall what affectation is in all its forms. From the moment that I become preoccupied about the effect I want to produce on the other person, my every act, word and attitude loses its authenticity; and we all know what even a studied or affected simplicity can be.

Here, however, we must note something of capital importance. From the very fact that I treat the other person merely as a means of resonance or an amplifier, I tend to consider him as a sort of apparatus which I can, or think I can, manipulate, or of which I can dispose at will. I form my own idea of him and, strangely enough, this idea can become a substitute for the real person, a shadow to which I shall come to refer my acts and words. The truth of the matter is that to pose is always to pose before oneself. "To play to the gallery . . .," we are accustomed to say, but the gallery is still the self. To be more exact, we might say that the other person is the provisional and as it were accessory medium, through which I can arrive at forming a certain image, or idol of myself; the work of stylisation by which each of us fashions this image might be traced step by step. This work is helped by social failure as much as by success. When he who poses is scoffed at by his companions, he decides, more often than not, that he has to do with imbeciles and shuts himself up with jealous care in a little private sanctuary where he can be alone with his idol.

Here we are in line with the merciless analyses to which the anti-romantics have subjected the cult of the *ego*. "But," you may ask, "should we not take care not to go too far? Is there not a normal condition of the *ego* which should not be confused with its abnormalities or perversions?" The question is a very delicate one. It must in no way be mistaken for a problem of technical philosophy, with which we are not dealing here and which involves the question of the very existence of a superior principle of unity which guides our personal development. What concerns us here is only to know under what conditions I become conscious of myself as a person. It must be repeated that these conditions are essentially social. There is, in particular, every reason to think that the system of perpetual competition to which the individual is subjected in the world of today cannot fail to increase and exasperate this consciousness of the *ego*. I have no hesitation in saying that if we want to fight effectively against individualism in its most harmful form, we must find some way of breaking free from the asphyxiating atmosphere of examinations and competition in which our young people are struggling. "I must win, not you! I must get above you!" We can never insist enough upon how the real sense of fellowship which shows itself in such striking contrast among any team worthy of the name, has been rendered weak and anaemic by the competitive system. This system does in fact encourage each one to compare himself with his neighbour, to give himself a mark or a number by which he can be measured against him. Moreover, we must notice a thing which is essential in our argument: such a system, which makes self-consciousness or, if you prefer to call it so, self-love ten times worse, is at the same time the most depersonalising process possible; for the thing in us which has real value cannot be judged by comparison, having no common measure with anything else. Unfortunately, however, it seems as though people have taken a delight in accumulating every possible confusion concerning this point, and I have no hesitation in saying that the responsibilities of those who claim to celebrate the cult of the individual are overwhelming. Maybe there is no more fatal error than that which conceives of the *ego* as the secret abode of originality. To get a better idea of this we must here introduce the wrongly discredited notion of gifts. The best part of my personality does not belong to me. I am in no sense the owner, only the trustee. Except in the realm of metaphysics, with which we are not dealing today, there is no sense in enquiring into the origin of these gifts. On the other hand, it is very important to know what my attitude should be with regard to them. If I consider myself as their guardian, responsible for their fruitfulness, that is to say if I recognise in them a call or even perhaps a question to which I must respond, it will not occur to me to be proud about them and to parade them before an audience, which, I repeat, really means myself. Indeed, if we come to think of it, there is nothing in me which cannot or should not be regarded as a gift. It is pure fiction to imagine a pre-existent self on whom these gifts were bestowed in virtue of certain rights, or as a recompense for some former merit.

This surely means that I must puncture the illusion, infinitely persistent it is true, that I am possessed of unquestionable privileges which make me the centre of my universe, while other people are either mere obstructions to be removed or circumvented, or else those echoing amplifiers, whose purpose is to foster my

self-complacency. I propose to call this illusion moral egocentricity,
thus marking clearly how deeply it has become rooted in our very
nature. In fact, just as any notions we may have of cosmography do
not rid us of the immediate impression that the sun and stars go
round the earth, so it is not possible for us to escape completely here
below from the preconceived idea which makes each one tend to
establish himself as the centre around which all the rest have no
other function but to gravitate. It is equally true that this idea or
prejudice, no matter how becomingly it may be adorned in the case
of great egoists, appears, when we come down to a final analysis, to
be merely another expression of a purely biological and animal
claim. Moreover, the ill-starred philosophies which, particularly in
the nineteenth century, attempted to justify this position not only
marked a retrogression as far as the secular wisdom of civilised
humanity was concerned, but, it cannot be disputed for a moment,
have directly helped to precipitate mankind into the chaos where it
is struggling at the present time.

Does it, however, follow that this *egolatry*, this idolatry of the
self, must necessarily be met by a rationalistic and impersonal doctrine? Nothing, I believe, would be farther from the truth.
Whenever men have tried to put such a doctrine into practice we
must own that it has proved itself extremely disappointing. To be
more exact, such an experiment has never been and never could be
effective. Actually it is of the very essence of this doctrine that it
cannot be really put into practice, except perhaps by a few theorists
who are only at ease among abstractions, paying for this faculty by
the loss of all real contact with living beings, and, I might add, with
the great simplicities of existence. For the immense majority of
human beings, the entities which such a rationalism claims to set up
as the object of everybody's reverent attention are only shams
behind which passions incapable of recognising themselves take
cover. It has been given to our generation, as to that of the end of
the eighteenth century and that of the Second Empire, not only to
observe but to suffer the disastrous effects of the sin of the ideolo-
gists. This consists, above all perhaps, of infinitely intensifying the
inner-falsehood, of thickening the film which is interposed between
a human being and his true nature until it is almost impossible to
destroy it.

Moreover, this same point will enable us to understand the most characteristic elements in what today is commonly accepted as the meaning of the term "person." Nowadays, the individual allows himself, legitimately enough, to be likened to an atom caught up in a whirlwind, or, if you wish, a mere statistical unit; because most of the time he is simply a specimen among an infinity of others, since the opinions, which he thinks are his own, are merely reflections of the ideas accepted in the circles he frequents and handed round in the press which he reads daily. Thus he is only, as I have had occasion to write, an anonymous unit of that anonymous entity "one." But he almost inevitably has the illusion that his reactions are authentic, so that he *submits,* while all the time he imagines he is taking action. It is, on the contrary, in the nature of a person to face any given situation directly and, I should add, to make an effective decision upon it. But, it may be asked, is not this the *ego* appearing once more? I think not. Let us understand each other. There could naturally be no question of conceiving of the person as of something distinct from that other thing, the *ego*, as if they were in separate compartments. Such an idea would be completely fictitious. We must go further. The person cannot be regarded as an element or attribute of the *ego* either. It would be better to say that it is something compelling, which most certainly takes its birth in what appears to me to be mine, or to be me myself, but this compelling force only becomes conscious of itself when it becomes a reality. It can thus in no way be compared with a slight desire. Let us say that it is of the order of "I will" and not of "I would like . . . ." I claim to be a person in so far as I assume responsibility for what I do and what I say. But to whom am I responsible, to whom do I acknowledge my responsibility? We must reply that I am conjointly responsible both to myself and to everyone else, and that this conjunction is precisely characteristic of an engagement of the person, that it is the mark proper to the person. We will not stay any longer among abstractions where there is always a risk of becoming imprisoned by words. Supposing that I wish or feel bound to put a certain person on his guard against someone else. I decide to write him a letter to this effect. If I do not sign my letter I am still as it were moving in a realm of play, of pastimes, and I might readily add mystification; I reserve to myself the possibility of denying my action; I deliberately maintain my position in a zone as it were halfway between dreams and reality, where self-complacency triumphs, the chosen land of those who, in our time, have made themselves the champions of the gratuitous act. From the moment that I sign my letter, on the contrary, I have taken on the responsibility for it, that is to say I have shouldered the consequences in advance. I have created the irrevocable not only for the other person but for myself. Of my own free will I have brought into existence new decisions which will bear upon my own life with all their weight. This, of course, does not exclude the possibility that it was a reprehensible, perhaps even a criminal action to write the letter. There is nevertheless a radical difference of quality, or more exactly of weight, between this action and that of writing a letter without signing it. Let us repeat that I tend to establish myself as a person in so far as I assume responsibility for my acts and so behave as a real being (rather than a dreamer who reserves the strange power of modifying his dreams, without having to trouble whether this modification has any repercussions in the hypothetical outside world in which everybody else dwells). From the same point of view we might also say that I establish myself as a person in so far as I really believe in the existence of others and allow this belief to influence my conduct. What is the actual meaning of *believing* here? It means to realise or acknowledge their existence in itself, and not only through those points of intersection which bring it into relation with my own.

Person – engagement – community – reality: there we have a sort of chain of notions which, to be exact, do not readily follow from each other by deduction (actually there is nothing more fallacious than a belief in the value of deduction) but of which the union can be grasped by an act of the mind. It would be better not to call this act by the much abused term of intuition, but by one which on the contrary is too little used – that of synopsis, the act by which a group is held together under the mind's comprehensive gaze.

As I hinted just now, one cannot strictly say that personality is good in itself, or that it is an element of goodness: the truth is much more that it controls the existence of a world where there is good and evil. I should be inclined to think that the *ego*, so long as it remains shut up within itself, that is to say the prisoner of its own feelings, of its covetous desires, and of that dull anxiety which works upon it, is really beyond the reach of evil as well as of good. It literally has not yet awakened to reality. Indeed, it is to be wondered whether there does not exist an infinite number of beings for whom this awakening has never truly taken place. There is no doubt that direct judgment cannot be applied to such beings. I would go further: it seems to me that each of us, in a considerable part of his life or of his being, is still unawakened, that is to say that he moves on the margin of reality like a sleep-walker. Let us say that the *ego*, as such, is ruled by a sort of vague fascination, which is localised, almost by chance, in objects arousing sometimes desire, sometimes terror. It is, however, precisely against such a condition that what I consider the essential characteristic of the person is opposed, the characteristic, that is to say, of availability *(disponibilité)*.

This, of course, does not mean emptiness, as in the case of an available dwelling *(local disponible)*, but it means much rather an aptitude to give oneself to anything which offers, and to bind oneself by the gift. Again, it means to transform circumstances into opportunities, we might even say favours, thus participating in the shaping of our own destiny and marking it with our seal. It has sometimes been said of late, "Personality is vocation." It is true if we restore its true value to the term vocation, which is in reality a call, or more precisely the response to a call. We must not, however, be led astray here by any mythological conception. It depends, in fact, on me whether the call is recognised as a call, and, strange as it may seem, in this matter it is true to say that it comes both from me and from outside me at one and the same time; or rather, in it we become aware of that most intimate connection between what comes from me and what comes from outside, a connection which is nourishing or constructive and cannot be relinquished without the ego wasting and tending towards death.

Perhaps we might make this clearer by pointing out that each of us from the very beginning, appears to himself and to others as a particular problem for which the circumstances, whatever they may be, are not enough to provide a solution. I use the term problem absolutely against my will, for it seems to be quite inadequate. Is it not obvious that if I consider the other person as a sort of mechanism exterior to my own *ego*, a mechanism of which I must discover the spring or manner of working, even supposing I manage to take him to pieces in the process, I shall never succeed in obtaining anything but a completely exterior knowledge of him, which is in a way the very denial of his real being? We must even go further and say that such a knowledge is in reality sacrilegious and destructive, it does no less than denude its object of the one thing he has which is of value and so it *degrades him effectively*. That means – and there is nothing which is more important to keep in view – that the knowledge of an individual being cannot be separated from the act of love or charity by which this being is accepted in all which makes of him a unique creature or, if you like, the image of God. There is no doubt that this expression borrowed from the language of religion renders more exactly than any other the truth I have in view at the moment. It is, however, none the less necessary to remember that the truth can be actively misunderstood by each one of us at any time and that there will always be something in experience which seems to provide an argument for him who, following in the footsteps of the cynics of all time, claims to reduce his fellows to little machines whose every movement it is only too easy for him to examine and even to regulate according to his fancy.

It must be understood that these observations are just as directly applicable to the relationship which binds me to myself, the manner in which it is given me to apprehend my own being. It is indeed a fact that I also can conceive of myself as a pure piece of mechanism and make it my chief business to control the machine as well as possible. From the same standpoint, I can regard the problem of my life purely as a problem of tangible results. All that is perfectly consistent. The simplest reflection, however, shows that this mechanism must inevitably serve some purpose which I am at liberty to choose and which is recognised and established as a purpose by my own act. We know from experience, however, that this act can remain practically unsuspected by the very one who has made it. If, indeed, I passively accept a group of regulations which seem to be imposed upon me by the circle to which I belong by birth, by the party to which I have allowed myself to be attached without any genuine thought on my part, everything goes on as though I were really nothing but an instrument, a mere cog in the wheel, as if, in short, the supreme human gift of free action had been refused me. Nevertheless, on reflection we see that all the time this presupposes the act by which the person has failed to recognise himself, or more exactly, has alienated that which alone could confer the dignity which is proper to his nature.

What then is this principle which it is given him thus to fail to recognise or on the contrary to guard and promote? It is easy to discover it if we penetrate the meaning of the notion of availability to which I referred a little way back. The being who is ready for anything is the opposite of him who is occupied or cluttered up with himself. He reaches out, on the contrary, beyond his narrow self, prepared to consecrate his being to a cause which is greater than he is, but which at the same time he makes his own. Here, moreover, it is the order of creation, of power, and of creative fidelity which is borne in upon us. We go wrong when we confuse creating with producing. That which is essential in the creator is the act by which he places himself at the disposal of something which, no doubt in one sense depends upon him for its existence, but which at the same time appears to him to be beyond what he is and what he judged himself capable of drawing directly and immediately from himself. This obviously applies to the case of the artist and to the mysterious gestation which alone makes the appearance of a work of art possible. It is not necessary to insist on this. We must remember, however, that the creative process, though less apparent, is none the less effective wherever there is personal development of any kind. Only here what the person has to create is not some work in a way outside himself and capable of assuming an independent existence, it is his own self in very truth. How can we help seeing that the personality is not to be conceived of apart from the act by which it creates itself, yet at the same time this creation depends in some way upon a superior order? It will seem to the person that sometimes he invents the order, sometimes he discovers it, and reflection will moreover show that there is always a continuity between the invention and the discovery, and that no line of demarcation as definite as that ordinarily accepted by common sense can be established between the one and the other.

If this is so, it must be seen that the personality cannot in any way be compared to an object of which we can say *it is there*, in other words that it is given, present before our eyes, that it is part of a collection of things which can, of their essence, be counted, or again, that it is a statistical unit which can be noted in the calculations of a sociologist employing the methods of an engineer. Or again, if we no longer consider things from outside but from within, that is to say from the point of view of the person himself, it does not seem that strictly speaking he can say "I am" of himself. He is aware of himself far less as a being than as a desire to rise above everything which he is and is not, above the actuality in which he really feels he is involved and has a part to play, but which does not satisfy him, for it falls short of the aspiration with which he identifies himself. His motto is not *sum* but *sursum*.

We must be on our guard here. It certainly would not do to underestimate the danger of a certain romanticism which belongs to every age. This consists of systematically depreciating that which is, in favour of some vaguely imagined and wished-for possibility, of which the transcendent appeal seems to be bound up with the fact that it is not and perhaps never can be fully realised. There can be no question here of an aspiration of that kind, for such an aspiration really springs from the *ego* and not from the personality, it is still a mere form of self-complacency. Here, and indeed everywhere as I see it, the necessity for incarnation must be given an important place. What I have been trying to say is that the personality is only realised in the act by which it tends to become incarnate (in a book, for instance, or an action or in a complete life), but at the same time it is of its very essence never to fix itself or crystallise itself finally in this particular incarnation. Why? Because it participates in the inexhaustible fullness of the being from which it emanates. There lies the deep reason for which it is impossible to think of personality or the personal order without at the same time thinking of that which reaches beyond them both, a supra-personal reality, presiding over all their initiative, which is both their beginning and their end. Here it would be well, if I had the time, to mark as clearly as possible the opposition – difference is not a strong enough word – between this supra-personal reality and its rivals, I should rather say its caricatures, which are no more than idols, and have led to the incredibly numerous false religions so prevalent, alas, in our time.

Here comes the great question to which I would draw your attention in ending this paper: What is the sign by which we can discover whether the personality is indeed surpassing and transcending itself or whether, on the contrary, it is falling back in some degree and sinking below its true level? This question is tragically acute today in presence of the fascinated and fanatical multitudes who, taking their orders without a shadow of enquiry or reflection, rush singing to their death. Can we really speak of a transcendence in this case? Has that which is personal reached its fulfilment in the supra-personal? I do not think we can reply by a pure and simple yes or no to this question. Most certainly there is as it were a promise or aspiration in this sacrifice which confers an undeniable nobility upon it and places it infinitely above any conduct based on selfish calculations. Yet, at the same time, we cannot avoid seeing that this sort of collective heroism, in so far as it partakes of the nature of an intoxication, looks most disquietingly like various kinds of sub-human behaviour, and as such falls outside the order in which any true values find their expression. It seems to me that it is precisely from the point of view of these values – and of these values alone – that the indispensable discrimination, of which I just now pointed out the necessity, can be made. It is the property of these values, however, to be universal, and, if for the moment we do not consider the case of the artist as such, for he must be judged by a special metaphysical set of rules, we shall notice that among these universal values there are two which stand out above the rest. They are the value of truth and that of justice. Equally, I dare to claim that any "religion" which tends to obliterate them, even momentarily, proves by that very fact that it is tending to be degraded into idolatry. I scarcely need to insist upon the terribly concrete corollaries following from these propositions, which bear the stamp of such harmless generalities. It is clear in particular, that every concession made either to racialism or to the Nietzschean or pseudo-Nietzschean ideology which grants the *masters* the supreme right of treating facts like a plastic substance, easy to manipulate to suit their will, it is clear, I repeat, that every step taken in such a direction would be in no way a transcendence but a retrogression. We cannot be severe enough towards those who at the present time have thus confused men's minds.

Of course, you must not misunderstand these suggestions. There is no question of returning to the dismal and bare rationalism which, alas, has for some forty years formed our official gospel. The claim of universality is impossible to define. True Christian philosophy and theology have the imperishable glory, not only of having never been mistaken about it, but of having honoured it and established it in the indefeasible foundations of our being. It is merely a question of incorporating this claim in the most concrete forms of human experience, without ever despising them, but, on the contrary, recognising that the most humble of them, if it is fully lived, can go immeasurably deep. You will, I know, allow me to end this lecture with some words of Gustave Thibon whom you heard in this very place only a few days ago, and who seems to me to have admirably expressed the need for incarnation from which the personality cannot escape without betraying its true mission, without losing itself among the mirages of abstraction, without paradoxically reducing itself to one impoverished indigent form of the very *ego* it falsely claimed to surpass in every way.

"You feel you are hedged in; you dream of escape; but beware of mirages. Do not run or fly away in order to get free: rather dig in the narrow place which has been given you; you will find God there and everything. God does not float on your horizon, he sleeps in your substance. Vanity runs, love digs. If you fly away from yourself, your prison will run with you and will close in because of the wind of your flight; if you go deep down into yourself it will disappear in paradise."

Le Peuch.
November, 1941.

To Heniu Pourrat

SKETCH OF A PHENOMENOLOGY AND A METAPHYSIC OF HOPE[1]

In a study such as the one I am here undertaking there can be no
question of starting from a particular definition and endeavouring
to explain its content progressively. I propose rather to appeal to a
special experience which it must be supposed you have. This experience, which is that of "I hope . . . ," must, like the fundamental
experience of faith, "I believe . . . ," be purified; or, more exactly, we
must pass from this experience in its diluted or diffused state to the
same experience, touched – I do not say absolutely conceived – at
its highest tension or again at its point of complete saturation.

You must not therefore be surprised to find me starting from an
"I hope" of a very low order which will constitute a negative point
of departure.

"I hope that James will arrive in time for lunch tomorrow and
not just in the afternoon." This, of course, means that I hope so
because I should like to have James with me for as long as possible;
and I have reason to think that what I want will come about: I know
that he does not intend to return to his office and could therefore
catch an early train, etc.

We can already detect two elements here which are always
found together: there is a wish and a certain belief. I am, however,
right in calling this a diluted condition, because in such a case I am
near to what we can term the point of indifference. After all, it is not
very important if James only arrives at five o'clock; there is nothing

1   Lecture given to the *Scolasticat de Fourvière* in February, 1942.

there for me to *take to heart* – notice this expression which we shall need to remember. Moreover, I observe that the reasons for hoping are here exterior to myself, they are outside my being, far from having their roots in the very depths of what I am. In reality it is merely a calculation concerning certain chances I am considering, a practical little problem of probabilities. Moreover, if I find James boring or his visit is inconvenient, I might quite easily say: "I am afraid he will arrive in time for lunch."

Now let us suppose, on the contrary, that I am going through a time of trial, either in my private affairs or in those of the group to which I belong. I long for some deliverance which would bring the trial to an end. The "I hope" in all its strength is directed towards salvation. It really is a matter of my coming out of a darkness in which I am at present plunged, and which may be the darkness of illness, of separation, exile or slavery. It is obviously impossible in such cases to separate the "I hope" from a certain type of situation of which it is really a part. Hope is situated within the framework of the trial, not only corresponding to it, but constituting our being's veritable *response*. I have used the metaphorical term of darkness, but this metaphor has nothing accidental about it. It is, indeed, true that throughout a trial of the kind I have in mind, I find I am deprived for an indefinite period of a certain light for which I long. In fact, I should say that every trial of this order can be considered as a form of captivity.

Let us try to get a closer view of the meaning of the word captivity, or rather let us examine the characteristics of any state which can be described as "being a captive or prisoner." A special kind of endurance is, of course, involved, but what are the conditions under which endurance becomes part of the experience of captivity? Here we must emphasise the part played by duration. I should consider myself a captive if I found myself not merely precipitated into, but as it were pledged by external constraint to a compulsory mode of existence involving restrictions of every kind touching my personal actions. In addition, that which characterises all the situations we are evoking at the moment, is that they invariably imply the impossibility, not necessarily of moving or even of acting in a manner which is relatively free, but *of rising to a certain fullness of life, which may be in the realms of sensation or even of thought in the strict sense of the word.* It is quite clear, for instance, that the artist or the writer who suffers from a prolonged sterility has literally a sense of being in prison, or, if you prefer, in exile, as though he had really been taken out of the light in which he normally has his being. We can, therefore, say that all captivity partakes of the nature of alienation. It may be in reality that, in tearing me out of myself, it gives me an opportunity of realising far more acutely than I should have done without it, the nature of that lost integrity which I now long to regain. This is illustrated in the case of the invalid for whom the word health arouses a wealth of associations generally unsuspected by those who are well. Yet, at the same time, we must determine not only what is positive but what is illusory in this idea of health which the sick man cherishes. A similar problem is presented when the beloved being whose disappearance I deplore seems to me more real and distinct now he is no longer with me than when I was able to enjoy a mutual and direct relationship with him.

I will not elaborate the details of the discussion which would take us away from our subject. I will merely remark that this method of reasoning does not seem to open the way for hope to us: quite on the contrary it is likely to land us in an anguish whence there is no escape, to make us prisoners of an experience which tears our hearts, where *fact* and *memory* are endlessly opposed and, far from merging together, are bound to contradict each other unrelentingly. All that we can say is that this form of reasoning brings into stronger relief the fundamental situation to which it is hope's mission to reply as to a signal of distress. But, it may be objected, are not some situations, where the tragic element seems to be absent, of such a nature as nevertheless to encourage or even to invite the exercise of hope? The woman who is expecting a baby, for instance, is literally inhabited by hope. It seems to me, however, that such examples, and I would even include that of the adolescent who anxiously awaits the coming of love, only seem to confirm what was said above. As a matter of fact, the soul always turns towards a light which it does not yet perceive, a light yet to be born, in the hope of being delivered from its present darkness, the darkness of waiting, a darkness which cannot be prolonged without dragging it in some way towards an organic dissolution. And might we not say in passing that it is from this point of view that such peculiarities as the aberrations frequent in adolescents and expectant mothers are to be explained?

In reality, we should probably go a step further in this direction and, interpreting the phenomena somewhat differently from Plato and the leaders of traditional spiritualism, recognise that there is quite a general aspect under which human existence appears as a captivity and that, precisely when it takes on this form, it becomes so to speak subject to hope. It would actually be easy to show, and as we proceed we shall probably realise more fully, that there is also an ever-present possibility of degrading this same existence to a state in which it would gradually lose all capacity for hope. By a paradox which need surprise only the very superficial thinker, *the less life is experienced as a captivity the less the soul will be able to see the shining of that veiled, mysterious light*, which, we feel sure without any analysis, illumines the very centre of hope's dwelling-place. It is incontestable, for instance, that free-thought impregnated with naturalism, however it may struggle, alas with increasing success, to obliterate certain great contrasts and to flood the world with the harsh light of the lecture hall, however it may at the same time advertise what I have elsewhere styled the category of the *perfectly natural* – it is, I repeat, incontestable that such a dogmatically stan-dardised free-thought eventually runs the risk of depriving souls of the very rudiments of secular hope.

But with what kind of hope are we really concerned? What exactly is its object?

It seems very important to me to stress here, in connection with what I have just said about existence in general being a captivity, that hope, by a *nisus* which is peculiar to it, tends inevitably to tran-scend the particular objects to which it at first seems to be attached. Later on we shall have to recognise clearly the metaphysical impli-cations of this remark. But even now it is possible to appreciate the distinction in tone between "I hope . . . ," the absolute statement, and "I hope that . . . ." This distinction clearly runs parallel to that which obtains in all religious philosophy and which opposes "I believe" to "I believe that."

The philosopher must also consider another point of an equally decisive nature. It bears on the fundamental characteristics of the subject in "I hope . . . ." This subject is indeed in no way identical with the "I myself . . . ," who is nevertheless present, or at any rate is likely to come to the surface whenever there is a question not of hope but of certainty or even doubt. Here I must refer back to a group of ideas which I worked out a little while ago on the subject of the *Ego and Its Relation to Others.* The *ego,* I said, very often, in fact almost invariably, needs to refer to some other person felt or conceived of as an opponent or a witness, or again merely summoned or imagined as an echo or a rectifier. "You have your doubts, because you are ill-informed or because you lack inner stability, or for any other reason; as for me, I am sure – and (be it understood) I am proud of the fact." Or, on the contrary, "You are quite sure of this because you are simple, or badly informed, or for any other reason; as for me, on the other hand, I have a more critical sense than you, therefore I am in doubt."

Naturally, I do not mean that *I am sure* or *I doubt* inevitably implies a position accentuated in this way; but what is certain is that the underlying meaning which animates the *I am sure* or *I doubt* is not really distorted, it does not lose its actual nature through such an accentuation. The case is quite different with *I hope.* Here there is not, and there cannot be the note of defiance or of provocation which, on the contrary, so easily becomes essential to *I doubt* and *I am sure.* What is the cause of this difference? It is surely due to the fact that "I hope" is not orientated in the same way: there is no statement directed towards, and at the same time against, some other person either present or imagined. Of course there is nothing to prevent me from saying in certain cases, "For my part, I hope, whilst you do not." But there would be none of that suggestion of aggressive self-complacency which, on the contrary, so often characterises "I am sure" or "I doubt."

This will be elucidated, I think, if we take the trouble to examine the difference between hope and optimism. It is a difference which may seem to be more of a musical than a logical order and which accordingly is easy enough to misunderstand. Its importance, however, should not be overlooked.

The optimist is he who has a firm conviction, or in certain cases just a vague feeling, that things tend to "turn out for the best." This may concern some definite situation, some precise difficulty: it may have to do with difficulties, conflict and contradictions in general. It goes without saying that optimism can take very different forms. There is a purely sentimental optimism and an optimism with pretensions to reason (which to tell the truth is perhaps merely a camouflaged sentimentality). There are some kinds of optimism which maintain that they are based on practical experience; others, on the contrary, claim to rest on metaphysical or even religious arguments. I am inclined to think, however, that these differences are far less weighty than one might be tempted to believe at first. It is by no means certain that optimism does not always indicate the same disposition, the same *habitus*. Perhaps such a thing as deep optimism does not exist. The metaphysics of Leibnitz are deep, no doubt, but not in so far as they are optimistic, in so far as they are presented as a theodicy. When we come down to a final analysis, the optimist, as such, always relies upon an experience which is not drawn from the most intimate and living part of himself, but, on the contrary, is *considered from a sufficient distance* to allow certain contradictions to become alternated or fused into a general harmony. The optimist does not hesitate to extrapolate the conclusions which we are led to if only we are willing to "consider things" thoroughly, from a sufficient distance and over a wide enough stretch. "It always comes out right in the end. . . ."; "We shall be bound to see. . . ."; "If only we don't allow ourselves to stop too soon. . . ." Such are the formulæ which constantly recur in the speeches of optimists. Notice that the word "speeches" is important here. The optimist is essentially a maker of speeches. There is in the natural and favourably directed development to which he so complacently clings something which readily lends itself to oratorical sequences and written expression. In parenthesis we note that there is a pessimism which is the exact counterpart of such optimism. It is oratorical in the same way, and there is no fundamental distinction between them. They are like the inside and outside of the same garment.

To go on from what has already been stated, we should say that this optimism (or, for the matter of that, this pessimism which does not really differ from it) remains strictly in the province of the "I myself." The optimist introduces himself indeed as a spectator with particularly keen sight. "If your vision is as good as mine, you are bound to see . . ."; "As your eyes are not as perfect as mine, do not hesitate to trust to my testimony and to my clear-sightedness. . . ."

To be sure, the fact must be recognised that in the case of a given individual (seen in concrete reality and not through the writings of a theorist, be he economist or metaphysician), optimism cannot always be separated from an indistinct faith which cannot be shared by the spectator as such: but what is important for us here is optimism in its essence, that is to say precisely in so far as it does not include the intervention of faith, or even the direct participation, the engagement, which comes into being as soon as life is regarded as something other than purely external. But we have already seen, and we recognise more and more clearly, that he who hopes, in as much as his hope is real and not to be reduced to a mere platonic wish, seems to himself to be involved in some kind of a process; and it is only from this point of view that it is possible to realise what is specific, and, I should add super-rational, perhaps also super-relational, in hope. For, to use once again the expression I have so often employed, hope is a mystery and not a problem. We might point out from the same point of view that hope is very difficult to describe. Indeed, when I try to represent it to myself I am almost inevitably led to alter its true nature and to consider it as presumption. It is thus that we come to substitute "to flatter myself" for "to hope." But in reality if we succeed in learning its meaning more accurately or, which comes to the same thing, in imagining vividly enough what hoping amounts to in one of the situations described further back, we shall recognise that "I hope" cannot ever be taken to imply: "I am in the secret, I know the purpose of God or of the gods, whilst you are a profane outsider; and moreover it is because I have the benefit of special enlightenment that I say what I do." Such an interpretation is as unfair and inaccurate as it is possible to be, it does not take into account all that there is of humility, of timidity, of *chastity* in the true character of hope. The difficult task of the philosopher is precisely to react strongly against such an interpretation, and at the same time to understand why it is so difficult to avoid making it. How can we fail to see that humility, modesty or chastity, by their essence, can never consent to be defined, that is to say they will never deliver their secret to the mercy of rationalistic investigation? Hence the fundamental insufficiency, the clumsy inadequacy of the interpretations we generally have to fall back upon in seeking to understand what I term the mystery of hope. For instance, adopting the realistic point of view, people are ready enough to say, "Does not the hope of the invalid, the prisoner or the exile boil down in the end to a sort of organic refusal to accept an intolerable situation as final? The amount of vitality which the individual retains can be measured by this refusal, and do we not find that, if he has been worn down to a certain point of exhaustion, he will become incapable of exercising the hope which supported him in the first stages of his trial?"

It must be acknowledged that the notion of vitality here referred to is vague enough in itself. But what is extremely characteristic is the tendency of the argument to belittle hope: "Let us have no illusions, hope is not anything but . . ., etc." In this way its specific nature is disputed. It is a matter for reflection to discover the origin of this anxiety to depreciate. We shall return to this point further on. But at the same time it is to be noted that without any doubt the soul can be in a state of drowsiness which tends to paralyse every kind of reaction; it is quite clear, for instance, that cold or hunger can reduce me to a state in which I cannot concentrate my attention on any idea, or *a fortiori* use my powers of reflection; it would be no less absurd to draw materialistic conclusions from this as to the nature of attention or thought. As it happens, experience seems to establish that hope is able to survive an almost total ruin of the organism; if then it is vitality in some sense, it is very difficult to determine what that sense is, for it has nothing in common with the meaning we attribute to the word in speaking of the vitality of a healthy body. At any rate, the principle must be laid down that any physical theory of hope is absurd and, according to all appearances, contradictory; perhaps we might be justified in maintaining that hope coincides with the spiritual principle itself. Thus we must be careful not to think that we can understand it by psychological suppositions; these as a matter of fact are always imagined *a posteriori*, to explain something which is an abiding mystery by its nature. To convince ourselves of this it is enough to observe that we are quite unable to tell before an ordeal what that ordeal will do to us and what resources we shall find we possess with which to face it.

The truth is that there can strictly speaking be no hope except when the temptation to despair exists. Hope is the act by which this temptation is actively or victoriously overcome. The victory may not invariably involve any sense of effort: I should even be quite ready to go so far as to say that such a feeling is not compatible with hope in its purest form.

What then does it mean to despair? We will not stop short here with symptoms and signs. What is the essence of the act of despair? It seems as though it were always capitulation before a certain *fatum* laid down by our judgment. But the difference between capitulation and non-capitulation, though certain, is hard to define. Let us suppose that I develop some incurable illness and that my condition shows no improvement. It may be that I say of myself, "I cannot be cured," or that it is the doctors who tell me, with or without tact, that there is no possible prospect of my recovery (they are, for instance, warning me in order to spare me from disappointments which would wear me out to no purpose). In the first case it seems as though I decide and defy any real or possible contradictions. "You, who claim to know something about it, say that I can get better; but I myself, who know how I feel and who have inner experience of all my symptoms, I tell you that you are mistaken and that I cannot recover." In this way, I pronounce my own sentence, and at the same time my relations and my doctor will no doubt feel that I have made conditions as unfavourable as possible for my constitution to put up an effective resistance. Is there not now every chance that, discouraged by this sentence, it will feel obliged to confirm it? So it comes about that, far from merely foreseeing my own destiny, I shall really have precipitated it. Strangely enough, things may very well happen quite differently in the second case we are considering. It may be that the verdict communicated to me, coming from outside, will arouse in me not merely the strength to deny it, but to prove it to be wrong in fact. At least we can say that in this second case I do not appear in principle to be furthering my non-recovery, unless I ratify and thus make my own the sentence which has been communicated to me. But it remains true that a certain margin is left me, a certain possibility of contradiction, precisely because it was someone else and not I who declared my recovery to be impossible.

However, it is still necessary here to distinguish between two inner attitudes which are very different and which help to decide the event itself. To capitulate, in the strongest sense of the word, is not only, perhaps is not at all, to accept the given sentence or even to recognise the inevitable as such; it is to go to pieces under this sentence, to disarm before the inevitable. It is at bottom to renounce the idea of remaining oneself, it is to be fascinated by the idea of one's own destruction to the point of anticipating this very destruction itself. To accept, on the contrary, can mean to hold on and to keep a firm hold of oneself, that is to say to safeguard one's integrity. Because I am condemned never to recover from this illness, or not to come out of this prison I do not mean to give up, I do not consent, from this very moment, to be the useless creature which my illness or my captivity may finally make of me; I will counter the fascination which the idea of this creature might have for me with the firm determination to remain what I am. It may thus come about that by accepting an inevitable destiny which I refuse with all my strength to anticipate, I will find a way of inward consolidation, of proving my reality to myself, and at the same time I shall rise infinitely above this *fatum* to which I have never allowed myself to shut my eyes. Herein without any doubt lies the power and greatness of stoicism, but, at the same time, it must be recognised that the stoic is always imprisoned within himself. He strengthens himself, no doubt, but he does not radiate. I would go as far as to say that he affords us the highest expression, the greatest degree of sublimation of the "I myself." He bears himself – and that means that above all he controls his interior life – as though he had no neighbours, as though he were concerned only with himself and had no responsibility towards anyone else.

It is obvious that in hope there is something which goes infinitely further than acceptance, or one might say more exactly that it is a non-acceptance, but positive and hence distinguishable from revolt. Non-acceptance can indeed be a mere stiffening or contraction. When it is this it is powerless and can be, in the same way as its opposite, abdication, a manner of working out one's own defeat, of relinquishing control. The important question for us is to know how it can take on the positive character. How, if I do not accept, can I avoid tightening myself up, and, instead, relax in my very non-acceptance? We might compare this with the supple movements of the swimmer or the practised skier. But our difficulty is that it is very hard to conceive how there can be a suppleness and grace in something which, on the face of it, appears to be negation. We can begin to see the solution of this strange problem by reflecting that tightening up or stiffening, on whatever physical or spiritual level we may be considering it, always suggests the presence of the same physical factor, which, if not exactly fear, is at any rate of the same order, a concentration of the self on the self, the essence of which is probably a certain impatience. If we introduce the element of patience into nonacceptance we at once come very much nearer to hope. It seems then that there exists a secret and rarely discovered connection between the way in which the *ego* is either centred or not centred in itself, and its reaction to the duration of time, or more precisely to the temporal order, that is to say to the fact that change is possible in reality. A simple expression borrowed from everyday language is a help here: *to take one's time.* He who stiffens and rebels does not know how to take his time. What exactly do these words, so foreign to the vocabulary of technical philosophy, mean? "Take your time," an examiner would say, for example, to a flurried candidate. That means, do not force the personal rhythm, the proper cadence of your reflection, or even of your memory, for if you do you will spoil your chances, you will be likely to say at random the first words which come into your head. It may seem that we have wandered very far from hope in the strict sense of the word. I do not think so, and this is how I am going to try to explain the analogy, or more exactly, perhaps, the secret affinity between hope and relaxation. Does not he who hopes, and, as we have seen, has to contend with a certain trial comparable to a form of captivity, tend to treat this trial and to proceed in regard to it as he who is patient towards himself treats his inexperienced young *ego*, the *ego* which needs educating and controlling. Above all he never lets it contract but, on the other hand, he does not allow it to kick over the traces or take control prematurely or unwarrantably. From this point of view, hope means first accepting the trial as an integral part of the self, but while so doing it considers it as destined to be absorbed and transmuted by the inner workings of a certain creative process.

Further back I spoke of patience with oneself; perhaps it is still more instructive now to consider patience with others. This most certainly consists in never hustling or being rough with another person, more exactly, in never trying to substitute our own rhythm for his by violence. Neither should the other person be treated as though he lacked an autonomous rhythm, and could accordingly be forced or bent to suit us. Let us say positively this time that it consists in placing our confidence in a certain process of growth and development. To give one's confidence does not merely mean that one makes an act of theoretical acceptance with no idea of intervention, for that would, in fact, be to abandon the other purely and simply to himself. No, to have confidence here seems to mean to embrace this process, in a sense, so that we promote it from within. Patience seems, then, to suggest a certain temporal pluralism, a certain pluralisation of the self in time. It is radically opposed to the act by which I despair of the other person, declaring that he is good for nothing, or that he will never understand anything, or that he is incurable. That is, of course, the same despair which makes me proclaim that I shall never be cured, that I shall never see the end of my captivity, etc. It seems, strangely enough, that, in hoping, I develop in connection with the event, and perhaps above all through what it makes of me, a type of relationship, a kind of intimacy comparable to that which I have with the other person when I am patient with him. Perhaps we might go so far as to speak here of a certain *domesticating* of circumstances, which might otherwise, if we allowed them to get the better of us, frighten us into accepting them as a *fatum*. If we look no further than its etymological meaning, patience appears to be just a simple letting things alone, or allowing them to take their course, but if we take the analysis a little further we find that such non-interference is of a higher order than indifference and implies a subtle respect for the other person's need of time to preserve his vital rhythm, so that it tends to exercise a transforming influence upon him which is comparable to that which sometimes rewards love. It should moreover be shown how here and there pure causality is utterly left behind. Of course patience can easily be degraded; it can become mere weakness, or mere complacency, precisely in so far as it betrays the principle of charity which should animate it. But can it be overlooked that hope likewise is liable to degradations of the same order, when, for instance, it is found in the mere spectator who, without being in the least involved in the game or race at which he is present, hopes that one or other of the competitors will succeed, and at the same time, in a confused sort of way, congratulates himself that he is running no risk and has no direct part to play in the struggle.

To tell the truth, I have no doubt that the comparison I have suggested will appear paradoxical and absurd. In the case of patience there is question of a being, but here we are not dealing with a being but a situation which in its essence has nothing personal about it. On reflection, however, the gap tends to narrow, perhaps because I can hope or not hope in the being of whom I am in a sense in charge, and we shall have to ask ourselves if "I place my hope in you" is not really the most authentic form of "I hope." But it is not everything; the trial affects me, it attacks my being so that I am likely to be permanently altered by it. Thus there is a risk that illness will make of me that deformed creature, a catalogued and professionalised invalid, who thinks of himself as such and contracts in all respects the *habitus* of illness. It is the same with captivity or exile, etc., and, I should say, with every sort of misfortune. In so far as I hope, I detach myself from this inner determinism which is rather like a cramp, threatening, when the trial is upon me, to change me into one of those degraded, abnormal, and in the end perhaps hypnotised expressions of human personality produced by despair, because it is above all things a fascination.

We come here, I think, to one of the vital centres of our subject. But immediately an objection presents itself which must be squarely faced. It does not seem possible to consider hope purely and simply as an inner action of defence by which I should be able to safeguard my integrity when it is threatened by an obsession: or more exactly, it is not the actual safeguard which we are aiming at; if this is secured by hope, it can only be indirectly. Everything goes to show that hope does not bear upon what is in me, upon the region of my interior life, but much more on what arises independently of my possible action, and particularly of my action on myself: I hope – for the return of someone who is absent, for the defeat of the enemy, for peace, which will give back to my country the liberties of which disaster has robbed it. If it is permissible to say, as I already implied above, that hope has the power of making things fluid, it remains to be seen exactly how and upon what this power is exercised.

Let us again this time make use of an example. For a long time
a father has been without news of his son. The boy had gone on a
mission to a distant country, telling his relations not to worry if he
did not write for some time, but his silence is unduly prolonged and
gives rise to the worst fears. Yet the father persists in hoping. Each
day he awaits the letter which would bring his anxiety to an end. To
despair would be to say, "I have been disappointed so many times
there is every reason to expect that I shall be again today"; it would
be to declare this wound incurable, this wound which not only is
inflicted by separation but which is separation. "I shall never again
be anything but the wounded, mutilated creature I am today. Death
alone can end my trouble; and it will only do so by ending me
myself. That is all destiny is able to do for me – destiny, that strange
doctor which can only cure the disease by killing the sufferer." The
despairing man not only contemplates and sets before himself the
dismal repetition, the eternalisation of a situation in which he is
caught like a ship in a sea of ice. By a paradox which is difficult to
conceive, he anticipates this repetition. He sees it at the moment,
and simultaneously he has the bitter certainty that this anticipation
will not spare him from living through the same trial day by day
until the extinction which, to tell the truth, he anticipates likewise,
not seeing it as a remedy but as a supreme outrage to the departed
for whom his mourning does at least ensure the shadow of survival.
Despair here appears as an enchantment, or more exactly as a kind
of witchcraft, whose evil action has a bearing on all which goes to
form the very substance of a person's life.

Let us be still more precise. Each instant, my impressions, in the
very general sense which Hume gives this word, stand out against
a certain "background" in which reflection alone is able to discern,
somewhat imperfectly perhaps, what belongs to the past or the
future or what is only a horizon of floating possibilities. Contrary to
what one is often tempted to admit, it is not true to argue that this
"background" contrasts with given facts, as though it were merely
imagined; it is also "given" in another form, that for instance in
which we anticipate the future, and rejoice, grow sad or worry
about a certain prospect. It is precisely because we place ourselves
unwarrantably on the "ground of facts" that we are led to formulate
the principle that the future is not given – and can therefore only be

imagined. It would be much nearer the truth to say that in anticipating I receive, I pocket in advance, I take a certain advance percentage, on a given fact which is to come, and is quite literally credited to me. Actually it does not greatly matter here if these advances are different from the rest which we shall effectively realise one day. What I just called the substance of life can now be separated from the act, almost impossible to describe, by which I am aware of this substance at a given moment as one is aware of the quality of a wine or the water of a precious stone. Reflective analysis will no doubt here suggest the idea of a relationship between the immediate, the anticipated and also the remembered which we might say backs the operation. If we kept to the idea of this relationship we should easily come to speak of a triangulation which each of us is making at every moment of his existence. That, however, would only be a very imperfect approximation, for by this triangulation I could never determine anything but my position at a given moment. Now, the appreciation which is here under discussion is something quite different from a simple registration, indeed it tends at each moment to convert itself into a global judgment, valid *ubique et semper* and thereby infinitely transcending everything which is limited to the *hic et nunc*.

The truth is that it is impossible to rest satisfied here with an interpretation expressed in terms of relationships. An amateur psychologist, whose name I have unfortunately forgotten, brought out in a paper, which I believe is still unpublished, the importance of what he very aptly called *"L'entrain à la vie* (enthusiasm for living)." The appreciation, or *a fortiori* the triangulation, of which I mentioned the possibility just now, is in reality nothing but the intellectualised and inadequate expression of that which is dynamically known to us as enthusiasm or ardour for life. This term of ardour, unphilosophical as it may be, has the merit of retaining and as it were incarnating a metaphor which we cannot reduce to abstract terms without thereby condemning ourselves to miss the essential and inescapable connection which exists between life and a flame. In passing, how can we help noticing like Dr. Minkowski, that certain metaphors furnish us with settings for the human experience "to exist" to such a point that we have the right to regard them as veritable concrete categories. It is on this flame, which is life, that

the malevolent action of despair is exercised. We might say to put it
in another way that ardour renders soluble or volatile what without
it would at every moment tend to prevent existence. It is turned
towards a certain matter in the personal *becoming* which it is its
function to consume. Where, however, "the evil spell" exists, this
flame turns away from the matter which is its natural food, to
devour itself. This is what we express admirably when we say of a
being "he preys on himself."[2] From this point of view, despair can
be compared to a certain spiritual autophagy. We must notice here,
and keep in mind for all that follows, the part played by the *self*, that
action which consists not only of reflecting but of making the self
the centre.

Do these indications throw any light on our problem? In the
example we were considering – that of the son of whom there is no
news – it is clear that the disappointing fact, the arrival of the post-
man who does not bring the longed-for letter, illustrates what I was
speaking of as something to be consumed or dissolved. The term of
liquefaction expresses the same process. But we must not forget the
criticism to which we have previously subjected the confused
notion of vitality. We might say that a natural optimism exists,
which reflects before everything else the perfect functioning of the
organism, but which may also correspond to a thoroughly egoistical desire to husband one's forces, to save oneself useless anxiety
for as long as possible; it goes without saying that this natural optimism is not to be confused any more than theoretical optimism
with hope. The latter appears to us as inspired by love, or perhaps
more exactly by a combination of scenes which this love conjures
up and irradiates. But an objection at once arises which we must
now face squarely and which seems likely to ruin any metaphysical
theory of hope.

The objection consists of questioning the value of the belief
implied in hope. If I wish ardently for a certain thing, it will be said,
I shall represent it to myself very distinctly, I shall realise it in my
imagination and immediately, by the same process, I shall believe it
is actually going to happen. If this be so, must we not admit that
hope implies an illusion of which critical reflection at once exposes

2   "*Il se consume.*"

the mechanism? This is exactly the illusion which makes us take our wishes for realities – our wishes or our fears: the mechanism is obviously the same in both cases.

We must now ask ourselves under what conditions it is possible to save hope, that is to say to recognise a value in it which such criticism cannot diminish, pertinent as it may be in a great number of particular cases.

It is here no doubt that we must remember the distinction made above between "to hope" and "to hope that." The more hope tends to reduce itself to a matter of dwelling on, or of becoming hypnotised over, something one has represented to oneself, the more the objection we have just formulated will be irrefutable. On the contrary, the more hope transcends imagination, so that I do not allow myself to imagine what I hope for, the more this objection seems to disappear.

It might, however, be asked whether that is not just an evasion. Indeed, from the very moment that I am called upon to endure some trial such as illness or exile, what all my wishes are bent upon is my liberation. I may represent more or less precisely the exact way in which it will happen, but in any case I realise it intensely, and by that very fact I tend to believe in it: it seems then that the psychological mechanism functions in the same way even where my consciousness is not hypnotised by a certain precise image.

But it must be answered that in reasoning thus we arbitrarily simplify an interior situation which includes, as has been expressly stated, the essential element of temptation to despair. The stifling conditions which surround and as it were hedge us in, tend to appear unchangeable to us. We feel that there is no reason to suppose that a *miracle* will transform them into conformity with our desires. Notice that here another psychological mechanism is working in a precisely opposite direction from that which was shown to bring about the illusion exposed at the heart of hope. It must then be recognised that, in the situation and trials we have in mind, consciousness has to contend with two mechanisms which tend to work in opposite directions and this observation, coming at the end of what we have already noticed, leads us to recognise the secret connection between hope and liberty. Both take for granted the overruling action of the judgment.

Let us, for example, consider the example of the invalid; it is obvious that he has set his mind upon recovering by the end of a definite period; he is likely to despair if he is not cured at the appointed time. Here it would be the special function of the judgment to suggest that even if the time has passed without the expected recovery taking place, there is, all the same, plenty of room for hope. Here hope appears to be bound up with the use of a method of surmounting, by which thought rises above the imaginings and formulations upon which it had at first been tempted to depend. But, in this example, it depends no doubt on more than a question of dates. The very idea of recovery is capable, at any rate in a certain spiritual register, of being purified and transformed. "Everything is lost for me if I do not get well," the invalid is at first tempted to exclaim, naïvely identifying recovery with salvation. From the moment when he will have not only recognised in an abstract manner, but understood in the depths of his being, that is to say *seen*, that everything is not necessarily lost if there is no cure, it is more than likely that his inner attitude towards recovery or non-recovery will be radically changed; he will have regained the liberty, the faculty of relaxing to which we referred at length further back.

It really seems to be from this point of view that the distinction between believer and unbeliever stands out in its true meaning. The believer is he who will meet with no insurmountable obstacle on his way towards transcendence. Let us say again, to fix the meaning of the word obstacle more precisely, that in so far as I make my hope conditional I myself put up limits to the process by which I could triumph over all successive disappointments. Still more, I give a part of myself over to anguish; indeed I own implicitly that if my expectations are not fulfilled in some particular point, I shall have no possibility of escaping from the despair into which I must inevitably sink. We can, on the other hand, conceive, at least theoretically, of the inner disposition of one who, setting no condition or limit and abandoning himself in absolute confidence, would thus transcend all possible disappointment and would experience a security of his being, or in his being, which is contrary to the radical insecurity of *Having*.

This is what determines the ontological position of hope – absolute hope, inseparable from a faith which is likewise absolute, transcending all laying down of conditions, and for this very reason every kind of representation whatever it might be. The only possible source from which this absolute hope springs must once more be stressed. It appears as a response of the creature to the infinite Being to whom it is conscious of owing everything that it has and upon whom it cannot impose any condition whatsoever without scandal. From the moment that I abase myself in some sense before the absolute Thou who in his infinite condescension has brought me forth out of nothingness, it seems as though I forbid myself ever again to despair, or, more exactly, that I implicitly accept the possibility of despair as an indication of treason, so that I could not give way to it without pronouncing my own condemnation. Indeed, seen in this perspective, what is the meaning of despair if not a declaration that God has withdrawn himself from me? In addition to the fact that such an accusation is incompatible with the nature of the absolute Thou, it is to be observed that in advancing it I am unwarrantably attributing to myself a distinct reality which I do not possess.

It would however be vain to try to hide the difficulties, from the human point of view, of this position of which no one would dream of contesting the metaphysical and religious purity. Does not this invincible hope arise from the ruins of all human and limited hopes? Must not the true believer be ready to accept the death and ruin of his dear ones, the temporal destruction of his country, as possibilities against which it is forbidden to rebel? To go further: if these things come about, must he not be ready to adore the divine will in them? We cannot be enough on our guard against the softening processes to which some people have recourse in order to reassure those whose faith might fail in the presence of such terrible happenings. I have in mind particularly the allegations of those who claim to calm us by observing that God, being infinitely good, cannot tempt us beyond our strength by driving us to despair which he has actually forbidden us. I am afraid that these are no more than verbal tricks; we know neither the real extent of our powers nor the ultimate designs of God; and, if the arguments were really possible to accept, it would in the long run amount to an implicit and as it were hypocritical way of laying down conditions which would bring hope once more within the limits of the relative.

But then must it not be agreed that the absolute hope to which we are invited tends to become identified with despair itself – with a despair however which it is no longer even permitted for us to indulge in, and which is perhaps no more than an infinite apathy?

On the other hand, it is to be wondered whether, in claiming to establish himself beyond the reach of any possible disappointment in a zone of utter metaphysical security, man does not become guilty of what might well be called treason from above. Does he not tend to violate in this way the fundamental conditions under which he is introduced into the world? To tell the truth, in falling back upon the idea of what I have called absolute hope, it seems that I elude my problems far more than I solve them and that I am juggling with the given facts.

But are we not then losing our way again in the inextricable? Here I take the example once more of the patriot who refuses to despair of the liberation of his native land which is provisionally conquered. In what, or in whom, does he place his hope? Does he not conditionalise his hope in the way which just now we decided was unwarrantable? Even if he recognises that there is no chance that he will himself witness the hoped-for liberation, he carries beyond his own existence the fulfilment of his desires, he refuses with all his being to admit that the darkness which has fallen upon his country can be enduring, he affirms that it is only an eclipse. Still more: it is not enough to say that he cannot believe in the death of his country, the truth is much more that he does not even consider he has the right to believe in it, and that it would seem to him that he was committing a real act of treason in admitting this possibility; and this is true whether he is a believer or not. In every case he has made a judgment, which lies outside all his power of reflection, that to despair would be disloyal, it would be to go over to the enemy. This judgment rests on a postulate which is actually very likely to remain implicit but which we must examine. It consists in the affirmation that in hoping for liberation I really help to prepare the way for it, and that, inversely, in raising a doubt about its possibility I reduce the chance of it to some degree. It is not that strictly speaking I impute a causal efficacy to the fact of hoping or not hoping. The truth is much rather that I am conscious that when I hope I strengthen, and when I despair, or simply doubt, I weaken or let go of, a certain bond which unites me to the matter in question. This bond shows every evidence of being religious in essence.

Here we come up, however, against a difficulty. Where the matter in question is strictly speaking my own fate, can we speak of a bond or indeed of religion? It is probably necessary here to introduce a distinction which we have previously had occasion to bring out. When I tremble for my own existence, it may be that I am giving way to the simple instinct of self-preservation: it is very doubtful if one can legitimately designate by the word "hope" the kind of organic attachment to myself which makes me imagine final liberation in the midst of danger, even where the future seems most threatening. It is different when piety towards oneself intervenes. By this I mean a reference to a certain spiritual interconnection at the heart of which my existence can preserve its meaning and its value. We are not dealing here with an abstraction, an impersonal order: if I inspire another being with love which I value and to which I respond, that will be enough to create this spiritual interconnection. The fact of the reciprocal love, the communion, will be enough to bring about a deep transformation in the nature of the bond which unites me to myself. Where the matter concerns me alone, or more exactly when I consider myself as though I were the only one concerned, the question of knowing what is going to happen to me may strike me as practically without interest or importance. This, however, will not prevent the instinct of self-preservation from remaining active in me with all that it entails. It is obviously not the same if I know that he whom I love is in some way dependent on me, and that what happens to me will affect him vitally. We might say in the manner of Hegel that my relationship to myself is mediated by the presence of the other person, by what he is for me and what I am for him. But it is of capital importance for our subject that we see at the same time that this spiritual interconnection of which I have only examined the simplest example here, invariably appears as veiled in mystery to him who is conscious of having a part in it. Here again, let us be as concrete as possible. To love anybody is to expect something from him, something which can neither be defined nor foreseen; it is at the same time in some way to make it possible for him to fulfil this expectation. Yes, paradoxical as it may seem, to expect is in some way to give: but the opposite is none the less true; no longer to expect is to strike with sterility the being from whom no more is expected, it is then in some way to deprive him or take from him in advance what is surely a certain possibility of inventing or creating. Everything looks as though we can only speak of hope where the interaction exists between him who gives and him who receives, where there is that exchange which is the mark of all spiritual life.

But perhaps, without sinning through excessive subtlety, it might be pointed out that this delicate interplay of relationships can exist internally wherever there is genuine creation. In that case we need only put outside the category of hope the blind attachment which impels us simply to go on living, carrying out day by day the functions, organic or otherwise, which are exercised for ourselves alone without any superior object in view, be it intellectual, moral or aesthetic. If this is so, the ancient distinction of the Stoics upon which any critical examination of hope is invariably founded, the distinction between things which depend, and do not depend, upon ourselves, will lose a great deal of its significance. Further, how can we fail to recall the connection established above between hope and liberty? Not only does voluntary action not presuppose an objective judgment already formed by which I should see in advance what was in my power to do and what was beyond it, but it must on the contrary be maintained that the authentic formula of willing is *I will*, therefore *I can*; in other words, I decide that it is in my power to do a certain thing, to obtain a certain result precisely because it is my will (or because it is necessary) that this thing should be done and this result obtained. Actually we only have to remember that to act freely is always to innovate, in order to see that there would be a contradiction in admitting that I should be obliged in my willing to depend simply on the knowledge of what I had done before. It is, however only by starting from such knowledge that I could proceed to an objective setting of limits between what is in my power and what is beyond it.

It is not difficult to see how a positive philosophy of hope can be arrived at from these observations. We are actually going to find that all our foregoing remarks will come together as into a sheaf. When we said that hope was the very opposite of pretension or defiance, we were ready to recognise that it is essentially silent and modest, that it bears the mark of inviolable timidity except where it develops in the department of the *us,* that is to say in fellowship. We talk to each other of our common hope but hate to express it before those who do not share it, as if it were really – and perhaps indeed it is – a secret. If hope is not a defiance, perhaps it is nevertheless conscious of appearing defiant or provocative in the eyes of those who claim that they are established on the firm rock of experience: "It has always been seen that . . ." or, on the contrary, "It has never been found that . . . ." Hope with scandalously carefree grace undertakes to prove these assertions false; by what right?

It seems as though hope is linked to a certain candour, a certain virginity untouched by experience. It belongs to those who have not been hardened by life. We are impelled to introduce a notion here which, from the point of view of objective knowledge, will appear to be devoid of sense: it is that of a sullying or withering which is connected with experience. The notion of experience itself is ambiguous. On the one hand there is an established and catalogued experience in the name of which judgments are pronounced by the pronoun "one." On the other hand there is an experience in the making which is only possible precisely when all the other kind of experience has been set on one side, even if finally and after having been duly desiccated, it is given a place in the herbarium of universal wisdom. It is quite evident that hope is intimately bound up with experience in the second sense and perhaps it might be claimed that hope is its spring. In the name of accepted experience people claim to trace some kind of circle of Popilius round us; "There is no way out" – that is the formula to which the experts of established experience fly. But postulated at the very basis of hope is the non-validity of such assertions, the truth that the more the real is real the less does it lend itself to a calculation of possibilities on the basis of accepted experience. Hope quite simply does not take any heed of this sum total. It might be said that in a sense hope is not interested in the *how:* and this fact shows how fundamentally untechnical it is, for technical thought, by definition, never separates the consideration of ends and means. An end does not exist for the technician, if he does not see approximately how to achieve it. This, however, is not true for the inventor or the discoverer who says, "There must be a way" and who adds: "I am going to find it."

He who hopes says simply: "It will be found." In hoping, I do not create in the strict sense of the word, but I appeal to the existence of a certain creative power in the world, or rather to the actual resources at the disposal of this creative power. Where, on the other hand, my spirit has been as it were tarnished by catalogued experience, I refuse to appeal to this creative power, I deny its existence; all outside me, and perhaps within me also (if I am logical) appears to me as simple repetition.

We have arrived then at the important conclusion that what is specific in hope is lost sight of if the attempt is made to judge and condemn it from the point of view of *established experience*. It misunderstands the teaching of such experience with insolent ingenuity, though it is actually definite enough. The truth is much more that hope is engaged in the weaving of experience now in process, or in other words in an adventure now going forward. This does not run counter to an authentic empiricism but to a certain dogmatism which, while claiming to be experience, fundamentally misunderstands its nature, just as a cult of the scientific may stand in the way of living science in its creative development.

It is not difficult to see that hope thus understood involves a fundamental relationship of consciousness to time which we must now try to analyse.

If we accept the perspective of established experience, we are led to suppose that time will bring nothing new beyond an illustration or an added confirmation, actually superfluous, of the pronouncements engraved on the tables of universal wisdom or merely of common sense. It is as much as to say that we are here in a world where time no longer passes, or, which comes to the same thing, where time merely passes without bringing anything, empty of any material which could serve to establish a new truth or inspire a new being. How can we help remembering here the impression, rightly termed *hopeless*, which every child and adolescent has received when his elders pronounce one or other of those axioms which claim to express *truths which are indisputable* and duly established. Such axioms seem to strike out of existence all the dreams, all the confused aspirations of him who not having had *his own* experience refuses to accept a so-called proof with which he is in no way associated. We actually have grounds for wondering by what strange optical illusion the axiom which appears as hopeless and discouraging to him who is supposed to be instructed by it, causes such vanity and self-satisfaction in those who give it out. The reason is surely to be found in the sense of superiority which, rightly or wrongly, fills those people who imagine that they represent universal wisdom to youngsters whose wild presumption needs to be mortified as much as possible. We see the antagonism between the older and younger as an antagonism between someone who is trying to feel his way in life as we feel our way along a road, and who only has a flickering light to guide him, and someone who claims to be at the other side of this same life (and of his own life as well) and to be able to give out, from some abstract spot, truths acquired at a great price. It goes without saying that this conflict is at the heart of what is often called the problem of the generations and that no truly logical or rational solution can be found for it, because the antagonists are on different levels in time, because they have no real communion with each other and neither of them discusses with the other, but with a certain idea a certain *eidôlon* of the other.

All then prepares us to recognise that despair is in a certain sense the consciousness of time as closed or, more exactly still, of time as a prison – whilst hope appears as piercing through time; everything happens as though time, instead of hedging consciousness round, allowed something to pass through it. It was from this point of view that I previously drew attention to the prophetic character of hope. Of course one cannot say that hope sees what is going to happen; but it affirms as if it saw. One might say that it draws its authority from a hidden vision of which it is allowed to take account without enjoying it.

We might say again that if time is in its essence a separation and as it were a perpetual splitting up of the self in relation to itself, hope on the contrary aims at reunion, at recollection, at reconciliation: in that way, and in that way alone, it might be called a memory of the future.

One cannot however disguise the impatience, one might say the uneasiness, which such glimpses give rise to in spirits dominated by an anxiety for truth: "Is there to be nothing in these explanations," it may be asked, "which enables us to discern if hope is anything but an illusion, if it is in any possible degree a light thrown upon a certain subsoil of things? And yet is not this, when we come down to the final analysis, the only question which matters?"

To reply to such a challenge, it will be well, I think, to introduce the idea of a certain human condition which we cannot hope to transcend by thought, for reflection shows that in trying to rise above it we make it unreal and impoverish it. The unpardonable mistake of a certain rationalism has consisted precisely in sacrificing the human as such, without anything to take its place, to certain *ideas*, whose regulative value we certainly should not think of questioning, but which lose all their meaning if we attempt to make of them a world existing by itself where "the human as such" will be counted as nothing but dross and rubbish. This general remark seems to me likely to throw light on the debate, which arises between those who want to save hope and those who on the contrary seek to banish it to the world of mirages.

The term "condition" is one which needs very careful definition. Perhaps we should see in the human condition a certain vital and spiritual order which we cannot violate without exposing ourselves to the loss not only of our equilibrium, but even of our integrity. As, however, the term condition may also be taken sometimes in a slightly different sense which is very nearly that of nature, we must recognise that it is a characteristic of man's condition in the second sense that he is able to fall short of his condition in the first sense. The condition-order implies a joint working which is always precarious between our nature and an acquired wisdom, infused into our will – a wisdom actually in no way bound to be explicitly conscious of itself. Again we must of course be careful not to confuse this wisdom with the dogmatic empiricism of which I have already pointed out the sterilising effect. Perhaps the human condition is characterised not only by the risks which go with it and which after all are bound up with life itself, even in its humblest forms, but also, and far more deeply, by the necessity to accept these risks and to refuse to believe that it would be possible – and, if we come to a final analysis, even an advantage – to succeed in removing them. Experience teaches us, as a matter of fact, that we can never refuse to take risks except in appearance, or rather that the refusal itself conceals a risk which is the most serious of all, and that it is even possible for us finally to condemn ourselves in this way to lose the best of the very thing which by our avoidance we had intended to safeguard.

But it must be noticed that the attitude of those who in the name of reason take up their position against hope is in all points comparable with that of the people who claim to avoid risks. In both cases what they want to avoid is disappointment. But perhaps it is of the nature of disappointment that we have no right to anticipate it, as we do when we become preoccupied about its prevention. Perhaps, on the other hand, we have not sufficiently noticed that disappointment appears to him who undergoes it as a sort of breach of confidence on the part of – whom, or what? The reply usually remains uncertain, but in every case we tend to personify the experience which has failed to fulfil our expectations. I counted on *such a thing* happening: it did not happen: I seem to myself to be a creditor facing an insolvent debtor: why? It seems that in *counting on* I have given something, or I consider that I have given something, of my own: literally I have given credit – and the event or the mysterious source of the event has failed in its obligation towards me. Disappointment will then leave the soul all the more sore if in its depths it has had the presumption, or given way to the temptation, of somehow chaining reality down in advance as one binds a debtor with the agreement one forces upon him. But we have never ceased to insist that this claim, this presumption, is definitely foreign to hope which never stipulates the carrying out of a certain contract (which is, strangely enough, always a strictly one-sided contract). Perhaps it is simply that hope shows the originality and, I must add, the supreme dignity, of never claiming anything or insisting upon its rights. And it is permissible to consider the analogous situation of a being who is awaiting a gift or favour from another being but only on the grounds of his liberality, and that he is the first to protest that the favour he is asking is a grace, that is to say the exact opposite of an obligation.

Here the relationship which the words "hope in" express, appears in its originality and, I should add, in its perfection. It seems as though a philosophy which revolves round the contractual idea is likely to misunderstand the value of the relationship. I should however add that here, as everywhere for that matter, a certain slipping or degradation inevitably tends to come about. "To hope in" becomes "to expect from" then "to have due to me," that is to say "to count on" and finally "to claim" or "to demand." The perpetually recurring difficulties which a philosophy of hope encounters are for the most part due to the fact that we have a tendency to substitute for an initial relationship, which is both pure and mysterious, subsequent relationships no doubt more intelligible, but at the same time more and more deficient as regards their ontological content.

Furthermore, it must be owned that the evolution of mentalities which we observe around us seems to follow the same slope, the same line of degradation. Men in general seem less and less capable of "hoping in"; it is indeed difficult to interpret as hope the idolatry which immense, fascinated masses show for leaders who have previously, by ceaseless propaganda, succeeded in paralysing not only any critical spirit in their minions, but all true sense of values. All that we can say is that this idolatrous attachment is the miserable substitute, I should be ready to say the toxic succedaneum, of the hope for which those same multitudes no doubt still have a nostalgic longing in the depths of their hearts, even if they show themselves actually incapable of exercising it. To be quite fair it must however be noted that democracy, considered not in its principles but in its actual achievements, has helped in the most baleful manner to encourage *claiming* in all its aspects, the demanding of rights – and indeed to bring a mercenary spirit into all human relationships. I mean by this that the democratic atmosphere tends to exclude more and more the idea of disinterested service born of fidelity, and a belief in the intrinsic value of such service. Each individual claims from the start to enjoy the same consideration and the same advantages as his neighbour; and, in fact, his self-respect tends to resolve itself into an attitude which is not only defensive but ever claiming rights from others. Thus he considers it beneath his dignity to do anything whatever for nothing. The abstract idea of a certain justice is here oddly connected with the anxiety not to be duped, not to allow another person to take advantage of his simplicity or his good nature. But in this perspective how can the spirit of mistrust – mistrust not only of others, but of life itself – not tend to make the human soul less and less a possible dwelling place for hope, or indeed for joy? We seem here to touch the metaphysical roots of a denaturalisation which seems almost as though it were coextensive with a certain type of civilisation. It may be said in passing that the very fact that a certain belief in progress, far from arresting this evolution, has, on the contrary, helped to precipitate it, suffices to show how far such a belief is opposed to true hope, in spite of the fact that in its far distant origin it may have been a confusedly rationalised derivative of it.

We should not however hide from ourselves that all these considerations would not yet be enough to convince those who, under the influence of a stoicism or a more or less distorted form of the philosophy of Spinoza, persist in refusing to allow that hope has any metaphysical value. "Do you not," they say, "merely arrive at the very insignificant conclusion, for which it is really superfluous to use such complicated arguments, that hope is a tendency which constitutes the inner spring of human enterprises because it is calculated to stimulate usefully those who engage wholeheartedly in them?" This is as much as to say that in the last resort hope is only a subjective tendency, that by itself it would never be able to throw any light upon the inner meaning of things, and brings with it no guarantee that it will be realised.

But it must be replied that it is precisely such an opposition as we have here imagined that we have to repudiate or to transcend. Certainly there is no question of denying that this opposition has a meaning where an enterprise with some material aim is under consideration; the building of a port, or a pyramid; the hollowing out of a tunnel, or the damming of a river. Just because it is simply a question of producing certain material results, the inner disposition of the agent – or it would be better to say the instrument – can and should be regarded as a contingent fact in relation to the result to be produced. This in reality seems as though it could well be arrived at by pitiless masters driving a multitude of terrorised slaves with whips. But let us remember that such results do not in reality involve any genuine creation, any love of the thing created. Now it is precisely where such love exists, and only where it exists, that we can speak of hope, this love taking shape in a reality which without it would not be what it is. When this has come about it is untrue to claim that hope is merely a subjective stimulant; it is, on the contrary, a vital aspect of the very process by which an act of creation is accomplished.

"But," they will say again, "the hope we are discussing here is surely strangely different from that which was previously defined as a response to a situation which entailed captivity?" It may be taken that, in spite of appearances, this difference conceals a fundamental identity. Do not let us forget that, as a matter of fact, the general condition of man, even when his life appears to be quite normal, is always that of a captive, by reason of the enslavements of all kinds which he is called upon to endure, if only on account of the body, and more deeply still because of the night which shrouds his beginning and his end. We can be certain that all creative activity, whatever it may be, is bound up with this condition, in the double meaning which we have given to the word, and that it is in reality the only means given us of causing light to shine forth in our prison. It may be asked whether this is not to make of creation a diversion as Pascal would have understood it. I do not think so really, for the notion of Pascal involves the idea of the utter solitude of the creature struggling with the agony of his destiny, whereas we have seen, and we must return to it again, that hope is always associated with a communion, no matter how interior it may be. This is actually so true that one wonders if despair and solitude are not at bottom necessarily identical.

From this point of view the essential problem to which we are seeking to find the solution would be whether solitude is the last word, whether man is really condemned to live and to die alone, and whether it is only through the effect of a vivid illusion that he manages to conceal from himself the fact that such is indeed his fate. It is not possible to sit in judgment on the case of hope without at the same time trying the case of love.

It is curious to notice that a purely objective philosophy, in the name of which it is claimed to denounce the mirage of hope, is so near as to become identified with the radical subjectivity of a Proust, for whom love is a mis-knowing and resolves itself into nothing but illusions of perspective. There is every reason to think that it is by one and the same action that it is possible to free ourselves from these two philosophies which are only opposed outwardly, that is to say in the formula given to them, but which agree in their negative aims. For the rest, Proust himself puts us on the way of truths to which he becomes more and more blind as his work develops and as he comes to propose to himself an image of life which is at the same time more systematic and impoverished. The subjective conception of love, with the justification it confers upon despair (since only the pure artist possesses the key of salvation) appears all the more unimpeachable as the being becomes increasingly the prisoner of an obsession of which the other being is less the object than the excuse, since he evades the grasp not only of intuition but of all knowledge worthy of the name. I *see* a being so much the less the more I am obsessed by him, for my obsession tends to substitute itself for him. It must be added that this obsession itself becomes all the more tyrannical the more I claim to possess him, to monopolise him, the more obstinately I set my mind to break all the bonds which unite him to other beings, in the hope of making him totally mine. This is the illusion of Arnolphe, and it is to be wondered whether Moliere did not forestall and surpass Proust. One of two things must happen. Faced with this determination to monopolise him, the other person either makes his escape by flight or lying, or else he loses his own nature and becomes a nonentity. In either case it follows inexorably that, because love has thus failed in its mission and become perverted, it consummates its own loss.

But it is to be asked whether a logical process of the same kind, though far less clearly and easily discernible, is not working itself out wherever the fundamental relationship uniting the human soul and the mysterious reality which surrounds and at the same time confronts it becomes perverted. This relationship, when grasped in its truth, is a participation. This means that we do not only become guilty of an usurpation but that, in spite of all appearances, we become strangers to ourselves, in so far as we treat the reality as something which can be won and placed at our disposal. We might say again that this reality thus referred and enslaved to selfish ends loses its true nature also, and becomes a sham and an idol. But shams and idols always appear, to those who view them with enough penetration, as milestones, marking the road to despair.

Perhaps we can now feel authorised to formulate a few general propositions which will sum up most of the observations we have been able to make in the course of our all too winding journey.

In face of the particular trial, whatever it may be, which

confronts me and which must always be but a specimen of the trial of humanity in general, I shall always be exposed to the temptation of shutting the door which encloses me within myself and at the same time encloses me within time, as though the future, drained of its substance and its mystery, were no longer to be anything but a place of pure repetition, as though some unspecifiable disordered mechanism were to go on working ceaselessly, undirected by any intelligent motivisation. But a future thus devitalised, no longer being a future for me or anybody else, would be rather a prospect of vacancy.

A systematised empiricism, crystallised into impersonal and permanent formulæ, would confer upon what is in truth only a movement of the soul, a retraction, an inward disloyalty, the theoretical (and fallacious) justification which such a step needs in order to establish itself in its own eyes.

Against this combination of temptations there is only one remedy, and it has two aspects: it is the remedy of communion, the remedy of hope. If it is true that man's trial is infinite in its varieties and can assume the innumerable forms under which we know privation, exile, or captivity, it is no less certain that by a symmetrical but inverted process, each one of us can rise by his own special path from the humble forms of communion which experience offers the most despised, to a communion which is both more intimate and more abundant, of which hope can be equally regarded as the foreshadowing or the outcome.

"I hope in thee for us"; such is perhaps the most adequate and the most elaborate expression of the act which the verb "to hope" suggests in a way which is still confused and ambiguous. "In thee – for us": between this "thou" and this "us" which only the most persistent reflection can finally discover in the act of hope, what is the vital link? Must we not reply that "Thou" is in some way the guarantee of the union which holds us together, myself to myself, or the one to the other, or these beings to those other beings? More than a guarantee which secures or confirms from outside a union which already exists, it is the very cement which binds the whole into one. If this is the case, to despair of myself, or to despair of us, is essentially to despair of the Thou. Avowedly, it is conceivable that there is some difficulty in admitting that I form with myself a real community, an *us:* it is, however, only on this condition that I have my active share as a centre of intelligence, of love and of creation. This absolute Thou in whom I must hope but whom I also have always the possibility of denying, not only in theory but in practice, is at the heart of the city which I form with myself and which, as experience has given tragic proof, retains the power of reducing itself to ashes. It must be added that this city is not a monad and that it cannot establish itself as a distinct and isolated centre, without working for its own destruction, but that on the contrary it draws the elements of its life from what is brought to it along canals, often very badly marked out, from friendly cities, of which however it often scarcely knows the name or the situation. It is to a consciousness of these reciprocities, of this mysterious and incessant circulation, that I open my soul when I hope – a prophetic consciousness, as we have said, but vague and in danger of becoming obliterated to the extent that it seeks to pass itself off as second sight. If this is so, it must be said that to hope, as we have already hinted, is to live in hope instead of anxiously concentrating our attention on the poor little counters spread out in front of us which we feverishly reckon up over and over again without respite, tormented by the fear of being foiled or ruined. The more we allow ourselves to be the servants of Having, the more we shall let ourselves fall a prey to the gnawing anxiety which Having involves, the more we shall tend to lose not only the aptitude for hope, but even I should say the very belief, indistinct as it may be, of its possible reality. In this sense it is no doubt true that, strictly speaking, only those beings who are entirely free from the shackles of ownership in all its forms are able to know the divine light-heartedness of life in hope. But, as far as we can judge, this liberation, this exemption, must remain the privilege of a very small number of chosen souls. The vast majority of men are, as far as we can see, destined to remain entangled in the inextricable meshes of Having, and there are actually the gravest reasons for thinking that it is on this condition, burdensome as it may be, that humanity is able to discharge, well or badly as the case may be, the tasks, often so thankless and obscure, which have been assigned to it. A final condemnation of Having would amount basically to the rashest repudiation of finite existence by finite man himself. Such could not be uttered without an excessive humility which would look so much like the most inordinate and blasphemous pride as to be confused with it. What, however, we might perhaps dare to say is that if, however feebly, we remain penetrated by hope, it can only be through the cracks and openings which are to be found in the armour of Having which covers us: the armour of our possessions, our attainments, our experience and our virtues, perhaps even more than our vices. Thus, and only thus can the breathing of the soul be maintained, but under conditions, alas, of irregular action and a dangerous uncertainty often on the increase so that it is always in danger of being blocked like the lungs or the bowels.

But in expressing ourselves thus, are we not led to make hope appear too much as a natural faculty? To go still deeper, what position should we adopt on the question as to whether it depends upon us or whether, on the contrary, it is either the fruit of an innate disposition, or a pure grace, and in final analysis the result of supernatural help? I will take care here not to venture upon theological ground. In the region of philosophic reflection, however, it seems as though it is equally true, and consequently equally false, to say that hope depends or does not depend upon me.

The meaning of this question does indeed become more obscure when it bears upon that which is most intimately myself. Does it depend upon me whether I am in love or whether I possess a certain creative faculty? Certainly not, but precisely because it does not depend upon me to be or not to be such as I am. Let us admit, on the contrary, without troubling about the philosophical controversies on free will with which we are not concerned, that it depends upon me whether I take a certain step, or make a certain journey, visit, gesture, etc., which anyone else in my place could equally well do. We are then led to the paradoxical conclusion that what depends upon me is the very thing which does not form part of me, which remains in a sense exterior (or indifferent) to me. It must however be added that a gift, whatever it may be, is never purely and simply *received* by a subject who has nothing to do but make a place for it in himself. The truth is much rather that the gift is a call to which we have to make response; it is as though a harvest of possibilities had to be gathered from us, among which we had to choose, or more exactly it is as though we had to actualise those which accorded best with the urgency interiorly felt which is, in reality, only mediation between us and ourselves.

It is from this general observation that we must start if we would recognise that it is both true and false to say that it depends on us whether we hope or not. At the root of hope there is something which is literally offered to us: but we can refuse hope just as *we* can refuse love. Moreover, we can no doubt deny hope, just as we can deny or degrade our love. Both here and there the role of *Kaïros* seems to be to give our liberty an opportunity of exercising and spreading itself as it could never do if it were left to itself – a hypothesis which is probably contradictory, anyway.

We see from this why it is legitimate to consider hope as a virtue; the truth is that all virtue is the particularisation of a certain interior force, and that to live in hope is to obtain from oneself that one should remain faithful in the hour of darkness to that which in its origin was perhaps only an inspiration, an exaltation, a transport. But there is no doubt that this faithfulness cannot be put into practice except by virtue of a co-operation, whose principle will always remain a mystery, between the goodwill which is after all the only positive contribution of which we are capable and certain promptings whose centre remains beyond our reach, in those realms where values are divine gifts.

Perhaps, if we would elucidate the nature of hope more completely, at least, as far as such elucidation is possible, we should now tackle directly the question of the relationship connecting hope with our reasons for hoping. It may be best to state the problem in its most extreme form: can one hope when the reasons for so doing are insufficient or even completely lacking?

Let us notice first of all that this question must inevitably be asked by anyone who treats hope as an external phenomenon and wonders under what conditions it can appear. I will call such a one the observer in what is to follow.

Reflection soon shows us, however, that thinking in these terms of hope is the very way to stifle it.

First of all, the meaning of the word *can* is ambiguous.

(a) Can it in fact happen that anyone hopes without any reasons for hoping? Or on the other hand

(b) Is it permissible to hope where the reasons are insufficient or lacking?

Let us notice first that in both cases we admit implicitly that the proposition "there is no reason, or at least no sufficient reason, for hope," has some meaning. We must not however be taken in by words; we cannot speak of the non-existence or existence of such reasons as of the non-existence or existence of something which could form part of anyone's experience. Here "there is" or "there is not" is necessarily related to a definite subject. We mean that in the eyes of X there is or there is not good enough reason for hope. But in the statement of our problem what subject is implied? Let us consider in particular question (a). Do we mean "Can it in fact happen that someone hopes under conditions which, for me who am asking the question, afford no grounds for hope?" or "under conditions which *for the subject himself* afford no grounds for it?"

We must obviously answer the first question in the affirmative: it is quite clear that the other can keep on hoping where the observer considers that reasons for hope do not exist, that is to say where they are invisible to him. This first question then is insignificant and idle.

Has the second a more precise meaning? Can anyone, in fact, hope where he himself admits that the reasons are insufficient or lacking? But, if he truly recognises in all sincerity that these reasons are non-existent or insufficient, he himself admits that he does not really hope (unless, of course, he has succumbed to human respect by granting to some interlocutor what he does not believe in his own heart; but such a case is outside our hypothesis). Moreover, the use of the word "sufficient" implies a contradiction, for, if the subject hopes, it would surely seem that the reasons for hoping are sufficient for him, whatever the observer may think about them.

But in reality the question which the subject is supposed to ask himself, and in this particular case to answer in the negative, does not arise for him unless he detaches himself in some degree from his hope. Actually, it comes into a different register and springs from a calculating faculty of the reason which, with the very approximate means at its disposal, proceeds to carry out a regular balancing up of chances. Without any doubt it may happen that, on consideration, hope gives in for a variable space of time to those calculations of the reason; above all if the subject is engaged in a discussion with someone whom he wants to convince: It is none the less true, however, that hope and the calculating faculty of reason are essentially distinct and everything will be lost if we try to combine them. On the other hand, in the statement *(b)*, when we bring in the idea of a right to hope we are entering precisely upon this very process of reasoning by computation which at bottom means a calculation of probabilities. It is as though to hope were to argue in a certain way and as though there were a possibility of enquiring into the validity of the arguments. Looked at from this point of view, the answer to the question is obvious. It is absurd to claim that it can be legitimate to hope without sufficient reasons for hope. But we must repeat once more that here the meaning of the word hope has been completely distorted.

It seems as though we shall thus be led to an utterly negative conclusion and that we shall have to deny that the words "reasons for hoping" have any meaning whatsoever. If so, in this matter we shall have to subscribe to an irrationalism or a radical fideism. But faced with the facts of experience, such a thesis appears nothing short of absurd.

Take, for instance, a mother who persists in hoping that she will see her son again although his death has been certified in the most definite manner by witnesses who found his body, buried it, etc. Is not the observer justified in saying that there are no reasons for hoping that this son is still alive?

However subtle and irritating in certain respects the distinction I am going to introduce here may appear, perhaps we should reply to the objection in the following way: In so far as the hope of the mother is expressed as an objective judgment, "It is possible that John will come back," we have the right to say: "No, objectively speaking, the return must be considered as impossible." But at the root of the mother's objective judgment, which, as such, cannot be accepted, she has within her a loving thought which repudiates or transcends the facts, and it seems as though there was something absurd or even scandalous in disputing her right to hope, that is to say to love, against all hope. More exactly, what is absurd is the very idea of a right which we can recognise or dispute.

We are not at the end of our difficulties, however. Common

sense will retort that it is not permissible to identify hope and love here. "Whatever may be the love which I feel for a certain individual, it cannot be admitted that in virtue of this love, I can assume the right to exceed the limits of logic." It is a mere sophism to say, "I cannot bear the idea that he will not come back, therefore it is possible that he will." But here again, hope is considered from outside and entered in a register where it does not belong. What hope gives us is the simple affirmation, "You are coming back." And this "you are coming back" is beyond the reach of objective criticism. Such criticism could only deal with it legitimately if it were translated into the language of prevision or of a judgment based on probabilities.

It cannot be denied that each of us is exposed to the temptation of carrying out such a substitution on our own account. We have already seen how hope loses its true nature by the very fact that it tends to offer itself for the approbation of the subject himself and also of other people. In this way it loses its essential elasticity, but it only loses it because it denies its own nature and this denial is a fall.

This, which at first appears very paradoxical, seems to me to be elucidated if we keep in mind the fundamental distinction between hope and desire and if we recall the observations which were made further back. We might say that hope only escapes from a particular metaphysical ruling on condition that it transcends desire – that is to say, that it does not remain centred upon the subject himself. Once again we are led to draw attention to the indissoluble connection which binds together hope and love. The more egoistical love is, the more the alluringly prophetic declarations it inspires should be regarded with caution as likely to be literally contradicted by experience; on the other hand, the nearer it approaches to true charity, the more the meaning of its declarations is inflected and tends to become full of an unconditional quality which is the very sign of a presence. This presence is incarnated in the "us" for whom "I hope in Thee," that is to say in a communion of which I proclaim the indestructibility. No doubt, as always, critical thought will immediately take up its position against this assertion. It will invoke the evidence of experience, and of the spectacle of endless visible destruction which it presents to us. But this evidence itself can only be challenged in the name of a certitude which we have already seen is not based on established experience – the certitude that all such arguments are only true in a very fleeting sense, and that the incessant changes to which critical pessimism claims to give so much importance, cannot touch the only authentic reality. This assertion is precisely what we discover when we reach the intelligible core of hope; what characterises it is *the very movement by which it challenges the evidence upon which men claim to challenge it itself.* We must add that this conception of hope is both symbolised and supported by all experiences of renewal, not considered in their philosophical or even physical processes, but in the infinite echo which they awaken in those who are called upon either to live through them directly, or to share sympathetically in the blessings they bring. So what we said above about the relationship which hope establishes between the soul and time is elucidated and completed. Might we not say that hope always implies the super-logical connection between a return *(nostos)* and something completely new *(Kaïnon ti)*? Following from this it is to be wondered whether preservation or restoration, on the one hand, and revolution or renewal on the other, are not the two movements, the two abstractly dissociated aspects of one and the same unity, which dwells in hope and is beyond the reach of all our faculties of reasoning or of conceptual formulation. This aspiration can be approximately expressed in the simple but contradictory words: *as before, but differently and better than before.* Here we undoubtedly come once again upon the theme of liberation, for it is never a simple return to the *status quo,* a simple return to our being; it is that and much more, and even the contrary of that: an undreamed-of promotion, a transfiguration.

Perhaps after these considerations we might at last attempt to give the definition which we would not allow ourselves to place at the beginning of our analysis: we might say that hope is essentially the availability of a soul which has entered intimately enough into the experience of communion to accomplish in the teeth of will and knowledge the transcendent act – the act establishing the vital regeneration of which this experience affords both the pledge and the first-fruits.

Le Peuch.
January, 1942.

To JULIEN LANDE

THE MYSTERY OF THE FAMILY[1]

Clearly I owe you a few words of explanation concerning the title
under which this lecture has been announced. I must admit that it
is rather a surprising title, which may seem oddly sensational. Why
not have called our discussion "The Problem of the Family"? For
numerous reasons: first, the family does not suggest just one problem, but an infinity of problems of every description which could
not be considered as a whole; you have already heard several of
them discussed with a competence which I lack. But it is above all
because the family seems to me to belong to an order of realities, or
I should rather say of presences, which can only create problems in
so far as we are mistaken, not so much with regard to their special
character, as to the way in which we human beings are involved in
them. I apologise for being obliged to quote myself here; for I need
to employ a distinction which I attempted about ten years ago to
introduce into the domain of concrete philosophy and of which the
importance still seems to me considerable.

I said that there can only be a problem for me where I have to
deal with facts which are, or which I can at least cause to be, exteri-
or to myself; facts presenting themselves to me in a certain disorder
for which I struggle to substitute an orderliness capable of satisfying the requirements of my thought. When this substitution has
been effected the problem is solved. As for me, who devote myself
to this operation, I am outside (above or below, if you like) the facts
with which it deals. But when it involves realities closely bound up

1   Lecture given to *L'Ecole des Hautes Etudes Familiales* at Lyons and at
    Toulouse in 1942.

with my existence, realities which unquestionably influence my existence as such, I cannot conscientiously proceed in this way. That is to say, I cannot make an abstraction of myself, or, if you like, bring about this division between myself on the one hand and some ever-present given principle of my life on the other; I am effectively and vitally involved in these realities. This holds good for instance in the case of the union of body and soul, or, in more precise terms, the bond which unites me to my body. I cannot make of this bond a pure idea to be placed in front of me and considered as an object, without misunderstanding its essential nature. Thus it follows that every term by which I try to qualify it as a relationship or to determine its function will invariably prove to be inadequate: I cannot exactly say that I am master of my body, or that I am the slave of my body, or that I own my body. All these relationships are true at once, which amounts to saying that each one of them taken by itself is false, that it does not so much *translate* as it *traduces* a certain fundamental unity. This unity is less a *given* principle than a *giving* one, because it is the root from which springs the fact of my presence to myself and the presence of all else to me. Thus it encroaches upon its own data and, invading them, passes beyond the range of a simple problem. It is in this very definite sense that the family is a mystery, and it is for this reason that we cannot properly and without confusion treat it simply as a question to be solved. Anticipating what is coming later, I want to point out right away that there is a deep similarity between the union of soul and body and the mystery of the family. In both cases we are in the presence of the same fact, or rather of something which is far more than a fact since it is the very condition of all facts whatever they may be: I mean incarnation. I am not, of course, using this term in its theological sense. It is not a question of our Lord's coming into the world, but of the infinitely mysterious act by which an essence assumes a body, an act around which the meditation of a Plato crystallised, and to which modern philosophers only cease to give their attention in so far as they have lost the intelligence's essential gift, that is to say the faculty of wonder.

I assure you that I am not proposing to introduce anything in the nature of an exposition of doctrine here. I am dealing rather with a series of *enquiries* leading us towards a point which thought could not reach directly. Why? Because this point is situated at the same time too close up to us and too far away to be found in the strictly limited zone of objective knowledge. I have said too close and too far away, but, in reality, these contraries are found to coincide here, and I am inclined to think that this coincidence of that which is quite close and that which is infinitely far away is precisely what characterises every kind of mystery, even religious mysteries, which we are not dealing with here.

On the one hand, when I speak of my family, the primitive idea this word evokes is that of a certain pattern or constellation of which, as a child, I spontaneously take it for granted that I am the centre. Am I not the object of all those solicitous glances which sometimes touch me, sometimes overwhelm and sometimes irritate me, glances of which not a shadow escapes me for they all seem to be aimed at me personally in the same way as the voices whose inflections pass from gentleness to severity, from persuasion to threats. It is only little by little that I discern the relationships which bind these beings to each other, thereby discovering that each one has his own life, his inviolable relationships with all the others, and also that for some of them I am a cause of preoccupation and a subject of discussion when I am not present, so that, I only receive a partial presentation, an adaptation for my personal use, of the thoughts and feelings which I arouse in these beings of whom only one side, and that always the same, is turned towards me. From this moment, everything becomes strangely complicated, new relationships are formed between them and me. If I have found that they are hiding themselves from me, how can I avoid the temptation of hiding myself from them in my turn? But at the same time strange contours appear in my personal life, it becomes furrowed with valleys and split up into compartments as well. The simple unspoilt countryside of my first years becomes complicated and clouded over. My family draws away from me, while remaining as near and as much a part of myself as ever: a tearing process? Let us rather say a traumatisation as difficult to heal as possible. That is not all, it is not even the beginning. Under the abstract words of paternity and sonship, I have gradually come to guess at occult and forbidden realities which make my soul dizzy. They attract me, but because they attract me, and because I think I should commit a sacrilege if I gave in to this attraction, I turn away from them. At the very least, I come to believe that, far from being endowed with an absolute existence of my own, I *am*, without having originally wished or suspected it, I *incarnate* the reply to the reciprocal appeal which two beings flung to each other in the unknown and which, without suspecting it, they flung beyond themselves to an incomprehensible power whose only expression is the bestowal of life. I *am* this reply, unformed at first, but who, as I become articulate, will know myself to be a reply and a judgment. Yes, I am irresistibly led to make the discovery that by being what I am, I myself am a judgment upon those who have called me into being; and thereby infinite new relationships will be established between them and me.

On the other hand, I have to recognise that behind the lighted but much restricted zone which I call my family there stretches, to infinitude, ramifications which in theory at any rate I can follow out tirelessly. Only in theory, however, for in fact an impenetrable darkness envelops this *upstream* region of myself and prevents me from exploring any further. I can discern enough, however, to enable me to follow this umbilical cord of my temporal antecedents, and to see it taking shape before me yet stretching back beyond my life in an indefinite network which, if traced to its limits, would probably be co-extensive with the human race itself. My family, or rather my lineage, is the succession of historical processes by which the human species has become individualised into the singular creature that I am. All that it is possible for me to recognise in this growing and impressive indetermination is that all these unknown beings, who stretch between me and my unimaginable origins whatever they may be, are not simply the causes of which I am the effect or the product: there is no doubt that the terms cause and effect have no meaning here. Between my ancestors and myself a far more obscure and intimate relationship exists. I share with them as they do with me – invisibly; they are consubstantial with me and I with them.

By this inextricable combination of things from the past and things to come, the mystery of the family is defined – a mystery in which I am involved from the mere fact that I exist: here, at the articulation of a structure of which I can only distinguish the first traces, of a feeling which modulates between the intimate and the metaphysical – and of an oath to be taken or refused binding me to make my own the vague desire around which the magical fomentation of my personal existence is centred. Such is the situation in which I find myself, I, a creature precipitated into the tumult; thus am I introduced into this impenetrable world.

To evoke the mystery of the family is then far less to attempt to resolve a problem than to try to recapture a reality and to awaken the soul to its presence. The consciousness of this reality has become tragically obliterated during several generations, and its clouding over has been one of the contributory causes for the precipitation of men into the hell where they are struggling today.

But this evocation, which appears to be simple enough, is in reality extraordinarily difficult to accomplish. For a mysterious reality can only be made actual for him who not only rediscovers it but who has the sudden consciousness of having rediscovered it, simultaneously realising that previously he had entirely lost sight of it. I have to strive then to make you aware of this negative evidence, thankless as such an undertaking may appear.

Nothing seems to me to give more direct evidence of the blindness from which a great number of our contemporaries are suffering in the matters we are considering today than the increasing number of controversies of a strictly spectacular order which arose in the period between the wars, whether in the Press or in public meetings, in connection with marriage, divorce, the choice of a lover, the practices of birth-control, etc. For whom, before what sort of spectators, did this ceaseless and all too often poisonous controversial stream flow? Before idlers, more and more incapable of living, I will not say their life, but *a* life of any sort, who led a ridiculous and sinister existence on the margin of reality, waifs without knowing it, shipwrecked mariners who did not even know that their ship was lost. These puppets made no effort to grasp a truth and derive nourishment from it, but they had an unhealthy craving to hear what they called a discussion of ideas. A discussion, that is to say a clash of ideas, not dealing with experience, for all experience worthy of the name has a certain weight and value – but professions of faith, challenges, prosecutions. Everything that happened in this realm seemed to show that a flow of words and argumentation were the actual sign of a total absence of experience and genuine thought. No doubt I shall be stopped here: "Are you not tending," it may be asked, "to exaggerate arbitrarily the importance of discussions which have never held the attention of the sane and healthy elements in our country? The family is not an institution which has lost its meaning, it is still a living reality. We only need to look around us. How many families, even during this lamentable period, kept their vitality and preserved their unity!" I think that we must stop here and fearlessly face some very painful truths. Certainly there is no question of denying for one moment that a great number of people – mainly but not exclusively Christians – have preserved the meaning of family life in spite of the unwearied efforts of propaganda of every description which tried systematically to weaken it. Nevertheless we cannot fail to recognise the seriousness of the crisis which has begun in our time, a dangerous and perhaps in the long run a mortal crisis, as is proved by incontestable statistics: the huge increase of divorce, the general spreading of abortive practices, etc. These are facts which force us to penetrate deeper in order to expose the roots of these "social facts," roots which are to be found at the actual level of belief, or more exactly, *unbelief* where, for my part, I am inclined to see a cardinal principle of the spiritual biology of our era. These are the roots which the philosopher has to discover with the cool self-possession of a surgeon making an incision into a wound.

May I at this point be allowed a short digression, which actually is not a digression at all?

When I recall my experience as a member of the university and that of some of my friends, I see that it had become increasingly difficult to deal with problems concerning the family before a class of young students. I remember very well the embarrassment I felt on a particular occasion when it fell to me to speak of divorce, not simply as a recognised fact but as a practice which, taken all round, is disastrous and blameworthy. I knew quite well that I had in front of me the sons of divorced parents and that there was a risk of their bringing all the weight of my judgments against their parents, unless they revolted, as indeed they had a right to do, against strictures involving their most private feelings – feelings which indeed had to be respected. On these grounds, what a temptation there was to maintain a prudent reserve and to keep to vague and meaningless generalities! But on the other hand how can we help seeing that if these great realities of marriage, generation, etc., are not approached directly and with fearless sincerity, they degenerate into nothing but material for rhetorical arguments. Conventionality is thus substituted for life, conventionality of which for my part I shall never weary of denouncing the poisonous influence, for it will never be anything but a waste product of thought, something which cannot be assimilated. This then is the dilemma confronting so many of those responsible for education at the present time. Should we, with no fear of appearing dogmatic, courageously tackle these questions while in so doing we risk upsetting and scandalising impressionable young beings; or should we confine ourselves to the hollowest of phrases or to historical or so-called historical facts and thus, in the latter case, help to encourage the loose relativity which has tended in our day to weaken all real moral judgment so prejudicially? If I insist thus on a difficulty which only seems to affect specialists, it is because I see in it a symptom revealing a state of things so grave that we can no longer shut our eyes to it. If we took the trouble to consult the textbooks of morals and sociology which for twenty years or more were in favour with the high priests of official teaching, we should see to what an extent they encouraged the tendency to view problems in an almost exclusively historical setting and to emphasise the changing character of family institutions ever destined to grow more flexible. This tendency cannot be compensated for by what is at bottom no more than the wordy and superfluous reiteration of a few general principles earmarked by an out-worn rationalism. We might already notice at this point, so that we can probably return to it later, that, by a paradox worthy of our attention, these sociological moralists came in the end to preach the most disintegrating individualism, whilst all the time proclaiming and heralding the establishment of a socialism which was to subordinate personal initiative, in every field, to State control.

It will doubtless be objected that I am referring here to a period of our history which is happily passed and that for the last two years a vigorous and healthy reaction has taken place concerning this point and a great many others in favour of what we sometimes rather ingenuously term "right-mindedness." I most certainly do not wish to underestimate the importance and value of this reaction. It seems to me, all the same, that we must be careful to avoid an optimism which might have many disappointments in store for us. The multiplication of catchwords and well-known slogans in official speeches and in the Press should not mislead us. There is nothing there to lead us to believe in an effective conversion of hearts and minds: it is certainly not by mere methods of publicity that we shall succeed in reaching the most deep and hidden springs of individual wills. It is even permissible to fear that there may be a serious relapse and that the evils, from which we have already suffered so much, will reappear later with increased violence.

What is needed first of all is that by reflection, the only weapon at our disposal, we should project as clear a light as possible upon the tragic situation in which so many are living. These people are unable to explain to themselves a vital uneasiness, an anguish of which it is only in their power to grasp the most exterior causes or the most superficial symptoms. It seems to me that we should indeed be setting to work in the wrong way if we started merely from a moral crisis, from the increasingly deliberate repudiation of general principles which would have been accepted without question up to a certain time in history. I should prefer to say that these principles are in themselves nothing but the approximate and imperfect expression of a certain mental attitude towards life. It is in reality this attitude itself which has been transformed. In order to make the meaning of the words I am using more precise, I suggest that what has come about is much more a vital weakening than a transgression, or a denial. In a fine passage, recently quoted by Mr. Albert Béguin, the great Swiss author Ramuz, writing some years ago, spoke of a certain sense of holiness "which is the most precious thing the West has known, a certain attitude of reverence for existence – by which we must understand everything which exists, oneself and the world outside oneself, the mysteries which surround us, the mystery of death, and the mystery of birth, a certain veneration in the presence of life, a certain love, and (why not acknowledge it?) a certain state of poetry which the created world produces in us." It is precisely this sense of holiness, this fundamental reverence for life and for death, itself considered as the nocturnal phase of life, it is this state of poetry produced in us by the created world which, during the last decades, and more particularly of recent years, has given way to the pressure of pride, of pretentiousness, of boredom and despair; and for reasons, which will very easily appear on analysis, it is in the domain of family reality that the dire consequences of this giving way have first become apparent, actually threatening more and more directly the integrity of the individual considered in his structure and his own particular destiny.

He who refuses to face the danger goes on obstinately repeating that the family exists. But the word to exist is here the most equivocal and therefore the most deceptive of terms. If the family is a reality it cannot be simply expressed or objectively established like a simple succession. Let us even insist that it is infinitely more than what appears from pure and simple entries in civil registers. It exists only on condition that it is apprehended not only as a value but as a living presence.

A value first of all. I think that here we must make an attempt to relive – but in such a way that we think it out and elucidate it – an experience which was shared by most of us when we were children, an experience which it is actually very difficult not to distort when we try to express it, because it includes a certain pride. This pride if we are not careful might seem to be confused with vanity, but this is a degradation of it. We are proud to belong to a certain community because we feel that something of its lustre falls upon us. Pride, as I recently had occasion to write, is a certain response made from the depths of my being to an investiture of which it behoves me to prove myself worthy. Such pride is experienced on my own account. It in no way aims at impressing some other person with the awe and fear which would flatter me. Thus it is a constructive sentiment, helping to give me inner foundations on which to establish my conduct. Vanity, on the other hand, by the very fact that it is turned outwards towards the rest of the world, is essentially sterile, or even, in the last analysis, disintegrating. But it is through this sentiment of pride that we can trace in what way the family is a value. It is a recognised hierarchy, and I do not merely have to integrate myself into it by recognising the authority vested in its leader; I have actually been caught up in it from the origin. I am involved in it, my very being is rooted in it. This hierarchy cannot fail, this authority cannot be abolished without the family bringing about its own destruction as a value. After that, in my eyes, it can no longer be anything but a net in which I feel I have been caught by mistake and out of which there is nothing left for me but to extricate myself as soon as possible.

In speaking of a presence, I introduce a somewhat different shade of meaning here, which it will be as well to explain more precisely. Again in this case each one of us must refer back to his childhood memories which, when we are dealing with realities of this sort, seem to me to play the part belonging to reminiscence in the philosophy of Plato. Each of us, with the exception of a few rare and unhappy individuals, has, at least on certain occasions, been able to *prove by experience* the existence of the family as a protective skin placed between himself and a world which is foreign, threatening, hostile to him. And there is no doubt that nothing is more painful in the destiny of an individual than the tearing away of this tissue, either by a sudden or a slow and continuous process, carried out by the pitiless hands of life or death, or rather of that nameless power of which life and death are but alternating aspects. The similes associated with and alas! abused by a feebly sentimental or didactic kind of poetry, the similes of cocoon, nest or cradle are those which most exactly illustrate what I should be ready to term the downy element in the reality of the family.

But here by an analytical effort we must free ourselves from metaphors themselves. We must make ourselves aware of the primitive *us*, this archetypal and privileged *us* which is only normally realised in family life. This *us* is in general inseparable from a *home of our own*. It is certainly not by chance if all the forces which have been working towards the destruction of the family house have at the same time been preparing for the overthrow of the family itself. This privileged *us* cannot, even on the humblest levels of this life of consciousness, be separated from a permanent habitation which is ours and which in the course of our existence has gradually become consubstantial with us. The spontaneous and immediate consciousness of an *always*, a perpetual life, is associated with the familiar objects among which we live, with the setting in which daily tasks are carried out, with the feelings which can scarcely be formulated of a tutelary presence incarnated in these things and in this background and which, as it were, deepens and colours the daily outlook. All this seems to me in principle indissolubly bound up with the existence of the family considered both as a fact and a value. I want no other proof than the one (negative it is true) afforded by the mental upheaval, and often the heartbreak, so frequently brought upon a child by the common enough event of a house-move. It is brought upon a child and often enough even upon an adult if he has kept the childlike character, the tenderness of tissue which persists in some people throughout all the battering and bruising of personal experience. But inversely we must recognise that all which tends to destroy the sense of a habitation and of permanence in the surroundings of a being in process of formation will contribute directly to the weakening of his consciousness of the family itself. In passing, I may say that I am convinced that therein lies one of the chief causes of the disappearance of family consciousness among the working population of the great industrial centres, where nomadic life, not of tent and caravan, but of lodgings and furnished rooms, is the order of the day. The family tends to become simply an abstract idea instead of the very essence of the atmosphere a human being almost unconsciously inhales, an essence which imperceptibly impregnates and saturates his thinking, his appreciation and his love.

You may say that all these remarks only bear upon the outward and temporary conditions of life. But the more one strives to understand the meaning of existence, the more surely one is led to the conclusion that the outward is also the inward, or rather to the realisation that this distinction has no meaning where the actual growth of a being is involved. It is moreover obvious that the disappearance of the settled habitation, or rather of the home, is inseparable from the fading away of traditions. Actually these traditions are to the inner man what the family setting is to the visible one. We cannot just say they are his environment; they help to form him. Without them there is a risk of his becoming the plaything of every chance influence; his development is exposed to all the dangers of incoherence. But the traditions of which I am here thinking bear upon the continuity of the family itself: they are first of all the records and examples which secure the bond between the generations. But there is yet another thing: every family which has real vitality produces a certain ritual without which it would be in

danger of eventually losing its solid foundations. It is all this delicate architecture which is compromised and which, for nearly a
century, has been cracking. Why? The reasons for this decrepitude
appear to me to be very varied and to go very deep. Some are obvious. They have to do with ideology, with the diffusion of a mythology of which revolutionary spirits of every description have made
themselves the channels. Some of them can scarcely be analysed.
But we can say with certainty that the amazing transformation of
the material conditions of life brought about by the industrial revolution tends to relegate to an almost legendary distance those who
lived, thought and struggled before it. This upheaval was in reality
too complete, too massive to be understood by those very people
who witnessed it, and who became its victims instead of gaining
anything from it. It was first of all a change of rhythm. Men were
not able to recognise it; rather, they submitted to it by an inner
adaptation, and this was not effected without causing the most serious psychological damage in many cases, and bringing about a real
deterioration of the mental fibre. It was inevitable that this extraordinary acceleration of the rhythm of life should tend more and more
to prevent the slow sedimentation of *habitus* which seems surely to
have been from all time the essential condition at the origin of all
realities connected with the family. Still more, such an acceleration
could not take place without a reckless waste of the reserves slowly accumulated by living. Gustave Thibon in some illuminating
passages has brought out most marvellously this tragic aspect of
contemporary life. He denounces the fearful squandering of
reserves which has taken place before our eyes; he points out most
clearly that we are in danger of causing the worst possible confusion by preaching the duty of improvidence; for it is essential to
make "the distinction between the improvidence of the saint who
does not worry about the future because he has laid up his treasure,
the source of eternity and life, within him, and the improvidence of
the decadent man whose unstable soul has become the plaything of
the moment and of every passing temptation, and who, equally
incapable of waiting or of making a decision, constantly yields to
the *immediate* suggestions of an egoism without sequence or unity.
For the least economical person is also the most selfish. To
economise in the sane and strict sense of the word means above all:

to keep in order to give more effectively. No doubt there is a fore-sight which is miserly and self-contained, which is opposed to true human exchanges. But its legitimate child, absolute improvidence, is perhaps even more the enemy of giving and communion. In the material order, as in the spiritual, liberality and munificence are only possible for him whose strict vigilance has been able to create large reserves within and around himself. Such virtues have died out today."

Let us here notice that the great contemplative, in whom reflection and vision have become fused, is capable of unlocking doors which are hidden from the vulgar gaze. Technical progress, considered not in itself, not of course from the point of view of the principles which made it possible, but as we see it incorporated into the daily life of individuals, has not been effected without the loss of human substance. This loss is indeed its none too easily detected counterpart. It is on the plane of craftsmanship that this loss of substance appears most clearly. But where it is a question of secret relationships between people, the ravages brought about by the technical revolution are harder to recognise and to understand. It is certain that they are due in great measure to the growing standardisation of individuals for which the first responsibility is to be laid at the door of far too uniform an education, having much too little respect for local customs and peculiarities. Then there is the Press, whose degraded character can never be denounced resolutely enough. In addition there is a close connection between the acceleration of the rhythm of life and the appearance of a humanity which is inwardly more and more impoverished, more and more interchangeable. A metaphor, or rather an analogy will show what I mean. To take some region full of an inner soul, such as Brittany, for example; is it not noticeable that when we cross it rapidly it seems to be emptied of this spiritual quality, this mystery, which however we rediscover if we take the trouble to go through the country in a leisurely manner? The phenomenon which I have in mind here is of the same order, but it touches on human reality where being and appearing can never be truly separated. Moreover, even the mystery of places always conceals a human presence, maybe diffused; things are impregnated with the feelings they once awoke in souls. It is from the point of view of a philosophy of duration that we can succeed in understanding the unity, I would even go so far as to say the identity, of two phenomena which, for a superficial observer appear at first to be distinct. I mean to say on the one hand the depopulation of the country, and on the other the dissolution of the family. I think then that I shall not be wandering from my subject, if I try to expose the tragic inner reality of which these two phenomena are but two inseparable aspects.

Let us notice, first of all, that existence in towns makes a certain pretension, at any rate implicitly, of triumphing over the laws of alternation to which living beings are subject. The town-dweller strives, without the slightest success be it well understood, to inaugurate an order of life wherein there are no seasons. It is a lamentable and ridiculous application of the fateful sentence, *eritis sicut dei:* you shall be *as* gods, you shall be set free from the vicissitudes to which the animal world is subject. The large American cities are, as it were, the prototypes of a world where preservative processes, forcing and fakes are employed to provide specious satisfactions for the need we have developed to escape from the cosmic rhythm and to substitute for it I know not what inventions caricaturing the eternity for which we still yearn nostalgically. But hard experience seems to show that this exclusively human rhythm tends in fact to become that of a machine or an automaton, for it is a rhythm which is not super-organic but sub-organic. Thus the danger arises of a most fatal disorder invading the very heart of existence, for the man who is apparently striving to become a machine is nevertheless alive, although he ignores more and more systematically his condition as a living being. The inexpressible sadness which emanates from great cities, a dismal sadness which belongs to everything that is devitalised, everything that represents a self-betrayal of life, appears to me to be bound up in the most intimate fashion with the decay of the family. This sadness is sterility, it is a disavowal felt by the heart; a disavowal which, as we shall see more and more clearly, concerns the very conditions of life. It is really a question of what we might be tempted to call the very colour of existence; but yet we must understand that a colour can be looked at and as it were absorbed by the eye, whilst what we are dealing with is lived experience as such. In order to make my meaning clearer I will ask you to think of those changes, at first almost imperceptible, which tend to weaken the ties between us and our near ones. Each of us knows from experience how an intimacy can lose its transparency, how the current bearing two beings and uniting them dynamically can lose its fluidity, so that the individualities, which a moment ago still felt themselves to be fused and enveloped in the bosom of a tutelary and vivifying element, are now separated, colliding with each other in a succession of instantaneous clashes, each as brutally hurtful as a blow. I cannot help thinking that during the last centuries of our civilisation a dislocation of the same kind has taken place between man and life, and it is related to the obscure and organic misunderstandings in which so many married existences come to ruin. Thus the family has been attacked in the double spring whence it derives its special vitality: fidelity and hope.

The idea which I want to bring out here is difficult and from the rational point of view almost impossible to grasp, so, in order to avoid expressing it in academic terms which might distort it, I propose to say quite simply how it was recently borne in upon me in a concrete form.

We had just been through one of those almost completely depopulated villages which are to be found in hundreds in the departments of the south-west. A woman with whom we had exchanged a few words had complained to us of the quietness of the place, of the monotony and lack of amusements. Suddenly my thoughts were concentrated on everything which this word amusements stands for. "Assuredly," I said to myself, "it is above all the search for amusements which sends the villagers away to the towns. On the other hand, as these out-of-the-way places become more and more empty, life in them becomes more and more boring so that in a way the exodus creates its own justification. But in reality what do we mean by amusements? Amusement is diversion, a turning away, but what from? And how does the need for diversion show itself? This is the real problem. It is only too clear that the town with its 'amusements' has exercised a regular power of suction over the country districts; we might also say that the town dweller has brought about a gradual contamination of the peasant. But all the same, the soul of the peasant, which held out so long against this infection, had to become open to it. It is said, not without reason, that the uncomfortable conditions which are so frequent in the country, the lack of air and of light in the cottages, etc., have helped to depopulate the fields. But why have the inhabitants not devoted their energy to improving their rural dwellings as in certain mountainous districts such as the Grisons or the Tyrol? It is not enough to speak here of a certain natural laziness, there had to be a preliminary disaffection before this disastrous diversion could take place. And once more the question confronts me with an irritating persistency; diversion? Why do they seek it, from what do they turn away? How can we help seeing that the question is identically the same as that which confronts us when we enquire into the causes of the breaking up of the family?" Immediately, however, I saw the answer with a clarity which since that time has never been eclipsed. The need for amusement, as each of us knows from his own experience, is bound up with a certain ebbing of life's tide. But this is still insufficient and even ambiguous. It may indeed happen that vitality decreases without the manifestation of this need, and on the contrary this decrease may even result in the disappearance of all curiosity: indifference settles down on the soul, the being reacts less and less, he gives himself over to debility, he covers himself with veils. The ebb of life of which we are thinking here is quite different in character. The being imagines he regains his life by seizing every occasion of experiencing violent sensations of no matter what order. But these so-called stimulants afford but precarious protection against boredom. What then is this boredom? One of the most intelligent men of our time who held an important post in the government until these last weeks, said to me shortly before the war: "France is suffering from a metaphysical malady: she is bored." It was a diagnosis which went deep and which I have never forgotten – a diagnosis which has been tragically confirmed by our misfortunes. At the origin of diversion, of the will to be diverted or amused at any price, there is an attempt to escape, but from what? It can only be from oneself. The *ego* is without any doubt faced with a dilemma: to fulfil itself or to escape. Where it does not attain fulfilment, it is only conscious of itself as of an unendurable gaping void from which it must seek protection at any price. Anyone who is absorbed does not know this void; he is as it were caught up in plenitude, life envelops him and protects him. Boredom, on the contrary, is not only bound up with inaction but with a dismantling process. Thus we can very well understand that in the country the woman is far more subject to it than the man. If it is true to say that she suffers more than he does from discomfort and inconvenience, it is because she has more time to think about such things, unless she is continually taken up by the incessant occupations of motherhood, which actually means that these tasks are not only a burden but a support for her. "One is borne along only by one's responsibilities," Gabriel Séailles said most excellently. If we start from this point we can understand the causes of the ebbing of life or rather of consciousness, wherein this consciousness comes gradually to repudiate its fundamental commitments. What then are its commitments? Here we are coming down to essentials.

It seems as though it were necessary to postulate the existence of a pact, I should almost say a nuptial bond, between man and life; it is in man's power to untie this bond, but in so far as he denies the pact he tends to lose the notion of his existence. What is exactly to be understood by this bond? I may be accused of being led away by a metaphor, of unduly exaggerating abstractions. But however we interpret this fact philosophically, we must recognise that man is a being – and the only one we know – capable of adopting an attitude towards his life, not only his own life, but life in itself. He is then not a mere living being, he is, or rather he has become, something more, and we might say that it is through this faculty for adopting an attitude that he is a spirit. M. Jean Lacroix in his fine book *Personne et Amour* very rightly reminds us that one of the essential characteristics of man is his ability to expose himself voluntarily to death. This is, however, only a particular expression, the most striking of all, of a much more general truth – the truth of his transcendance over life and death. A human act, whatever it may be, presupposes it. It is this which makes it really possible and even legitimate to speak of man and of life as of two realities which are not confused or which have ceased to be confused. From this it follows that in speaking of a pact between man and life we have in mind on the one hand the confidence which man promises life and which makes it possible for him to give himself to life, and on the other hand the response of life to this confidence of man. But it is precisely the family, considered in relation to the act by which it is constituted, which shows us the working out of this pact, for it is in fact the pact's incarnation.

And it is inversely in the acts by which families are disunited that the breaking of this same pact takes place before our eyes. It is not difficult to illustrate this very general idea by concrete examples.

The essential act which constitutes marriage is obviously not the pure and simple mating which is only a human act, common alike to men and animals; it is not just a momentary union, but one which is *to last*; it is something which is established. A family is founded, it is erected like a monument whose hewn stone is neither the satisfaction of an instinct, nor the yielding to an impulse, nor the indulgence of a caprice. From this point of view we should probably not hesitate to say that there are innumerable false marriages (of course, I am not using these words in the sense of "faux ménages"). I am thinking here of those unions which are perfectly legal, but where there is nothing in the inward depths of character, nothing in the very centre of the will which corresponds to the socially binding form or even, alas, to the strictly sacramental character of the union entered into. It is more than probable that in a society where divorce is not only accepted, but regarded in many circles as a more or less normal contingency, a time must inevitably come when the irresponsibility with which so many unbelievers lightly and heedlessly get married, is communicated from one to another until it infects even those who by tradition, human respect or some remnant of faith are still impelled to take a vow of fidelity in the presence of God, only to find out too late that by this contradiction they are themselves caught in a trap from which it is not possible to escape except at the price of a scandalous renunciation or dishonourable subterfuge.

Here we must also touch on the difficult question of knowing whether the bond of marriage can really be compared with a simple contract. I must own that on this point the opinion of jurists matters little to me, for it seems very probable that reflection should here be free of the categories which they employ. Indeed, the more marriage is regarded as a simple contract, the more one must logically come to admit that it can be renounced by common accord, that it can even become no more than a temporary promise. The more one forms an exclusively rational idea of marriage, the more one is led, not perhaps theoretically but in fact, not only to admit divorce as, at the most, a possibility in exceptional cases, but to

incorporate with one's notion of the marriage bond the idea that it
can be revoked. Or alternatively one may proclaim that in the interests of society the individual should be sacrificed in this as in many
other matters to the agonising pressure of convention. But this solution which may perhaps satisfy the legislator or the sociologist has
the serious defect of setting up the most tyrannical heteronomy in
the realm where the individual person seems most justified in
claiming his inalienable right to be an exception.

The only condemnation of divorce which can be justified, at
least in theory, in the eyes of those very people who suffer most
under it, is the condemnation which they must recognise as being
pronounced in the name of *their own* will – a will so deep that they
could not disown it without denying their own natures. If one postulates that in principle the conjugal union finds its consummation,
and even its sanction, in the appearance of a new being in which the
husband and wife fulfil and pass beyond themselves, it becomes
obviously absurd to consider it quite natural that this same married
couple should become free again whenever the sentiments which
prevailed at their union change for some reason or another. They
are no longer simply united by a reciprocal act which by common
accord they can annul, but by the existence of a being for whom
they are responsible and who has rights over them which cannot be
set aside – unless we are cynically to argue from the fact that in the
animal species there comes a moment when male and female lose
all interest in their offspring because it no longer needs them. One
can scarcely deny, I fear, that the innumerable human beings who
today invent for themselves the most loose conception of the married state, argue from the example of the animals to justify themselves. Moreover it is worth noticing how easy it is to slide from
what professes to be a completely rational notion of marriage to the
grossest form of naturalism which claims to remove all lines of
demarcation between man and other living creatures, in order that
he may enjoy all the licence which goes with the natural state. But
we know only too well the aberrations people can fall into when
they claim to draw positive conclusions concerning what can and
should be considered natural and consequently justifiable, particularly in matters of sex, from their observations of animal habits.

We can in reality be certain that where the mind oscillates

between an abstract formalism and an animalism with pretensions of a pseudo-scientific or poetically mystical nature, it condemns itself to lose sight of the unity apart from which it is impossible to think of the mystery of the family. "The heads of families, those great adventures of the modern world," said Péguy. What does this mean except that a family is not created or maintained as an entity without the exercise of a fundamental generosity whose rightly metaphysical principle must be examined. We must, of course, leave on one side the man who generates by chance, who produces his offspring like the animals without accepting the consequences of his act. He does not found a family; he produces a brood. In the true head of a family, the harmony which is attained between consciousness and the life force is established in a sphere which is not easily accessible to us by analysis. Perhaps there is even a danger that such a method might prevent us from understanding how this harmony is possible. As is so often the case, our thought has to work negatively and can only reach its objective by exclusion.

It is obvious on the one hand, as we have seen, that where the family is conceived as a reality any idea of marriage as a mere association of individual interests must be ruled out. It seems as though the marriage must in some way regulate itself in relation to the offspring, for whose coming preparation has to be made; but it is not less certain, and this observation is of the greatest importance here, that a marriage concluded simply with a view to procreation is not only in danger of degeneration because it does not rest on a firm spiritual basis, but, still more, it is an attack upon what is most worthy of reverence in the specifically human order. There is something which outrages the very dignity of the person when the joining of two beings is envisaged merely as a means of reproduction. The operation of the flesh is thus degraded and terrible revenge is in process of preparation for the time when the misunderstood and stifled powers in the depths of the human soul shake off the yoke which has been tragically imposed upon them. So it is certainly not true to say that procreation is the end of marriage. We must rather admit that both form complementary phases of a particular history which each one of us has to live out and through which he accomplishes his destiny as a creative being. The meaning of this word "creative" is very precise here: it denotes the active contribution each soul is at liberty to bring to the universal work which is accomplishing itself in our world and doubtless far beyond it. In this connection the condition of a human being of whatever kind is not essentially different from that of the artist who is the bearer of some message which he must communicate, of some flame which he must kindle and pass on, like the torch-bearers of Lucretia. Everything seems to happen as though on the human level the operation of the flesh ought to be the hallowing of a certain inward fulfilment, an out-flowing not to be forced since it springs from an experience of plentitude. Perhaps I should make myself better understood by saying in a way which actually is not exclusively Christian that the operation of the flesh loses its dignity and degenerates from its true nature if it is not an act of thanksgiving, a creative testimony. But, from this point of view, what a deep difference we must establish between husbands and wives who prudently secure for themselves an heir to succeed them, an heir who is nothing but a representative or a substitute for them – and those who, in a sort of prodigality of their whole being, sow the seed of life without ulterior motive by radiating the life flame which has permeated them and set them aglow.

These observations, which actually should be infinitely shaded, make it possible to catch a glimpse of the meaning of the sacred bond which it is man's lot to form with life, or, on the other hand, to stretch to a breaking-point after which he remains alone in a darkened and defiled universe.

There is assuredly a sense in which it is absolutely true to say that in such a realm all generalisations are deceptive. It is not even enough to remember that there are only particular cases. The truth is rather that there are no cases at all, each soul, each individual destiny constitutes a microcosm, governed by laws which, at least to a certain degree, are only valid for that soul. Hence it follows that in questions concerning particular people, such as a certain childless couple, or a family centred upon an only child, we have no right to judge. We never know – it is not our business to know – what disappointments, what secret trials underlie that which we might at first be tempted to condemn as selfishness, cowardice or voluntary sterility. And indeed we can be glad of it, for in principle it is intolerable and undistinguishable from the most odious pharisaism that any of us should invade the privacy of others with our judgments. We regain our right to judge, however, in matters concerned with realities of a social order, such as the increase of divorce, the spread in the use of contraceptives or the practice of abortion. We can above all exercise our judgment with full knowledge and complete justice against an abominable propaganda which aims at making such methods appear rationally justifiable.

But from my own point of view, it will be understood that the question is not really one of proclaiming the immoral or anti-social character of any action or conduct. I have rather to discuss the symptoms in such action or conduct of a disaffection of beings from Being which, to tell the truth, does not imply the denial of an explicitly formulated promise, but the drawing back by which a spiritual organism dwindles, shrivels, cuts itself off from the universal communion in which it found the nourishing principle of life and growth. But what we should notice here is that by a serious perversion of the mind this sclerosis is interpreted as an emancipation, this atrophy as a blossoming. This is the unforgivable sin of which a certain ideology has been guilty; they imagined that they were liberating the person when all the time they were suffocating it. To borrow the famous comparison of Kant, I should say that thinking to lighten the weight of the atmosphere which presses upon human souls, they have transported them into a rarefied medium, where it is not possible for them to breath normally. But what is tragic in the world of the soul is that there is no clear indication of mortal dangers as on the physical plane, where unmistakable symptoms or sufferings afford the most imperative of signals and force the organism to react. Here, alas! the coma of the dying can last for generations without the patient, misled by his physicians, realising his condition even in his death agony. Actually this expression is not strong enough, for the threat here is not merely that of death, which after all is essentially a purification; it is one of degradation and perversion under the innumerable forms possible to human nature, and these forms, by the very diversity of their character, are the counterpart or countersign of the dignity and vocation of man.

Perhaps we shall now be able to discuss why the mystery of the family can truly be said to be a mystery of fidelity and hope. Analysis shows that the crisis in our family institutions can be traced to a deeper and deeper misunderstanding of the virtues through which the unification of our destiny both terrestrial and super-terrestrial is consummated.

First of all a fundamental error or illusion must be disposed of concerning fidelity. We are too much inclined to consider it as a mere safeguard, an inward resolution which purposes simply to preserve the existing order. But in reality the truest fidelity is creative. To be sure of it, the best way is to strive to grasp the very complex bond which unites a child to its parents. There we have a relationship which is always exposed to a double risk of deterioration. Some, professing a strict and narrow traditionalism, tend to consider the child as entirely in the debt of those who gave it life; others, on the contrary, minimising this debt, if they do not actually deny it altogether, will tend to treat the child as the creditor, for they view life not as a blessing but a crushing burden which the parents in their heedless selfishness have placed on the shoulders of an innocent creature. I have already had occasion to remark that the phenomena of the breaking up of families which is increasing so rapidly at the present day is probably connected with this systematic depreciation of life. The advocates of birth control claim more or less sincerely that it is out of pity for their possible descendants that they refuse to give them the chance of existence; but we cannot help noticing, all the same, that this pity which is bestowed at small cost, not upon living beings but upon an absence of being or nothingness, is found in conjunction with a suspiciously good opportunity for indulging the most cynical egoism, and can scarcely be separated from an impoverished philosophy which measures the value of life by the pleasures and conveniences it provides. It is no less certain that pure traditionalism presents an inacceptable position here as elsewhere. Life, as it is transmitted in the act of procreation, is really neither a blessing nor a curse in itself. It is a possibility, an opportunity, a chance for good or evil. But this possibility is only achieved in so far as the being to whom it is granted appears from the moment of his birth as a subject, that is to say as able to enjoy and above all to suffer, and capable of one day attaining to the consciousness of what he has at first only felt. This being has to be armed in such a way that the two-sided possibility which has been given him appears to him as a precious opportunity when, on reaching the stage at which he adopts his own attitude to life, he can appreciate it. It is, then, the sacred duty of parents to behave in such a way towards their child, that one day it will have good reason to acknowledge that it is in their debt. But if ever they are to be justified in considering that they have a *credit* here it will be exclusively in so far as they have succeeded in discharging a debt themselves, which to tell the truth cannot be likened to a payment of account but rather to the production of a work of art where their only share is the laying of the foundations. This amounts to saying that the debt and credit are strictly correlated and connected together on the child's side quite as much as on that of the parents. But is not this to recognise implicitly that such categories are too narrow, that they are no longer applicable except where the mystery of the family has been somehow desecrated from within by beings who have ceased to share its life and have transported themselves onto a plane where each one demands his due? In the same order of ideas it is very interesting to notice that though these notions of credit and debt tend sometimes, alas, to be accepted in limited families where a special function seems to be vested in the child by his parents through a pseudo-agreement in which he will always be justified in saying he has had no part, they will be found quite inapplicable to large families where the husband and wife, with no niggardly calculations and no pretensions to dispose of life as of their savings, have generously given themselves up to the creative spirit which penetrated them. It is still necessary, of course, that the children should share in the spirit of the family. Unfortunately, it does not always follow that they do. If they allow themselves to become infected with the prevalent individualism they will be tempted in many cases to pose as the victims of the blameworthy thoughtlessness of those who brought them into the world. So then in the end everything comes back to the spirit which at the same time is to be incarnated or established, and maintained, the spirit spreading beyond the self; and it is precisely this spirit which is expressed by the words "creative fidelity." The more our hearts as well as our intellects keep before them the idea of our lineage, of the forbears to whom we are answerable – because in the last analysis it is from them that we receive the deposit which must be transmitted – the more this spirit will succeed in freeing itself from the shroud of selfishness and cowardice in which a humanity, more and more cut off from its ontological roots, is in danger of becoming gradually enveloped. Inversely, the more the sense of a lineage tends to be lost in the fading consciousness of a vague and nameless subsoil, the less the human soul will be able to discern its ultimate responsibilities and the more the family will tend to be reduced to an association with common interests, a sort of limited company of which it is lawful and even normal that the constitution should become increasingly flexible.

I think that it is indispensable here to stress the fact that creative fidelity such as I am trying to define depends in no way upon the acceptance of any special religious belief, although Christian dogma gives it a transcendent justification and adds infinitely to its splendour. We must, I think, recognise on the one hand that there exists a form of Christianity, heretical no doubt but all the same unimpeachable, which, by the predominance given to the eschatological side can dangerously weaken or even undermine the soul's love of life. This love of life I should readily call the ethico-lyrical impulse which controls the human swarm. Many souls under Jansenistic influence have no doubt succumbed to the temptation of abjuring what is human and deserting the earth, without perhaps getting much nearer to heaven by so doing. But, on the other hand, I should be quite disposed to think that a *religio* exists of which the pagans themselves have left us admirable signs, a reverence for the dead and for the gods presiding over the home which apart from any essentially Christian spirituality gives evidence of the pact between man and the life-force to which I have so often had occasion to refer: and it is only too easy to understand that where this *religio* has given way to the pitiless pressure, not of technics but of a mentality fascinated and unsettled by the progress of technics, we see as at the present time an increasing number of violations of that natural morality and order still recognised as such by our forefathers. I am tempted to think that it is this *religio* which we must first restore and that unfortunately a Christian super-structure, which only too often is nothing but a camouflage, can very well disguise how fatally it is lacking. Unquestionably this point seems to me the most important in the whole tangle of considerations which I have tried to set before you today. The men of my generation have seen carried out before their eyes with extraordinary tenacity a work of systematic subversion which is no longer directed against revealed doctrines or principles hallowed by tradition, but against nature itself. Man, whatever brainless biologists may think about him, will never be on the same level as the animals. Wherever he is truly himself, wherever he is faithful to his vocation, he is infinitely above them. Wherever he deliberately renounces his true calling, he falls infinitely below them. As for the humanism for little Voltaireans on the retired list, offered by those who advocate a return to the just mean, to average virtues, to prudent calculations and methodical precautions, we now know with tragic certainty that it is the tremulous forerunner of the worst individual and national disasters.

This is not all: if so many souls today seem to be deaf to the call of creative fidelity, it is because these souls have lost all sense of hope. I must here briefly recall the fundamental ideas which I developed a few weeks ago on this theological virtue, the mysterious source of human activity. I said that hope cannot be separated either from a sense of communion or from a more or less conscious and explicit dependence on a power which guarantees this communion itself. "I hope in Thee, for us," such is the authentic formula of hope. But the more this "for us" tends to confine itself to what concerns the self instead of opening onto the infinite, the more hope shrivels and deteriorates, and, in the domain of the family, the more it tends to degenerate into a shortsighted ambition and to fix its attention on ways of safeguarding and increasing a certain Having which actually need not take a grossly material form. But I added that it is only by breaking through Having that hope can effect an entrance into our soul. By the term Having I did not mean exclusively the visible possessions of which each of us can make an inventory, but rather the armour of good or bad habits, opinions and prejudices which makes us impervious to the breath of the spirit, everything in us which paralyses what the Apostle calls the liberty of the children of God. Perhaps in this connection it would be well to follow the example of one of the greatest thinkers of our day and to concentrate our attention on a central fact in the psychology of contemporary man; I mean anxiety, and particularly the anxiety which is less the result of bitter experience than a mortifying anticipation, the anxiety which is like the premature decay of those who have never lived. There is indeed scarcely one of the collective influences of this age which has not tended to mark the foreheads of our adolescents with the sign of this decay; school, the Press, forms of entertainment even, have helped to impair the youthful freshness, the candid voice, the limpid gaze, the purity of heart, without which youth ceases to be a quality and a grace and becomes no more than a title, a dimension entered on an identity card. It would be unpardonable to undervalue the reaction which has been taking place for the last few years in movements which are, or hope to be, the prelude to a renaissance in our unhappy country. But there is no disguising the fact that the task is crushing and is far beyond the power of the movements in question. The atmosphere is still saturated with germs of decay which can only be swept away by an entirely new spirit. I think it is clear that on the one hand such a renewal can only spring from a religious principle but that on the other it cannot surely be the work of Christians alone, if by that we mean those who are regular members of a definite church. Finally, I am persuaded that though we certainly do not want public authorities to be patrons, since this only too often compromises a movement, we can at least ask them not to paralyse the initiative of people of all complexions, as they unite in a common effort to stimulate and revivify society. It is very much to be feared, indeed, that the State, the modern State, all of whose organs have been successively overdeveloped, will tend finally to kill everything which it claims to sanction or foster in the human being, for it is beyond its power either to give life or to reveal and recognise it.

Life: I confess that I have doubtless misused this word, the ambiguity of which I am the first to acknowledge and deplore. But whatever may be the confusion to which this ambiguity exposes loose or untrained processes of thought, it none the less has the special positive merit of revealing to us, like a drop of water in the desert, the existence of the mystery of incarnation to which I drew your attention at the beginning. The family, in as much as it is the matrix of individuality, is really the meeting place of the vital element and the spiritual. Still more it is an evidence of our inability to separate them, unless it be when we claim to abide by the wager of a purely speculative reason which sets out, with an arrogant disregard for the conditions which follow from its introduction into the world of beings, to throw off the shackles proper to the state of a creature. In the last analysis it is on this elementary yet generally misunderstood notion of the state of a creature, the condition of a creature, that we must here place the decisive accent. By a paradox which well deserves our attention, the more man, misled not by science but by a certain elementary philosophy of science, comes to regard himself as a mere link in an endless chain, or as the result of purely natural causes, the more he arrogates to himself the right of absolute sovereignty in all that concerns the ordering of his personal conduct. The more he is theoretically humiliated by a materialistic philosophy which claims to deny any special identity to himself or his actions, the more does he actually develop a practical pride which impels him to deny the existence of any human order to which he might owe obedience. It is natural that under such conditions the family should be choked between the claims of two systems apparently opposed, but actually converging and reinforcing each other. In fact, it only assumes its true value and dignity through the functioning of a central relationship which cannot be affected by any objective causality and which is the strictly religious relationship whose mysterious and unique expression is found in the words *divine fatherhood*. Certainly this analogy may seem very far from a natural fatherhood, which is established by methods belonging to positive consciousness. The analogy, however, is not simply a spiritual way of looking at things. It is of a constructive character; it provides a key. We are here approaching a paradoxical truth upon which all the metaphysical understanding of the family depends. Far as we may be from claiming that theology arbitrarily transposes natural relationship into the sphere of divine realities, we must undoubtedly recognise that, inversely, all the so-called natural relationships which, as we have seen, can never be reduced to simple experimental data, not only symbolise transcendental relationships towards which they direct our devotion, but they also tend to weaken and dissolve precisely in so far as these relationships are misunderstood and denied. In other words, contrary to the persistent humanistic illusion, we have good reason to assert that family relationships, like human matters in general, afford no consistency, no guarantee of solidity. It is only when they are referred back to a superhuman order, which here below we cannot grasp apart from its signs and indications, that their truly sacred character becomes apparent. Accordingly, as events have gone on showing for the last quarter of a century, wherever man betrays faith in man, wherever treason becomes a habit and then a rule, there can no longer be room for anything but insanity and ruin. It can scarcely be different wherever the claim is made to establish a way of private life which disregards the vow of fidelity. The truth is that humanity is only truly human when it is upheld by the incorruptible foundations of consecration – without such foundations it decomposes and dies. Do not let us say, however, that it returns to nothingness. If this word has any meaning, which is not certain, it is on a level of reality far below the human structure. When man, by denying the existence of God, denies his own, the spiritual powers which are dissociated by his denial keep their primitive reality, but disunited and detached they can no longer do anything but drive the beings of flesh and soul back against each other in a despairing conflict – those beings which, had their union been safeguarded and preserved, would have gone forward towards eternal life. What all this amounts to is that if, as is certain, we have to recover today the sense of a certain fundamental reverence towards life, it cannot be by starting from below, that is to say from a biology of racialism or eugenics infected with ill-will. On the contrary, only an affirmation which reaches far beyond all empirical and objectively discernible ways of living can gain for us a sense of life's fullness and, besides this, set the seal of eternity upon the perpetually renewed act of creation, that act by which the whole family preserves its being and grants to the soul, which it forms and guides, the fearful power of completing or, alas, of repudiating it.

Le Peuch.
March–May, 1942.

To JEAN DE FABREGUES

THE CREATIVE VOW AS ESSENCE OF FATHERHOOD[1]

The thoughts which I want to propose for your consideration today follow directly from those I put before you last year at Lyons and at Toulouse in my lecture on the *Mystery of the Family.* One might even say that in the last analysis I am only presenting an application of the general idea which formed as it were the framework of that lecture. I think therefore that as this idea can serve as a guiding thread through the sinuosities of the developments which are to follow, it will be useful to place it in abstract outline at the head of my talk. To-day, experience seems to show us clearly that the unbeliever is indulging in an illusion when he imagines that he only has to make a clean sweep, that is to say to demolish what he regards as the superstructures of religious consciousness, and he will have at his disposal a clear field, or let us say arable ground in which all he need do is to sow the good grain distributed by reason in order to see rich harvests of natural morality spring up before his eyes. In reality everything goes to show that the crumbling away of religious beliefs, which has been going on for the last century and a half in vast sectors of the western world, brings as its consequence *a weakening of the natural foundations* on which these beliefs had grown up. The philosopher, when faced with a fact of such dimensions, is obliged to seek an explanation and to wonder if the principle of these foundations does not contain a certain piety clearly religious in essence. This we might without any offence call sub-Christian, for it is the understructure upon which authentic

1   Lecture given to the *Ecole des Hautes Etudes Familiales* at Lyons, July, 1943.

Christianity is built. It is this understructure, or foundation, which is being destroyed before our eyes today, so that the work of reconstruction, of which all recognise the need, has to be carried out, not on the ground level, as is ordinarily imagined, but in an underground region which has to be examined and cleared. On this point I can only express my agreement with two of the most vigorous and penetrating minds of our time, two men who might appear to be opposed by temperament and formation, but who from their different standpoints reach identical conclusions with equal lucidity as they face the spectacle of a fallen world. They are Marcel Légaut, the author of *Prières d'un Croyant* and *La Condition Chrétienne*, and Gustave Thibon, the gifted observer of human nature whom certain people have tried vainly to enlist in the service of an official doctrine.

The simplest reflection is enough to show that fatherhood cannot be considered as a mere given fact, or even as an objectively determinable relationship between beings united to each other by laws which can be compared to those governing natural phenomena. Thus, to take only one example, it would be obviously absurd to conceive of fatherhood as a mode of causality or, for the matter of that, of finality. My child cannot be considered as an effect of which I am the cause, nor, though it is a little less absurd, can I say that he is the end in relation to which I must appear to myself simply as the means. The truth is much rather that fatherhood, like all the realities underlying the natural order, starting with incarnation, that is to say the fact of being united to a body, contains within it innumerable aspects which analysis can bring out only at the risk of unduly isolating and thus distorting what is organically united, thereby appearing to misunderstand the concrete unity with which it is concerned. If we try to define fatherhood in strictly biological terms, we are really not talking of it at all, but of procreation. If we introduce considerations of a judicial or sociological order, we expose ourselves to no less a danger; it is that of allowing fatherhood to be absorbed in a conception which is completely relative. From this point of view, it could only be defined in relation to a given historical civilisation whose religious and judicial institutions are purely transitory. But in an age such as ours should we not, on the contrary, resist as deliberately and persistently as possible the deadly fascination of relativism for intellects which are already uprooted, and should we not strive to recognise a constant element which can doubtless be covered up or misunderstood, but only at the cost of serious consequences for the whole spiritual economy. It is precisely for this constant element, considered, be it well understood, as a demand rather than a law, that I am here proposing to seek. The fact of living in a time of *crisis* and transition affords obvious advantages for such an investigation. Here, as always in life's domain, exceptions and anomalies are likely to guide our reflection and to help us to discern an order which we should be less likely to notice and of which we should not so easily understand the implications if it presented a more even and strictly regular character and thereby became more thoroughly incorporated in our consciousness. We have to insist tirelessly that this order not only presupposes the collaboration of a natural determinism whose detail escapes us, and of all that is most deliberate in the human will, but also, at the very root of such collaboration, an impulse of which the principle itself is metaphysical and evades our scrutiny. It belongs to faith alone, under whatever form it may attain consciousness, not indeed, and this by definition, to achieve knowledge of this principle, but to sense its mysterious efficacy and to bow to it humbly. This actually amounts to saying that, certain conditions being granted, or on the contrary eliminated, it is extraordinarily easy and tempting for man to start by ignoring it and then to deny it. Let us at the same time add that in a world where such ignoring and subsequently such denial have become systematic, it is only at the price of an heroic and seemingly desperate effort of reflection that what in other periods appeared as an evident fact, less to be considered than lived, can be regained as it were at the sword's point.

My aim here will be to mark what I think are the successive stages of this recuperative reflection – reflection of the second degree – to which the thankless but indispensable task falls of remaking, thread by thread, the spiritual fabric heedlessly torn by a primary reflection, a reflection not only unable to distinguish the universal implications of life, but further, and above all, obstinately opposed to gratitude and respect for what is sacred in any order whatsoever. From this point of view the words piety and impiety –

words well-nigh forgotten by philosophy for lack of use – will regain their irreplaceable value. A task such as the one we have all undertaken here is only conceivable under the sign of piety; but it goes without saying that I am not taking the word here in the vague yet narrow sense which is given it in the expression "works of piety" *(ouvrages de piété)*. Piety means neither devotion nor edification. No, we are here concerned with reverence, with the spirit of piety, or rather, to go more deeply, with a piety in knowledge, united to a notion which really concerns the hallowing of the real. It is the province of the most metaphysical thought to give its true value to this term, and it must be recognised that a second-rate intellectualism has helped with all its power to eradicate the notion of it from our minds. Moreover, it goes without saying – and I say this categorically to prevent any fatal mistake – that this piety in knowledge, if it is not to degenerate into a caricature of itself, not only permits, but demands the most lucid examination of the anomalies, or even the aberrations which a misunderstanding of his own particular condition entails for man.

Perhaps the best method of treating the problems which are going to engage our attention would be to start, not from human facts considered in their almost inextricable complexity, but from the facts of revelation, and in particular the dogma of the Trinity, seen once more in its amplitude and in the unfathomable wealth of its concrete manifestations. Indeed, contrary to what a humanism incapable of understanding its own metaphysical implications supposes, there is every reason to think that the relationship between God the Father and God the Son is not in any way the product of a sublimation of strictly human relationships. It seems much rather that these relationships themselves, in the course of history, have been deepened and renewed under the action of a transcendental idea, without which what we call our nature would never have been able to evolve fully. I own, however, that I did not consider that I had the right, or perhaps I simply did not feel able to adopt this method, so that I have chosen to proceed as usual to a phenomenological examination of concrete situations of which it seems to me thought cannot make abstraction without a danger of being lost in words. I will then take as my point of departure a very simple remark concerning what is fundamentally paradoxical, one might almost say absurd or scandalous, from the point of view of logical reasoning, in the way the act of procreation is accomplished. The act of procreation: it would seem theoretically that this should be the very act above all others by which it is given to the creature if not to equal the Creator, at least to accomplish in his sphere a reflection, an analogy of the divine act without which he himself would have no being. Experience, however, seems to show us that this is not the case. If, in order to catch a glimpse of what creation can be, we go to the only domain to which we have more or less direct access, that is to say to the realm of art or of thought, we shall be obliged to recognise that to procreate is not in the least to create. In the last analysis what is required of the male is not really an act, it is a gesture, which can be performed in almost total unconsciousness and which, at least in extreme cases, is nothing but a letting go, an emptying of something which is over-full. When we say that in generation the active part belongs to the man, it is only true if we play upon the word active to some extent, giving it the impoverished and vague meaning which it commonly bears in the natural sciences, instead of the full meaning which is associated with it when we are speaking of human action and its special value. There is no idea of disputing that a natural dynamism is introduced here by which extraordinarily powerful energies are freed. That would be absurd. What I want to say is that it is quite possible for this dynamism not to come to the surface on the plane of consciousness of effort or trial. The gesture of procreation can be accomplished under such conditions that the man only has an indistinct recollection of it and is able to wash his hands of all its consequences since they will take place outside him, in another world as it were, a world with which he has no direct communication. It must be well understood that I am here making abstraction both of social institution and of the demands of the affective side of our nature; but really these institutions are so imperfect and the demands are in many cases so vague that man can claim the privilege in this matter of a fundamental irresponsibility; a privilege, be it understood, in respect of the egoistical individuality which confuses liberty with the absence of obligations. Moreover, all this only takes on a meaning if we evoke in contrast the part which falls to the woman, a part,

humanly speaking, so much more active: gestation, which symbol-
ises creation in so direct a manner, not as it is in itself, but as we are
able to imagine it. After all, it is the woman, and she alone, who
brings children into the world. And it goes without saying that from
the biological point of view it would be absurd to put too strong an
accent on her onerous privilege. But this only shows that human
perspectives, which are all that interest us here, in no way coincide
with those offered for our consideration by an objective study of
life. We shall assuredly have to return later on to this non-agree-
ment, this asymmetry which will certainly be enough to prove the
impossibility of establishing a "biological morality." The sole object
of these preliminary remarks is to bring out the elementary fact, too
often hidden under words and prejudices, that the experience of
fatherhood, whatever it may be, or rather become, whatever its special characteristics and its almost innumerable varieties, develops
from what must certainly be called a nothingness *(néant)* of experience. It is exactly the contrary of what is true of motherhood. Let us,
however, notice in passing that everything here is still unavoidably
complicated by the existence of strictly sexual facts. I am thinking
here not of biological but of human sex, that is to say of the way in
which man and woman react as conscious human beings to the act
by which they are mated. It is only too clear that the intimate reaction of the woman to gestation and her feeling towards the child she
bears can be determined, in certain painful cases, by the servitude
and humiliation in which she conceived, and in others, on the contrary, by the exaltation of total self-giving which consecrates happy
unions. It might actually happen in the first hypothesis that the
child was cherished all the same as a compensation and a return –
or on the other hand detested as the permanent evidence of an
insult and a defeat; and it might also happen in the second hypothesis that the child should awaken feelings of adoration because love
found in it an extension and consummation – or else, on the contrary, feelings of bitterness and resentment because this same love
fretted against it as a permanent hindrance. As always in the psychological realm, any of these possibilities may occur. But what we
can perhaps be right in saying is that in general there is a network
of much closer connections and much more delicate innervation in
the woman than in the man between the strictly sexual modes of

experience and the special aspects of emotional activity opened up by the existence of the child. In this respect we should be tempted to say that the man is perhaps more naturally detached than the woman; or, more exactly, detachment which generally is of a morbid character in the woman, is on the contrary almost normal in the man, for in him it comes down to the originally distinct existence of modes of experience which can, and even, in a last analysis, should harmonise without encroaching on each other.

These preliminary observations will help to give our investigations an axis and a direction. If, as we have seen, the experience of fatherhood develops from a nothingness *(néant)* of experience, we have to ask ourselves not only how this development can take place and work itself out, but, going further and deeper, whether beyond this initial blank we have not to discover, at least in the man who is truly a man, to borrow the words of M. Blondel, a secret motion of the will which prepares for the initiative he is to take in the future. It will indeed be well to face the central question squarely. Why and under what conditions can a man wish to have children? And, secondly, how can it come about that this wish becomes weakened or even destroyed in him?

Let us first notice, and this is of capital importance, that the question does not suggest itself to man's consciousness during periods of great vitality any more than does the question of why he himself is in the world. It really only arises where, as in our own age, there is an ebbing of life's tide. We must add that from the moment when man has come to ask this question and to find it quite natural, he tends almost inevitably to establish a state of affairs, a way of living, which makes life more and more agonising and continually diminishes the possibility of finding a satisfactory or even a satisfying solution for it. It might be said that the question tends to become more difficult to answer from the very fact that we ask it. To search our minds here for the *why* is not, as in other matters, simply to formulate a question which had already arisen before we put it into words. It is much nearer the truth to say that this question had not previously arisen, and that consequently it did not need an answer. But man's inner attitude towards life, that is to say both towards the life which he has received and the life which he has to transmit, has undergone a deep change.

Some people will not fail to have recourse here to a theme which has been very thoroughly exploited by Malthusian propaganda. Is not this change of inner attitude simply the emancipation of the poor human race which has at last understood that it must itself shake off the despotic yoke of vital force and put this force to the service of far-seeing and deliberate thought? From the moment when, by means of a carefully elaborated hygiene and scientific methods based on reason, we find it possible to discipline those obscure powers which for such long ages held our ancestors in bondage, it seems to be normal and even indispensable that we should ask questions which it would have been useless to ask so long as we were helplessly at the mercy of the tyranny of sex.

We can leave a preliminary point which only interests historians on one side. There is every reason to think that the use of contraceptive practices is nothing new in the history of mankind. There is therefore no reason to speak of a decisive point which has been reached in the history of the emancipation of our species. What is far more important is to ask ourselves how far this destruction of the fundamental relationship between man and life really corresponds to an effective liberation. It will be as well to begin by examining very closely the meaning of the word *why* in the question under consideration: we shall thus be led towards the profound views of Bergson on the transcendence of life in relation to the world of causes and ends. As a matter of fact, the more circumscribed an action is, the more it consequently belongs to the order of those actions which can either be reproduced by the agent himself in identical circumstances, or imitated by others – the more it is obviously legitimate to wonder why it is performed, or in other words what calls for it. On the other hand, the more totally an action involves the personality of the agent, the more it is of the nature of a vocation, and the more it is unique by its essence so that there can be no question of the agent repeating it or of others imitating it from outside, the less the question under consideration can be asked without absurdity. Let us say more exactly that the answer does not appear to the questioner as capable of informing or instructing him; it therefore seems as unsatisfying as the terse *"Because . . . ,"* with which we reply to a question we think tactless or idle. This means that the act performed by vocation seems essentially gratuitous to him who judges it from outside, whilst on the other hand the subject himself experiences it as something absolutely necessary, as over-motivated and, indeed, too necessary to be explained or justified. But, from the moment when man asks himself why it is that he can possibly want to have children, we can say that he is establishing between his reflective consciousness and the living being he still remains in spite of everything, the same order of systematic incomprehension which prevails between the man who is animated from within by a vocation and the one who questions this vocation from outside and at bottom challenges it.

It will no doubt be retorted that it is not legitimate to compare the genetic instinct to a vocation. But this association only seems arbitrary if one forms an anæmic and colourless idea of vocation. If it were no more than an inclination or an aptitude it is clear that the comparison would not hold good. But if it is really a call the case is quite different. Here and there an individual is in some way commanded to immolate his immediate personal aims, or again to make a clean sweep of all the arrangements which might seem most in harmony with common sense and the demands of reasoning calculations. It would never enter anyone's head to claim that vocation, precisely because strictly speaking it cannot be justified by the very person who intimately recognises it as his own, is situated outside the realm where motives are expressed and formulated. Experience shows distinctly that the more imperious it is, the less easily can it be explained by some aim ordinarily recognised as good (money, for instance, power, security, fame, etc.). We might say that this transcendence of the vocation is always bound up with the presence of a generosity which cannot be confined by any possible self-interest: this is particularly clear in vocations such as that of the priest, the artist, the doctor or even the soldier, and is less so for that of the technician in whom the vocation tends to be confused with the exercise of a strictly specialised function. It is evident that to refuse to follow a vocation, whatever the motive and however reasonable the refusal may be, is in no way to emancipate or free oneself. It is exactly the opposite, and we cannot dispute the fact except in the name of a conception which amounts to the admission that wisdom for each of us consists in planning all our actions to fit in with some object which can be readily accepted by public opinion. But we see only too clearly to what actual degradation we should thus be exposed. The kind of plebiscite to which we should, virtually at any rate, be making our appeal would mark the triumph of a certain mediocrity and would consecrate a standardisation, bearing not only upon the externals of existence, but even upon our inner experience of it. Where we dared to speak of emancipation we should have to become able to discern the progressive narrowing of the human horizon, or, in other words, the systematic levelling of the vital soil on which a human existence is built up.

Thus in meditating on the obscure question of the why, one is led, if not to recognise, at least to have some sense of the junction which tends to occur in a centre which is beyond our reach, between what I shall call for the sake of simplification the *infra* and the *supra,* the intermediate space being that in which our interests are asserted and our calculations worked out. This middle zone is the one where understanding, that is to say a certain limited and repetitive experience, articulates with emotions which are reduced to their simplest expression, and it is centred on the satisfaction of the appetites. It is instructive to observe that the spontaneity of subconscious life as it spreads out beyond a world where the Calculable triumphs, corresponds to a vow which only becomes conscious of itself infinitely above this sphere, in a zone where thought, disengaging its special essence, proves to be pure generosity or utter disinterestedness.

It would of course be absurd and really scandalous to suggest from all this that we have any grounds for exalting, or indeed for approving, or even for merely excusing the man who gives free rein to his progenitive instinct – a Restif, for instance, boasting that he has peopled the whole of France with his bastards. It is simply a question of recognising that in performing this gesture, which at bottom he is incapable of understanding, man does at least place himself at the axis of his destiny, that is to say that he adopts a position in which he can face one of the essential tests he has to satisfy in order to be master of his own life. On the other hand, in opposing this instinct with the timid objections of calculating prudence, he avoids the test and tends to convert his life into a prison however well-appointed and comfortable it may be. In any case, in order to face the test it is still necessary that he should recognise that he is responsible for his child. We might even go so far as to say that the words "his child" only acquire a meaning which can be accepted when this responsibility is fully recognised and shouldered. It is precisely here that we see the abyss opening which separates pro-creation from fatherhood, and it is this responsibility whose nature we now have to elucidate.

It is quite clear that in a legally constituted family this respon-sibility of the father is of an objective character. It exists whether he is conscious of it or not. At least in principle he incurs definite penalities in so far as he avoids it. This is the case theoretically at least, for in fact each of us has probably known careless or even unnatural fathers who have never been proceeded against in any way and who have perhaps gone on living right up to the end with-out any suspicion of their own unworthiness. But the question which concerns us here is not really to know whether, in a civilisa-tion such as our own, a father is obliged to see that his child is fed and educated, etc. What matters to us is rather to know what such an obligation can inwardly correspond to for him, when, as we have seen, the carnal bond which unites him to his descendant is found to be almost non-existent. "But," someone will be sure to exclaim, "is it not absolutely natural that in the presence of this being, who without me would not exist, I experience a feeling of tenderness and compassion – a feeling later to change its nature, becoming transformed into a lasting affection as a precise consciousness of the duties which are incumbent upon me develops?" It is, however, well to be careful here to avoid a moral optimism which is so often flatly contradicted by experience. In reality, this tenderness, even where it is genuinely felt, is very likely to be superficial and pass-ing, and the feeling which in many cases has every chance of triumphing is a growing irritation in the presence of a mewling, unclean creature who demands ceaseless attention and exercises a veritable tryanny over its relations. Conjugal love in the frequent cases where it is only an egoism in partnership is likely, at any rate in the man's case, to turn against the child and to degenerate into a sort of organic jealousy, that actually one would loathe to admit because it is so unreasonable. It would certainly be going much too far to generalise and to disregard the humanising part often played here by a family spirit which is actually almost impossible to analyse, but it is still more necessary to recognise how this family spirit is jeopardised by the conditions of life which tend to prevail in an industrialised society, and we should be exposing ourselves to the worst disappointments by treating this family spirit as something unchanging, able to assert itself everywhere and always, and normally ensuring an atmosphere of mutual understanding and affection between parents and children. The truth is rather that men in general are so incapable of sincerity towards themselves and are still so dominated by prejudice – that is to say, by the idea of what it is fitting to feel – that they are not even conscious of the inadequacy of what they so ingenuously call their natural feelings.

Actually, to be sure, nobody would deny that ordinarily a sort of habit or familiarity creates strong enough bonds. But here again a definite question arises which cannot be avoided; it concerns the special character of the sense of fatherhood and the grounds on which the father can have authority over his children. Moreover, I must insist that we are not here concerned with the objective basis of this authority and with the powers which, it can be admitted, have been as it were delegated to him by society. No, what is in question here is the consciousness of a right, whether he uses it or not, to exercise special authority over the child, at least when it reaches the age of reason and starts to claim to control its life as it chooses. This question deserves our attention all the more since we cannot help noticing signs of growing disorder in this matter. It seems to me that we are becoming increasingly familiar with the case of a father who develops something amounting to a bad conscience, because he sees the authority, which in theory he knows to be vested in him, more and more in the light of arbitrary coercion. In general I have a sense of disorder when I have to face a situation on which I have no hold; let us suppose further that with the situation comes the perception of a special call which I feel clearly is being made to me but which it is beyond my power to reply to directly: yet I cannot take it upon myself to ignore it: some kind of vague human respect, some indistinct scruple prevents me. It follows that I have nothing left but to indulge in some kind of ineffective gesticulation, which I have not the courage to keep up for too long because in my heart I feel that it is inane and ridiculous. Thus

I am reduced to just hoping that things will somehow arrange themselves; but all the time the call I heard remains in my consciousness, not as a distinct idea but rather as a sense of uneasiness. I cannot succeed in persuading myself that it came to me by mistake and that I am therefore free to take no notice of it. I therefore go on being worried and obscurely dissatified with myself. Moreover, this dissatisfaction is liable to change into irritation with the other person, or to degenerate into a sort of diffuse metaphysical bitterness of which we see only too many examples around us.

I do not think I am mistaken in suggesting that many fathers, if they were clear-sighted enough, would find that what has just been said about the general disorder is directly applicable to their relations with their children.

I will describe for you a definite example, that of an artist I used to know, who, without being an unnatural father, lived as it were outside his children's world, showing no interest in what they said or did, treating them like creatures of another species whose behaviour one observes with a short-lived curiosity. Without his knowing it, his daughter suffered deeply from this detachment which she could not understand. One day she made up her mind to write to him asking the reason for his attitude and telling him how much she wanted to come nearer to him. She wrote the letter, made sure that it was delivered, and vainly awaited an answer. . . . Certainly that is a special case from which I would not dream of generalising. What remains true, however, is that for reasons which I do not think have been fully elucidated, fatherhood nearly always presents the character of a more or less hazardous conquest, which is achieved step by step over difficult country full of ambushes. At any rate it is like this (and I shall deal with the subject at length further on) wherever the child has not been really wanted, wherever its presence is regarded as an abuse of confidence on the part of hidden life-forces towards the two conscious beings who had intended to regulate their existence secure from such intrusions.

Would it not bring us nearer to a solution of the problem which concerns us, to observe that man tends to compensate for what we called his initial *néant* of carnal experience by forming for himself a preconceived idea, not so much of the individual being who is to be his child as of the part he is called upon to play? Moreover, this is above all true in the case of a son, and more essentially still of an only son. In a civilisation like ours the son normally appears to the father as his heir, as the one who is to continue the succession, or at any rate this was the current idea in the society of yesterday. And where the father does not expect his son to take his place and carry on his work, he often requires of him to succeed where he himself has failed, to carry off the palm of victory which an unkind fate has refused him. Hence very often a sort of tension is created on both sides, the father distrustfully watching over this new being, concerning whom he has very definite views, but who appears to be possessed of a will of his own, a strong and incomprehensible will, capable of bringing his wise and long-cherished plans to nothing; the son, on the other hand, unless he is a model of docility, or too stupid to be moved by anything, almost bound in the end to feel a dull irritation when he understands that his future is as it were mortgaged by his father's plans. All this, I repeat, is specially true for an only child, and still more for people in modest circumstances, where a good education calls for onerous sacrifices and where a more or less quick return is expected. Now I have no hesitation in saying that where the creditor-debtor point of view influences the relationship between father and son, this relationship is hopelessly compromised and loses its true character. I recall here, as an analogy, a play in which I once portrayed a woman, deserted by her husband, sacrificing herself, or thinking she was sacrificing herself, for her only son, but actually using the most odious form of sentimental blackmail against him. In a case of this kind a disastrous transfer is made in favour of the mother who thus acquires the double rights of herself and of the absent defaulter of a father. Because of her son she refuses to be married again to a man she thinks she loves, and in this way she adds still more to the weight of the debt oppressing the child. It is indeed to be doubted whether so unhealthy, so fundamentally perverted and destructive a relationship could ever exist between a father and son. Everything actually happens as though the carnal intimacy between mother and son here turned against itself, weakening the soul of the adolescent at its foundations and disintegrating it. It is none the less true that misunderstanding between father and son can also bring about the most fatal of consequences.

To be sure, there are cases which appear to be quite the opposite and which have gone on increasing as family ties have tended to become weaker and our way of life softer; cases where the father's chief aim is to enable his son to enjoy the fruit of his own labours to the full, and to spare him the hard toil which he formerly had to endure. Without even recalling the mythical figure of the elder Goriot, it is enough to think of all those fathers who, having suffered the greatest privations in their youth, doubtless find a compensation for their past hardships in the fact that they can give generously to their child what was pitilessly denied to themselves. We know well enough what ingratitude often repays a liberality which takes the form of adulation, and it is worth asking ourselves whether this ingratitude has not a deep meaning, whether it is not life's ironical and cruel reply to an improper complacency by which the father has, without knowing it, undermined the austere rule which it was really his duty to maintain. "Idolatry," Gustave Thibon says very strongly, "is only a projection of individualism; it wears the mask of love but knows nothing of love. For it is not enough to love (everybody loves somebody or something); we have to know whether the beings and things we love are for us doors leading to the world and to God, or mirrors which send us back upon ourselves." And he denounces with admirable clarity "a state of mind where the child is simultaneously adored and repulsed and can only be treated as a god or an enemy" (*Retour au Réel*, pp. 77, 81).

Two additional remarks are necessary here. First it must be noted that on the whole the father's feeling for his daughter is probably more likely to become intimate and to spread out in generosity – except in the tragic cases, perhaps less numerous today than they used to be, when the unmarried daughter is deliberately treated as an unpaid servant and practically enslaved. But it is to be thought that where she has every chance of leading her normal life as a woman she is generally more capable than the son of inspiring the father with a feeling whereby he forgets and consequently passes beyond himself. And this happens without any need for introducing psychoanalytic references to unfulfilled incest which have been so wearisomely misapplied for the last quarter of a century. We only need to remember that it is, alas, quite in accordance with human nature for the father, without actually admitting it to himself, to see his son not only as his successor or heir, but as the rival fatally destined to eclipse him. Hence comes an ambivalence whose principle lies at the very heart of our condition. Why should not many a domestic enmity originate from this hidden jealousy – a jealousy which takes root in the very essence of time and at the core of our existence?

The second point is infinitely more important. We can state without hesitation that the limitations and deformations to which the fatherly feeling is liable seemingly tend to disappear in large families, and one might say that this is like the reward, the immanent sanction, of the act of prodigality by which a man generously sows the seed of life, instead of sparingly doling out the smallest possible number of descendants compatible with his need of survival. In this matter it would be impossible to exaggerate the extent of the difference which separates a large family from a family of one or two children: a difference comparable to that which in the philosophy of Bergson separates the Enclosed from the Open. It is a difference of atmosphere in the first place: that which exists between fresh air and the air in a confined space. We must, however, go much further. By the multiplicity, the unpredictable variety of the relationships which it embraces, the large family really presents the character of a creation; there is a direct relation between the persevering and often literally heroic effort by which it is built up and the new wealth, the wealth of life which it receives. It must of course be understood that a reservation previously formulated must be again made here: wherever the parents, and specially the father, are oblivious of their duties and their responsibilities, the large family, which in this case is scarcely more than a brood, can degenerate into a veritable hell. Here as elsewhere: nature only gives its best fruits if an upright way of thinking and a courageous will succeed in directing it without forcing it by violence, in short, if a way is found to govern and to serve it at the same time.

"The fathers of families, those great adventurers of the modern world." These words of Péguy, which I have already quoted last year, come naturally to one's mind here. We should fail to go to the bottom of things if we did not at this point remember the acceptance of risk which the establishment of a large family involves –

and the horror of this very risk which prevails in an ever-increasing fraction of a country on the way to progressive devitalisation. The adventure here really implies a state of mind which scarcely attains to distinct consciousness and which is for that very reason hard to describe in precise words; it is at bottom an essentially religious state of mind, which can actually, though this is relatively rare, survive the loss of positive beliefs, but which can also be lacking where the practice of a faith is being sincerely maintained. It is certainly not enough here to speak of love of life. The Malthusian couple who go to the cinema twice a week and treat themselves to an expensive meal every Sunday at Pontoise or at Bourgival can no doubt claim that they love life, and it is precisely in order not to spoil it for themselves that they take such care, and if necessary efface the consequences of their amorous frolics without a scruple. But nothing brings out better how hopelessly ambiguous the words "life" and "loving life" are. "Those were the good old days; life was worth living then," exclaim innumerable French people of both sexes as they sigh for the era of the tandem and the Simca 8. It would be possible to say that they nursed in the depths of their being, and stored up for the time to come, the pretension of acquiring life as one puts electricity or central heating into a house. Life really seems to them like an element to be used in order to obtain a few patent satisfactions, without which the world would be nothing but a prison. But is it not clear that for the "great adventurer of the modern world" the relations between man and wife are precisely the opposite? For it behoves him to place himself at life's disposal and not to dispose of life for his own purposes.

We must however recognise that the man of today tends to establish, as far as he can, an order of things in which the words "to place oneself at life's disposal" have literally no meaning. This is true above all in so far as he asserts the primacy of technics and technical knowledge. As this may not be immediately evident, perhaps I may be permitted to insist upon it. Technics are seen *as* all the systematised methods which enable man to subordinate nature, considered as blind or even rebellious, to his own ends. But it must be noted that the point at which man's powers of wonder are applied is thus inevitably shifted: what now seems worthy of admiration is above all technical skill in all its forms, it is no longer in any way the spontaneous course of phenomena, which has on the contrary rather to be controlled and domesticated, somewhat as a river is by locks. This admiration is tinged with a shade of defiance of a truly Luciferian character, it can hardly be separated from the consciousness of a revenge taken by emancipated humanity upon Nature whose yoke it has borne so long and so impatiently. This is particularly clear with regard to living nature; without even receiving a scientific grounding worthy of the name, men's minds are so saturated with naturalism that they tend to see human life as a particularly complicated and baffling case of the nature of living beings in general. As a result, without any given reason, they agree to regard life itself as a *"sale blague"* (rotten humbug), or at least as the rumbling of threatening possibilities against which it would be impossible to take too many precautions, whereas formerly it was hailed as a revelation, or at the very least a promise and pledge of a marvellous and unlimited renewal. It is perfectly clear that the obsession concerning possible illness and the preventive measures to be taken against it has in the last century become far more virulent than ever it was in the days when the science of prophylactic medicine was practically non-existent. It is to be noticed in passing that the development of prophylactic methods and of systems of insurance, because at bottom these correspond to analogous inner tendencies, have helped to foment in souls a spirit of suspicious vigilance, which is perhaps incompatible with the inward eagerness of a being who is irresistibly impelled to welcome life with gratitude. Let us consider this word for an instant. We feel gratitude for a gift we have received; but from the moment when we are no longer at all sure that we have literally received anything, when we wonder whether we have not rather been enticed into the trap of existence, and moreover that this does not result from the decision of some superhuman will, but from the play of blind forces with no possible consciousness, there can really no longer be any question of gratitude. Gratitude? To whom? For what?

It seems very much as though this radical and generally unformulated pessimism constitutes the foundation on which an ever increasing number of existences are building themselves up today. We should, moreover, take our analysis further and ask ourselves under what conditions an existence can justify itself, by which I mean recognise that it is worth the trouble it costs. Trouble here stands for the ceaseless and thankless effort by which we daily climb the slope which it would be so tempting to let ourselves slide down towards a total relinquishment and death. I am inclined to think that those people are becoming ever more numerous whose existence coagulates round a few satisfactions which from outside seem almost incredibly petty: the daily bridge party, the football match, some recreation connected either with love or food. They would not miss these pleasures *for anything in the world.* If for some reason or another they have to do without them, existence itself becomes a desert, a blank night of gloom. There is, of course, the most direct relation between the exaggerated value which is given to them and the insipidity which characterises the general substance of life – an insipidity which can in an instant become nauseating. In every department the passage from what is insipid to what is unendurable is imperceptible. We must not forget that a man's work ceases to have any attraction or even any meaning for him in so far as he has lost his relish for life. Normally it is in our work and through it that we become aware of this relish – which all the same does not rule out of existence the halo of leisure and holidays without which the daily prospect would become hard and gloomy. But the conditions of life deteriorate to the point of perversion when, as Thibon has said, that which was only the aureole tends to become the heart.

I should like now to gather together the conclusions we have reached in the course of our wanderings. Fatherhood, we have seen, cannot by any means be restricted to procreation which, humanly speaking, can hardly be considered as an act. It only exists as the carrying out of a responsibility, shouldered and sustained. But on the other hand we see that it degenerates as soon as it is subordinated to definitely specified purposes, such as the satisfaction of ambition through the medium of the child treated as a mere means to an end. It utterly denies its own nature when it is the mere blind generation of a being not only incapable of providing for his progeny and guiding their spiritual development, but of realising and acknowledging the obligations he has undertaken towards them. It is probably in contrast with such inertia and blindness that we can best understand what the pure act of fatherhood should be. By that

I mean a self-spending which can be compared to a gift, because it prepares and requires an engagement and because without this it is nullified. This pure act is inconceivable without what I propose to call the *vœu créateur*. But here a preliminary analysis is necessary, the notion of the *vœu* being one which very often contains a confusion, sentimental in its essence.

When we say to anyone, "I am making *des vœux* for your wife's recovery," we merely mean that we wish for this recovery, that it would please us. There is no active participation on our part, we are not involved. But here, on the contrary, the *vœu* cannot be reduced to a simple wish, it is an engagement. We must further notice that an engagement made in the presence of a transcendental authority is always liable to be degraded in so far as it takes on the character of a bargain and by so doing imposes conditions. "If you grant me this favour, I undertake to accomplish such and such an action calculated to please you." But this really comes to the same as saying: "To get this action you want out of me, you must agree to grant me the favour for which I am asking." The *mu* is seen here as a bribe. But of course bribery is quite impossible in the religious order, or more exactly that which is genuinely religious is to be recognised from the very fact that it is essentially opposed to any attempt of such a kind. Suppose that I undertake to respond to the favour, when I eventually receive it, by an action which proves my gratitude, this visible action should only be the sign of the invisible act by which I consecrate myself to the power which has helped me. There is still something equivocal, however, in this interpretation. Does it not actually seem as though I said "I will only consecrate myself to you on condition that you first give me this proof of your benevolence towards me"? Thus the defective reaction denounced above still persists here. I should not even say: "If you reveal yourself to me by granting this favour, I will consecrate myself to you in return." But rather: "If you reveal yourself to me, you will give me the strength to consecrate myself to you." Or again: "The act by which I shall respond to the favour you grant me will be, as it were, the pledge of the revelation I receive, not so much of your special benevolence towards me as of your essence which is pure liberality." The best formula for the *vœu* would then be to offer it as a prayer: "I beg you to reveal yourself to me, to make your presence real for me, so that it will be possible for me to consecrate myself with a full understanding – since in my present state I can only see you through the clouds of uncertainty which encircle me. Moreover, I do not claim that you should attach any value on your own account to this consecration which can add nothing to what you are; but if you love me, if you consider me as your son, it seems to me that, not for your own sake, of course, but for mine, you must want me to know and serve you, since, if it is not given to me to know and serve you, I am doomed to perdition."

Such seems to me to be the significance of this appeal which is of the very essence of the *væu*. We easily see that this appeal has a mediatory function here, in relation to a certain process of inner creation which actually can never be understood if we approach it as a matter governed by the will alone.

On the other hand, it seems to me essential to notice that, in spite of appearances, the *væu* does not in any way imply a dogmatic theory, nor, *a fortiori*, any definite idea of the power to which it is offered. If we reflect upon æsthetic creation, particularly that of the novelist and the dramatist, we shall realise this. The *væu* only takes shape after the artist has as it were been possessed by some form of reality which is revealed less by sight than by a sort of inward touch: but reality thus apprehended appears to him at the same time (and this is a paradox and a mystery) as independent in relation to his personal will and as nevertheless subject to the act by which he makes it pass into existence. The *væu créateur* is no other than the *fiat* by which I decide to put all my energies at the service of this possibility which is already imposing itself upon me, but only upon me, *as* a reality, so that I may transform it into a reality for all, that is to say into an established work. This means that the *væu*, far from being reduced to a mere wish, has the character of an engagement and a decision. But this engagement or this decision is not made simply within my own being, something transcendent is involved, however indistinct my consciousness of it may as yet be.

At the root of fatherhood, if I am not mistaken, we can discern something which is obviously analogous to this *væu créateur,* and it is by this alone that fatherhood can be considered as a human act, or even as an act at all, and not as the special term given to the biological process of procreation. It must however be added that this *væu créateur* cannot here by separated from a general attitude taken by man as he faces life or, to be more exact, the operation of life. This attitude is, first and essentially, an acquiescence by which man adopts and makes his own the words at the opening of Genesis: "God saw all that He had made, and behold it was very good." Moreover, we must be careful not to interpret this acquiescence purely as a judgment of worth. It would be better to recognise that judgment of worth is an intellectualised and for that reason an imperfect translation of something which is much more like admiration or simple wonder. It is this reaction, originally springing from the consciousness, which is expressed in the father's act as he falls in adoration before his newly born child. It goes without saying, of course, that this adoration is always in danger of degenerating into sheer idolatry, and that when this degradation comes about fatherhood *loses its special essence.* I insist on the paradox expressed by these words. In the order of concrete philosophy the essence is always liable to be defective. It has nothing in common with those entities, those unalterable *ousiai,* which classical metaphysics fixed in the pure heaven of speculation, thereby putting itself outside the conditions which alone can enable us to understand human existence and the place which failure in all its forms occupies in it.

Under these conditions, as we have already suggested, we must certainly recognise that a shaking of the metaphysical order, a severing of what last year I called the nuptial bond between man and life, is at the root of the crisis in fatherhood and paternal authority which is apparent even to the most superficial observer. But in our perspective today it seems to me still easier to explain what we should understand by this bond. It is at bottom a question of spontaneous confidence in life which can almost equally be regarded as a call or as a response. It is this, and this alone, which enables man to establish his roots in the universe and to develop to his full stature. We should moreover be mistaken if we spoke here of optimism, for we are dealing, as we have seen, with a far more fundamental tendency which lies hidden, as it were, deep below the work of the intellect. But from the moment when this confidence becomes dissolved in the poisonous secretions of superficial thought, aroused by the sight of suffering and failure, it is quite clear that man no longer knows what attitude to adopt regarding the act by which he is continued in other beings who would not exist without him. This act is less and less wished for, it is considered as the troublesome and theoretically avoidable complement of an act with quite another object – an act which takes and at the same time, if possible, gives pleasure without looking beyond the mere enjoyment of the moment. From this point of view, I repeat, the child tends to appear as an accident which has acquired shape, which has acquired not only a body but a soul. Hence the kind of pity tinged with remorse which will probably be felt in the presence of the child by him who engendered it without any idea of a *vœu créateur*. This means, I repeat once more, without the slightest consciousness of participating in a work of life, infinitely beyond him and yet requiring his contribution as an essential element which nothing can replace. Let us reiterate that he who wants a child to take his place or to make up to him one day for his personal inconveniences, cuts himself off by this very fact from all idea of transcendence, for this child is nothing for him but an element, or let us say a trump card, in the closed system which he has formed with himself. The situation is transformed from the moment when he really understands that what he has been allotted is in truth nothing but the reflection, the likeness of a creative gift which could not belong to him as such. I can no more give existence to someone else than I can to myself, and there is an obvious connection between these two impossibilities. But in so far as I refuse to allow myself to admit it, I am exposed to a double temptation. The first consists of organising my life as if I myself were the author of it, as if I did not have to answer for my actions to any person or thing; the second, of treating my children as though I had produced them, as though, strictly speaking, they were there for me, as though I had the right to decide what they were to become. That is precisely what is incompatible with the *vœu créateur* as I have tried to define it. Negatively this *vœu*, or this call, signifies that our child no more belongs to us than we do to ourselves and that accordingly, he is not there for our sake, nor, to go a degree further, is he there for his own sake either. It signifies, moreover, that for this reason he must not be brought up as though one day he would have to assert that in his turn he was responsible to no one but himself. It would indeed be contradictory on my part to admit for him what I deny for myself; I could not agree that he should one day be guilty of what on my own account I regard as an infringement of the deep law of life. Only one way remains open. We have to lay down the principle that our children are destined, as we are ourselves, to render a special service, to share in a work; we have humbly to acknowledge that we cannot conceive of this work in its entirety and that *a fortiori* we are incapable of knowing or imagining how it is destined to shape itself for the young will it is our province to awaken to a consciousness of itself. We can see clearly enough that the *vœu créateur* implies the combination of a deep personal humility and an unshaken confidence in life, conceived of not as a natural force but as an unfathomable order, divine in its principle. Now it is exactly the opposite combination which tends most often to be effected before our eyes, that is to say a maximum of personal pretension associated as we have seen with a radical agnosticism concerning life, its value and its meaning.

Here we must emphasise the close relationship which binds fatherhood not only to a special conception of love but to a definite way of experiencing and desiring it. Where love is degraded, fatherhood is degraded also. This degradation of love can take on two precisely opposite forms, according to whether the union of the couple is relaxed until it is no more than an engagement of short duration when no diversion is barred, or whether this same union becomes hardened and opaque, and is at the same time sterilised so that everything threatening to upset the routine of pleasure or simply of comfort, which eventually is the only law it knows, is excluded. Here again the only way of salvation is found in a transcendence which can alone prevent the couple from degenerating into an enclosed system. I will add that we can not give an opinion *a priori* on the idea of this transcendence which consciousness is able to form in any particular case. All one can assert is that the conception of the work of life which we attain to in the light of Christ frees us most surely from illusions and ambiguities. It is to these illusions and ambiguities that thought is still exposed when it claims to interpret this operation, either as a function of cosmological metaphysics, or, and for stronger reasons, of a racial, national and class philosophy, which in a last analysis invariably degenerates into idolatry. But this must not prevent us from recognising that it is quite possible for the Christian idea of the operation of life only to attain to an imperfect and relatively indistinct consciousness of itself, quite dissociated from any dogmatic profession of faith, without losing its genuine and stimulating value on that account.

Do all these considerations enable us to get a glimpse of how to set about solving the ethico-religious problem which here towers above all the others: the problem of knowing to what extent the father can and should regard himself as invested by God himself with the authority which he is bound to exercise over his own children? It seems as though the idea of the *vœu créateur* can help us to avoid the excesses of a fatherhood orientated in a theocratic direction. I will show you how.

In a profound study published in 1942 in the *Recherches de Sciences Religieuses,* Father Fessard drew attention to the fact that the formula *omnis potestas a Deo* is dangerously equivocal if taken by itself. "Most of the time," he says, "we only see in this union the relation of the human power to do all things to the divine power of the Almighty. Authority appears thus to be delegated from outside without any consideration of its special nature, as is the authority of a prince who confers all or some of his power to his lieutenants without reference to any law except his own good pleasure and, following from it as a sequel, theirs. So long as one remains at this feeble degree of reflection one can draw conclusions from this formula as contrary as possible to the essence of authority and of the common good. . . . Because the All-Power of God is only extended to bring about the rule of justice, a second degree of reflection leads to a recognition of authority not only as power which is fact, but as power which is righteous, and to make the universal ideal of Right the necessary end of all authority. Hence all power is required to tear itself away from its selfish ends and to reach out towards the universal in order to prove its divine origin." Yet, right or equity remaining still an indeterminate idea here, the conception of authority comes up against endless contradictions of fact and right, parallel with those which our reason perceives between the absolute power and the absolute justice of God. It is thus necessary that between fact and right the link should appear which forms the basis of their distinction, which gives meaning to their conflict and makes its end clear, In order that the contradictions of the All-Powerful and All-Just may be reconciled before our eyes, the All-Merciful has to be manifested. Through Him we are permitted to call the All-Powerful: *Father*, the All-Just *Son* and *Word*, whilst He finally reveals Himself as the *Spirit of Love*.

From a great height, too great for my liking, these dialectics illuminate the concrete situations which I have striven this morning to make clear to you. I think that personally I should prefer to express myself as follows: the father, as we have seen, is almost irresistibly inclined to treat his child as being *for him*, as being obliged to fill the place which he is reserving for him in a scheme of which one can easily say he is still the centre, since it is he who claims to establish its principles. A mortifying experience teaches him, however, in so far as he is capable of learning the lesson, that this scheme is as precarious as his own existence, if only because the son has the advantage of being likely, in the normal course of things, to outlive him and to have the power one day to upset the plan which he himself has worked out. Under these conditions, the father can reach such an excessive degree of humility that he treats himself as the mere means to an end, which he persuades himself lies beyond him and is incarnated in the autonomous will of the heir. Better thinking, however, leads him to transcend this double relationship, and to discern an organic unity where the imperfect and deceptive sequence which takes shape in the succession of generations is no more than the phenomenal and misleading expression of a substantial union which itself can only be consummated in eternity. In the last analysis it is in relation to this constitution of an organism, spiritual no doubt, but carnally rooted in the eternity of God, and in relation to this alone, that the *vœu créateur* can be defined, in so far as thereby a fidelity which is itself creative, the fidelity to a hope which transcends all ambition and all personal claims, takes a body. Yes, this word eternity, to which it is so difficult to give a positive, conceivable meaning, and which we can hardly translate into understandable language without becoming involved in insoluble difficulties, yet remains the key word here. Without it the whole human edifice will crack and in the end fall to bits in the horror of absolute absurdity.

It will be well to state here, explicitly and with force, that, as I have already suggested, fatherhood is not a mere function which is carried out blindly in order that a certain objective continuity should be secured. After all, there is no apparent reason why, taken by itself, the continuity of a progeny should have more ontological value or dignity than the life of a forest or a plantation. But it is quite different if this continuity of a human family is in truth one of the approaches by which the super-conscious and super-historical union of all in all is to be attained – the union in which alone creation can find its full meaning.

Let us notice something here, which, although it is only stated in passing, has very great importance in my eyes. It is that in this perspective it becomes possible to understand the metaphysical foundation of adoption, and to recognise that it is not merely a pale and bloodless copy of real fatherhood, but that it can be a means of grace, destined to make up for the deficiencies of biological filiation. Would there not, indeed, be something intolerable in having to admit that a purely accidental defect should utterly and inevitably deprive the human being of what is perhaps the most substantial of his attributes? But reflection shows us none the less clearly, that adoption must always be exceptional, that a society in which it became very frequent would be in danger of devitalisation, for it can only be a graft on the tree of life, sometimes marvellous and sometimes, alas, abortive.

From this general point of view, and probably from this point of view alone, it becomes possible to understand the fundamental nature of the *vœu créateur*, wherein we believe we have found the essence of fatherhood to lie. It is the quivering anticipation of a plenitude, of a pleroma in the bosom of which life, no longer an endless improvisation of disappointing variations on a few given themes, will be satisfied, concentrated and reassembled around the absolute Person who alone can give it the infrangible seal of unity.

Le Peuch.
June-July, 1943.

To BERTRAND D'ASTORG

OBEDIENCE AND FIDELITY[1]

It seems to me impossible to consider the spiritual decadence which has been going on for more than half a century in our own country, among others, without being led to emphasise the increasingly flagrant disrepute in which the value of fidelity has been held. It is therefore indispensable for anyone who wants to start upon the immense work of moral reconstruction which is necessary, to strive to re-establish this same value in the place which rightly belongs to it – that is to say in the very centre of human life, of life no longer degraded, alienated or prostituted, but lived in all the fullness of its true significance. As a matter of fact the code of ethics which is beginning to take shape in many places – above all, of course, in youth movements – is necessarily based on fidelity.

But there is no doubt that if we want to avoid dangerous simplifications and fatal confusions we must analyse the closely connected notions of obedience and fidelity as thoroughly as possible; otherwise an abuse is likely to be made of them by those who find it useful to exploit for their own ends a good will, degenerating little by little into a systematic docility and finally into a passivity of belief and intention.

I think it would be well to point out first of all the essential difference which separates obedience and fidelity: a difference which in fact tends to become obliterated by the somewhat vague use ordinarily made of the verb to serve.

Let us begin by noticing that the very meaning of the word serve is ambiguous, and that we must not forget the difference of

1   The publication of this article in a review was forbidden by Vichy in 1942.

spiritual level between *servir* (to serve) and *server à* (to be useful). If I come across a tool or machine of which I do not know the purpose, I ask: "For what does that serve?" In this context it is only a question of instruments used by beings endowed with a will, people working for the realisation of definite ends. There would, on the other hand, be something rather shocking about asking a human being, "For what do you serve?" This is precisely because it would be treating him as though he were a thing. Let us notice at this point that to represent the human being as an instrument inevitably leads at last to extreme consequences, such as the pure and simple doing away with old people and incurables: they no longer "serve any useful purpose," hence they are only fit for the rubbish heap: why should we take the trouble to keep up and feed machines which are past use?

There would, on the other hand, be nothing in any way shocking, at any rate if a certain degree of intimacy had been reached, if we asked the same human being, "Whom or what do you serve?" And if he took exception to such a question he would actually prove, by that very fact, that the deeper meaning of life had escaped him. It is clear, indeed, that all life is a service. This does not of course mean that it has to be devoted to some particular individual, but only that it is its essential nature to be *consecrated to* God, or some high purpose such as knowledge or art, etc., or even to some deliberately chosen social end. To serve in this second sense is to put oneself at the service of. Moreover here the accent should be put on the word "oneself," the reflective pronoun. To live in the full sense of the word is not to exist or subsist, to limit oneself to existing or subsisting, but it is to make oneself over, to give oneself.

It is unhappily too clear that these two meanings, of such distinctly different orders, have tended to become confused for minds more and more misinformed, or deformed. A crazy idea has taken possession of an increasing number of misguided individuals, the idea according to which to serve has something humiliating about it for him who serves. The person, considering himself more and more as a centre of claims and demands, such as "I, for my part . . . ," has thus hypnotised himself not only about his rights and prerogatives, but further about the feelings of envy inspired by the advantages with which others seem to him to be unduly favoured. "Why him?,

Why not me?" Resentment has without a doubt been constantly at work beneath a levelling process whose roots a detestable set of psychologists have too long omitted to expose. This has brought innumerable minds to reject the notion of any hierarchy whatever and to rebel against the idea of having to serve anyone at all. It is only just to add that those among the leaders or rulers who have allowed the sense of their responsibility to waste away in the depth of their being, have helped to an extent it is impossible to exaggerate to prepare the way for this crisis in the idea of service. What, however, is certain is that this anarchism, not violent but ill-tempered and full of sneering hatred, has terribly impoverished souls, and, even on the biological plane itself, has paved the way for France's devitalisation. The general lowering of the human tone, above all of course since 1918, probably constitutes the most outstanding fact of our recent history, the one perhaps which best explains our disaster. We must re-learn how to serve, but this does not simply mean we must re-learn how to obey, for to obey is only one way of serving. There are others.

Here a very simple remark will help to direct us. It is often said of a child that he is, or he is not, obedient. It would clearly be unfitting or even absurd to judge an adult in the same way. Why is this so? It is because the child has not the experience or the powers of reasoning which would enable him to decide for himself what has to be done, so that it behoves him to obey his parents, his teachers, in short all those who are qualified to make decisions about his daily existence. It follows that obedience is a virtue in the child, it is the mark not only of a way of behaviour but of an inner disposition which corresponds with his condition as a child. It is obviously different for the adult, if we consider his existence as a whole. An adult who was obedient in his whole manner of living, in all his acts, no matter whether they were connected with sexual or civic matters, would be unworthy of the name of man. One could consider him only as a being degraded to a state most adequately to be described as infantile. But it is no less clear that in certain special departments of his existence, the adult finds that he also has to obey. Only here, to obey does not mean to be obedient, it is the act by which he has to reply to the act of the chief, which is that of commanding. The function of the chief is to command, the function of the subordinate is to execute orders, that is to say to obey. I have said it is a function, hence the duty of obedience does not fundamentally and necessarily involve the being of him who obeys. This obligation only affects the definite actions which he is required to carry out, or from which he is required to abstain, whatever his personal feelings or his judgment may actually be. There could be no sense in claiming that on the level of feelings or judgment he *is* obliged to approve of the orders he has received. All that we can say is that he must not allow himself to show these feelings or this judgment, otherwise the obedience will be no more than a pretence, a sham obedience. We are not actually concerned at the moment with knowing whether the way the orders are given in any particular case is wise or not, or whether the prescribed action is good or not, neither are we wondering whether there are not some circumstances in which the refusal to obey would be justified. That is quite another problem which is quite outside the framework of these reflections. Here the question is solely to decide what the limits are within which the expression "to owe obedience" makes sense.

I should then be inclined to believe that obedience as such is given to the chief as chief, that is to say to the function. It is not given to the chief as a man, in so far as he is one man rather than another. Where the human quality of the chief is introduced it is a question of fidelity. Moreover, it goes without saying that in concrete experience – for instance, in a fighting unit – obedience and fidelity are very difficult to distinguish from each other; no doubt it is even highly desirable that this distinction should not reach the level of consciousness. None the less, from the point of view of reflection it is well to formulate it as clearly as possible. We might add that obedience bears with it a certain statute, whether explicit or not, defining the sphere in which it can be claimed. The more the frontiers of this zone of application tend to become obliterated, the more obedience is liable to be debased and to become confused with a general servility of which the degrading character ought not only to be recognised but proclaimed.

Fidelity presents problems of quite another order, which in the last analysis only the highest philosophy *is* capable not only of resolving, but of stating with exactitude.

In saying that obedience can and should be required (under

certain conditions) and that fidelity on the other hand should be deserved, we are preparing to discuss the originality of this virtue so discredited at the present time or so generally misunderstood. Let us observe to begin with that when we use the words *to be faithful to,* it is possible that we mean simply *to conform to* (a programme, for instance, or an intention), or negatively, *not to swerve from* (an allotted path). We only find here an impoverished meaning, obtained by diluting a far richer experience which we must try to grasp in its palpitating life.

Immediately the question arises: in the last analysis to what, or more exactly to whom, am I to be faithful? Must we not grant to idealism that the other person, as such, must always remain unknown to me and that consequently I cannot foresee what he will be: how under such conditions could I bind myself directly to him? Would it not be better on that account to recognise that the only true fidelity is fidelity to myself, and that it is by such fidelity alone that I can give proof of what is incorrectly regarded as fidelity to another? In other words, I may make it a point of honour to perform certain actions which are to the advantage of another person, but in the last analysis my only real obligation is to myself.

Let us, however, notice that we are starting from a postulate here. We take it as a matter of course that fidelity to oneself is not only justifiable but that it is clearly discernible and that we know exactly of what it consists. Is this really so? In the first place, what is this self to whom I undertake to be faithful?

To take the case of the artist – a case to which it is always useful to refer because it presents us with a strictly identifiable datum, his work: in what sense or under what conditions can the artist be said to be faithful to himself? Supposing that he conscientiously sets to work to imitate himself, that he strives to reproduce certain processes which enabled him to obtain the "effects" to which he owed his first successes. Should we say that he is faithful to himself? Certainly not, because really, in so far as he labours to reproduce these same "effects," he ceases to be himself. Instead of an artist, he becomes a manufacturer. He loses his identity among the patented productions which he sets out to deliver to his customers in as large quantities as possible. Notice in passing, that if in the actual act of creation, the artist tends to become merged in his work and to identify himself with it temporarily, he is none the less bound to detach himself from it in some sort when it is accomplished. This does not in any way mean that he disowns it; between him and it there will always be a sensual bond, a bond of affection and pain. Nevertheless, he will only continue to be himself on condition that he breaks free from it to some extent. From this privileged case, then, it appears that to be faithful to myself is to respond to a particular inner call which enjoins me not to be hypnotised by what I have done, but on the contrary, to get clear of it, that is to say to go on living and thus find renewal. There is no doubt that outsiders are inclined to express surprise and to take exception to this renewal. The artist had been catalogued as a painter of still-life, why does he now paint seascapes or portraits? And why has he changed his style which it was so gratifying to recognise at the first glance? What treason! All this comes to the same as saying that in such a case fidelity is difficult to appreciate from outside. Only the artist himself can know whether he has responded to the inner call or whether on the contrary he has remained deaf to it. Even he can only know this to a certain degree; for here it is not just a question of good intentions or a good will. It is only by an always imperfect comparison between the accomplished work and the indistinct consciousness of the work to be accomplished that he can decide whether he has been faithful or not.

In spite of appearances, the question is not very different for man in general. If I admit without discussion that to be faithful to myself means to be faithful to certain principles which I have adopted once and for all, I am in danger of introducing into my life as foreign, and we can even say as destructive, an element as the artist who copies himself does. If I were absolutely sincere I should have to compel myself to examine these principles at frequent intervals, and to ask myself periodically whether they still correspond to what I think and believe. How is it possible not to mistrust the natural laziness which prompts me to place these principles above all possible discussion? In this way I spare myself the always disagreeable test of a revision of my opinions. It may quite well happen that these principles or these opinions end by covering up and stifling my own special reality; in that case, how am I to be faithful to myself? I am no longer there, I do not exist any more. I have really been replaced by a machine. Moreover, the action of social life helps to further this substitution of the automatic for the personal. I am known, I am classified as professing such and such an opinion, and thus I am sure of having my special place on the social chess-board. In upsetting the accepted judgment of myself, however, I should be regarded as inconsistent, people would no longer take me seriously. Now I like people to attach importance to what I say, I want my opinions to have weight. Thus society, with which a whole section of myself is in league, tends to deter me from proceeding with this inner revision, though I should consider myself bound to proceed with it if I did not contrive to lose contact with myself. Moreover, it goes without saying that the spirit of contradiction, which sometimes impels me to defy other people's opinion and to disconcert them deliberately, is no better than this mediocre conformity.

So, then, everything obliges us to recognise that fidelity to oneself is both difficult to achieve and to discern. In order to be faithful to oneself it is first of all necessary to remain alive, and that is precisely what it is not so easy to do. The causes within and without us which militate in favour of sclerosis and devitalisation are innumerable. But these words are not perfectly adequate; it would be better to say that I tend to become increasingly profane in relation to a certain mystery of my *self* to which access is more and more strictly forbidden me. I should add that this unquestionably comes about in so far as the child that I used to be, and that I should have remained were I a poet, dies a little more each day. This profane self is a deserter, having adopted the point of view of "the outsiders." For such a self fidelity tends to be reduced to a stubbornly maintained agreement between myself and certain expressions, ideas, ways of living, to which I have fixed the label *mine*. But this agreement is only maintained at the expense of a certain intimacy, now broken and lost.

If, however, we make an honest enquiry, experience will force us to the paradoxical conclusion that the more I am able to preserve this intimacy with myself, the more I shall be capable of making real contact with my neighbour, and by neighbour I do not mean one of those depersonalised others whose jeers and censure I fear, but the particular human being I met at a definite time in my life and who, even though I may never see him again, has come for good into the personal universe which, as it were, wraps me round – my spiritual atmosphere, which perhaps I shall take with me in death. But, inversely, the more I become a profane outsider to myself, the more I condemn myself to nothing but the falsehood and mockery, beloved of comic authors, in my relations with others.

It is therefore well to remember that contrary to what might have been expected, my self-presence *(présence à moi-même)* is not a fact which we can take for granted. The truth is rather that it is liable to be eclipsed and must constantly be reconquered. You may ask what this presence is, and what is the self to which it is so difficult to remain faithful. The reply would have to be that it is the particle of creation which is in me, the gift which from all eternity has been granted to me of participating in the universal drama, of working, for instance, to humanise the earth, or on the contrary to make it more uninhabitable. But when all is said and done, such definitions are bound to be fallacious; whoever has loved knows well that what he loved in the other cannot be reduced to describable qualities – and in exactly the same way the mystery of what I am in myself is the very thing about me which is only revealed to love.

There is then no valid reason for thinking that fidelity to oneself should be more intelligible than fidelity to another and should clearly come first. It seems much rather that the opposite is true. I am undoubtedly less immediately present to myself than is the person to whom I have given my word. "Yet," you may say, "does not my fidelity to another person inevitably come down to the fidelity which I have vowed to a particular idea I have formed of him, and is not this idea simply myself once more?" We must reply that such an opinion has been arrived at *a priori*, and that experience distinctly disproves it. Does it not happen every day that one being remains faithful to another, although he has been forced to admit that he had formed an idealised representation of him? Should we say in this case that it is because of his pride that he determines to be faithful in spite of everything, so that no one can say that circumstances have been too much for him? Such an interpretation, although it may be right in certain cases, does not account for genuine fidelity. Is it not true that the most faithful hearts are generally the most humble? Fidelity cannot be separated from the idea of an oath; this means that it implies the consciousness of something sacred. I give you an undertaking not to forsake you, and I regard this undertaking as increasingly sacred in proportion to the freedom with which I give it, added to your own lack of power to use against me should I break it. I know, moreover, that from the very fact that I have thus bound myself absolutely, the means will be surely given me to keep faith; for although this oath in its origin and essence is my act, or to go deeper, *because* it is my act, it has become the most unyielding obstacle there could possibly be to everything in me which tends towards weakening or dissolution.

I have not, however, the right to bind myself thus except in very rare cases, on the basis of an intuition by which it is given me to recognise that I ought and I wish to place myself at your disposal, not only without lowering myself in my own eyes, but, on the contrary, honouring and as it were exalting myself by this very act. Fidelity then and the oath which seals it cannot be coined, they cannot be vulgarised. Perhaps it should further be said that in fact fidelity can never be unconditional, except when it is Faith, but we must add, however, that it aspires to unconditionality. It is as though my oath were accompanied by this prayer: "May heaven grant that I shall not be led into temptation, that is to say that no event shall cause me to think myself authorised to deny my promise on the pretext that the implicit conditions on which it rests have been changed in a way I could not foresee when I made it." I cannot perhaps go beyond this prayer without presuming too much on my own strength: but still it must be really sincere, and I must maintain within myself the will to fight against this temptation if ever it assails me.

It is true in a general way to say that the quality of a being can be recognised and proved by the fidelity of which he is capable. Yet we might well add that there are probably indiscernible fidelities, and that not one of us is authorised to assert that another person is entirely unfaithful. Moreover, fidelity cannot be humanly exacted, any more than love or life. I cannot force another to reply to me, I cannot even force him in reason to hear me, and it will always be possible for me to think that if he does not reply it is because he has not heard me. In such a domain prescriptions cannot go beyond the *as if (comme si)*, and only deal with behaviour. I charge you to behave towards me as though you had sworn fidelity to me. But it is impossible not to recognise the fragility of such a fiction. It is because fidelity is creative that, like liberty itself, it infinitely transcends the limits of what can be prescribed. Creative when it is genuine, it is so fundamentally and in every way, for it possesses the mysterious power of renewing not only the person who practises it, but the recipient, however unworthy he may have been of it to start with. It is as though it had a chance—it is certain that there is nothing final here—to make him at long last pervious to the spirit which animates the inwardly consecrated soul. It is in this way that fidelity reveals its true nature, which is to be an evidence, a testimony. It is in this way, too, that a code of ethics centred on fidelity is irresistibly led to become attached to what is more than human, to a desire for the unconditional which is the requirement and the very mark of the Absolute in us.

Le Peuch.
March, 1942.

To JEAN GRENIER

VALUE AND IMMORTALITY[1]

In reply to the invitation you so kindly gave me I have naturally been led to examine the nature of my journey ever since that far-off time where I first fearlessly addressed myself to the struggle which in the end all philosophy must involve. A journey implies both a starting point and a point of arrival. Now, although upon reflection I may to some extent manage to reconstitute the conditions under which my quest began and thus to mark the approximate point of my departure, I find on the other hand that it is absolutely impossible for me to state precisely, not only to others, but to myself, where I hope to arrive. There is nothing in my case which can be at all compared with that of a scholar whose researches follow a fixed line, who has drawn up a programme and is conscious of having reached a definite point in it. The truth is that the words *point of arrival* have no longer any meaning for me, and moreover it would probably be possible to show that there is also an illusion in picturing a point of departure. The really important thing is to rediscover what means one had at one's disposal, what equipment, and also what "the idea at the back of one's mind" was on setting out: but how can this be accomplished?

In reality here, as indeed everywhere, we have to get free from the claims and pretensions of an imagination which views everything in terms of space, and to recognise that on the philosophic plane at any rate (though probably wherever we have to do with creation) we must regard the image of a journey as misleading.

1   Lecture given in 1943 to the members of the Enseignement Catholique of Lyons.

Since we can hardly dispense with an introductory metaphor, I greatly prefer to ask you to imagine a certain clearing of the ground which takes place on the spot, which is indeed only effective on that condition, but of which the successful results can never be considered as finally consolidated. There is always a risk that weeds will spread in the furrows which have been so laboriously ploughed, there will always be swarms of pestilent insects to threaten future harvests. Hence comes the necessity for constant vigilance which cannot be relaxed without compromising everything. I do not claim that this comparison takes us very far, but, in my eyes, it does at least have the obvious advantage of not substituting a pseudo-idea for what is really at issue. We can never eradicate pseudo-ideas too resolutely or too methodically. It is extraordinary to see with what regularity, and I should be prepared to say with what cynicism, they take possession of the field every time that research of genuine profundity reaches the perilous second stage—that of publication, which only too often involves exploitation and vulgarisation. I am thinking here, for instance, of the very confused notion of existential philosophy which has become current.

I was saying that I can manage to form a retrospective idea of the initial conditions under which I began my inquiries. There are two points about which my memory is specially precise. I remember very clearly my exasperation when, in studying the thought of Fichte, I came to the conclusion that the German philosopher was claiming to deduce the empirical self from the transcendental self. "What an illusion," I thought, "or what a lie! Perhaps at a pinch it might be possible to establish that the self should figure as the empirical self in its own eyes, but in this case it could only stand for the empirical self *in general*. Now the empirical self in general is a fiction. What exists and what counts is such and such an individual, the real individual that I am, with the unbelievably minute details of my experience, with all the special features of the concrete adventure, assigned to me and to no one else as my particular life. How can all this be arrived at by deduction? It is not enough to say that the attempt would be impracticable, it would be absurd in principle. The reason is that this deduction which seemed to promise so much, stops just short of the essential, of the thing which alone matters for each one of us." By this, of course, I was definitely taking up my position against formalism of any kind, and moreover I went so far as to think that to apply methods of deduction in such a realm is arbitrary and even false, that it is the unlawful transposition into the metaphysical order of a requirement which only has value and meaning in certain definite departments of scientific thought.

Now, here is the second point. I remember having listened to the controversy which started in about 1906 or 1908 between Mr. Brunschvicg and Mr. Edouard Le Roy on the relations of science and religion, and having been somewhat shocked by the immoderate use which each of them seemed to make of a certain principle of immanence, which both showed to be an irrefutable law of the mind and for that very reason of reality. I remember saying to one of my companions – it may have been to Michel Alexandre: "That is a principle which I am prepared to attack directly and which ought at least to be subjected to a very thorough examination." In reality, from that time I tended to dispute the validity of this principle, rather in the same way as Chestov opposed the principle of identity.

I am therefore able to say that from the beginning my researches were explicitly directed towards what might be called the concrete examination of the individual and of the transcendent, as opposed to all idealism based on the impersonal or the immanent. We should doubtless mark, immediately afterwards, the valuable impetus given to me in my quest by experience of the tragic element in the universal drama, successively brought home to me in my private life and, of course, in the tremendous event which laid waste or maimed our existence from the year 1914.

It is not possible within the limits of this lecture for me to deal as fully as necessary with the part which the consciousness of tragedy played in the development of my thought. But it is quite evident that it was, for instance, at the root of the dispute (friendly, if one may say so) which brought me to grips with Léon Brunschvicg, and ended in our discussions in the *Société Philosophique*, the *Union pour la Verité* and the Congress of 1937. I shall actually be returning later to the last-mentioned debate and to the particularly serious question with which we dealt, far too briefly as a matter of fact. It is, however, possible to say in quite a general way that a consciousness of tragedy is bound up with a sharp sense of human plurality, a sense that is to say of communication and conflict at one and the same time, but above all of the irreducible element which no rational settlement can remove.

I have come across a note on a slightly different plane which, if I am not mistaken, has never been published in the *Journal Métaphysique*, though I do not quite know why.

"Metaphysical uneasiness. – It seems to me probable that metaphysics amounts to nothing else but the activity by which we define an uneasiness and manage partially (and, moreover, mysteriously) if not to remove it at least to transpose and transmute it, so that far from paralysing the higher life of the spirit it tends rather to strengthen and maintain it." What are we to understand, then, by this uneasiness? First of all, it is not a form of curiosity. To be curious is to start from a particular fixed centre, it is to strive to grasp or lay hold of an object of which one has only a confused or partial idea. In this sense all curiosity is turned towards the periphery. To be uneasy, on the contrary, is to be uncertain of one's centre, it is to be in search of one's own equilibrium. This is true in every case. If I am uneasy about the health of one of my relatives it means that the apprehension I feel on their account tends to destroy my inward stability. My curiosity is the more liable to become uneasiness the more the object which arouses it forms a part of myself, the more closely this object is incorporated into my own interior edifice. At the same time uneasiness is the more metaphysical the more it concerns anything which cannot be separated from myself without the annihilation of this very self. It is probably true to say that the only metaphysical problem is that of "What am I?" for all the others lead back to this one. Even the problem of the existence of other consciousnesses is reducible to it in the last analysis. A secret voice which I cannot silence assures me in fact that if others are not there, I am not there either. I cannot grant to myself an existence of which I suppose others are deprived; and here "I cannot" does not mean "I have not the right," but rather "It is impossible for me." If others vanish from me, I vanish from myself.

Can I say that I feel this metaphysical uneasiness as a state with a direct cause – such as the uneasiness one feels when waiting for a beloved being who is late? I do not think so; I should say rather that circumstances can, and even must, inevitably arise when I shall be conscious of an uneasiness which on reflection seems to me to reach

infinitely beyond these circumstances in themselves. It is of a permanent character in as much as it is not connected with such and
such a *now*. Still more, as soon as I formulate it, I extend it to all
whom it is possible for me to look upon as sharing in my own experience. It is an anxiety for all of us, and this amounts to saying that
it is in no way concerned with man in general (a pure fiction invented by a particular form of rationalism) but rather with my brothers
and myself.

Like all true uneasiness (that is to say uneasiness which is not
merely the indistinct consciousness of a functional disorder) metaphysical uneasiness can only find peace in knowledge. But of what
knowledge is there a question here? The metaphysician seems to
deny his own vocation if he does not proclaim that he is seeking
"truth"; but what is truth?

Perhaps we should first point out very distinctly that *the truth*
with which we are concerned here has nothing in common with the
truths which it is given to the scholar to bring to light as a result of
his patient investigations.

The property of a particular truth, of whatever order it may be,
is not only to be strictly definable, but furthermore to tend to identify itself with the statement in which it is formulated, or at least not
to make such an identification in any way difficult. In so far as it is
taken in itself, that is to say without reference to the previous
researches of which its discovery is the crown, it tends to appear as
independent of whoever proclaims it. This means to say that it is of
the essence of particular truths to have nothing personal about
them, to lay claim to an intrinsic value of their own. In this respect
there is a remarkable analogy between particular truths and things.
The thing is there, ready to be observed by anyone, the particular
truth gives itself also, as though offered to whomever wants to
recognise and proclaim it. This undoubtedly is the origin of a certain illusion of scientists. We can amass or collect particular truths
as one collects pebbles or shells. But it should naturally be noted
that by the very fact of our doing so, these truths are devitalised and
degraded. To realise this, we only have to think of those lists of historical or physiological facts drawn up for the purpose of enabling
a candidate to face such and such an ordeal of school or university
examinations.

Is it, as I have appeared to imply, truth in general which we have to contrast with particular truths? On reflection the expression "truth in general" is in danger of appearing vague and meaningless. For my part, I should prefer to speak here of *the spirit of truth.* Whatever we may sometimes say about it in language which is far too inexact, it is not against truth, but against the spirit of truth that we are all constantly liable to sin. Moreover, the spirit of truth can totally inhabit a being who in the whole course of his existence has only had the chance of learning a very few particular truths, and for whom these truths have never been even formulated in terms which would make it possible to pass them on or *a fortiori* to teach them.

What then is this spirit of truth which sometimes takes possession of us and which opposes the "spirit of imprudence and error," spoken of by the tragic poet? Here the philosopher must repossess himself of a principle which he has been leaving to the care of religious thinkers and even preachers to turn to account.

It seems clear to me that it is best to define the spirit of truth in relation to our condition, and here again there is a notion to reestablish. The idealist philosophers in particular have been far too much inclined to think of the condition of man as of certain contingent limits which thought could legitimately, and even ought to, ignore whenever it was fully exercised. Thus with such men as Brunschvicg or the thinkers of the Marbourg school everything which could not be reduced to mathematics lost all value. So a fatal duality is introduced into man's essence, and the idealist is always ready to hand over any residuary elements which do not seem to him to fit in with the essential pattern of all truth to a psychology which is nothing but a department of physiology or sociology.

The spirit of truth should be subjected to a phenomenological description. We should then see fairly easily that it cannot be confined within the limits of what is generally called the intelligence, or even the reason, in so far as the latter is fatally prone to become entirely divorced from reality. The spirit of truth is essentially incarnated in the act which terminates a game I can play with myself under any circumstances – a game always springing from a certain complacency. In relation to this game the spirit of truth appears to be transcendent, and yet its proper function might well be to restore me to myself. By its light I discover that in my vanity I have really been betraying myself. Here, surely enough, the words "more deep within me than myself," find their full meaning.

We might at first be tempted to identify the spirit of truth with liberty itself. But we have to be careful not to simplify our terribly complicated situation arbitarily. We might say that we are comparable with people whose goods are nearly all mortgaged and therefore not really at our disposal. To deny that we cannot dispose of them is once more to play with oneself, it is once more to violate the claims of the spirit of truth. What it is always within the power of each of us to accomplish is to draw up a balance sheet which is at least an approximation of our situation: it must further be added that we are, and always should be, much clearer about our debts than our assets. In drawing up this balance sheet it seems as though we should place ourselves in such a position that the spirit of truth which is certainly akin to inspiration would be able to pierce us as a pencil of light. What depends on us is in short to dispose ourselves favourably in relation to a possible grace. I use this word purposely here in the very same sense as Mauriac gives it in an admirable passage of *Ce qui Etait Perdu:* "Madame de Blénauge said, as though it was the most obvious thing, that he, Hervé, her son, had received among others one very great grace. 'I have?' – `Yes, the greatest grace of all; you see yourself for what you are; you know yourself; you call mud, mud; you know that mud is mud.'" This knowledge, however, if we can call it that, is at the same time a valuation; in this realm, truth and value cannot really be separated.

It is indeed of the nature of value to take on a special function in relation to life and, as it were, to set its seal upon it. An incontestable experiment, which can scarcely be recorded in objective documents, here brings us the most definite proof: if I dedicate my life to serve some cause where a supreme value is involved, by this fact my life receives from the value itself a consecration which delivers it from the vicissitudes of history. We must, however, be on our guard against illusions of all kinds which swarm round the word "value." Pseudo-values are as full of vitality as pseudo-ideas. The dauber who works to please a clientele, even if he persuades himself that he is engaged in the service of art, is in no way "consecrated"; his tangible successes will not deceive us. Perhaps, in a general way, the artist can only receive the one consecration that counts on condition that he submits to a severe test. This does not necessarily take the form of the judgment of others, for it may happen that for a long time the artist is not understood by those around him – but it means at least that with lucid sincerity he compares what he is really doing with what he aspires to do – a mortifying comparison more often than not. This amounts to saying that value never becomes reality in a life except by means of a perpetual struggle against easiness. This is quite as true in our moral life as in scientific research or aesthetic creation. We always come back to the spirit of truth, and that eternal enemy which has to be fought against without remission: our self-complacency. To return to our first example, the artist may even have to admit at a given moment either that he is incapable of achieving anything and that he would do better to give up a struggle in which he is wearing himself out in vain, or that he is condemned to remain an amateur, and that, if it is granted him to give pleasure to himself, he should have no illusions about the importance of this amusement.

It certainly does not follow from this that we should be justified in simply identifying value and truth, but only that the spirit of truth and the spirit of falsehood penetrate very far into a sphere from which a superficial analysis would at first be tempted to exclude them.

"Value," I said in a lecture given in May, 1938, at the *Cité Universitaire*, "is the very substance of exaltation, or more exactly it is the reality that we have to evoke when we try to understand how exaltation can change into creative force." In expressing myself thus I was making use of and expanding a passage of Charles du Bois: "For as long as it lasts," he said, "exaltation sustains us in our race, affording the strongest of spring-boards to increase our impetus: we feel its presence both in and around us at the same time, like the presence of a being greater and vaster but not of an essentially different nature from those other guardian presences which we could not do without. . . ." I must own, however, that it seems to me now that the word exaltation could lead to grievous confusion. What we are really aiming at is not an emotional paroxysm, it is an upward rising of the very being which may be expressed, and indeed most frequently is expressed, in an absolute self-possession, a calm in some way supernatural. This calm can only be established in the presence of ultimate realities, particularly of death. But let us take care not to deal only with words. What are we to understand by ultimate realities? Surely they are our limits.

A new discrimination has still to be made, however, and there is no doubt that this time it will be necessary to introduce the category of the existential in spite of the care which it is well to take in bringing it into any philosophical enquiry. The notion of limits is indeed ambiguous in itself. Our life considered from outside as a particular phenomenon, or as the ensemble of observable manifestations whose nature is not directly known to us, can obviously only subsist within certain limits (of temperature, atmospheric pressure, etc.). It is not, of course, such limits that we have in mind when we speak of ultimate realities. What interests us is at bottom the act by which what, objectively speaking, is only a certain given stopping place, is encountered by a being who at one and the same time recognises it and positively refuses to take any notice of it. Perhaps in this case we can use the verb *néantiser* which Mr. Sartre has recourse to so persistently and even injudiciously. You may, perhaps, object that the being does not really recognise the limit since he refuses to take any notice of it, but it must be answered that not to recognise it would mean that he was purely and simply blind; yet here there is perfect lucidity; risk is taken on, and this risk can in an extreme case, such as absolute sacrifice, be the complete acceptance of annihilation, this being considered as of no importance with regard to some special end. The word "sacrifice" is the one we have to keep above all; value is probably always related to a sacrifice which is at least possible; value is, however, only authentic when something incommensurable is not only granted but established, something beside which all the rest, at least for the time being, sinks into non-existence – all the rest, including myself, that is, if by myself I mean a being who appears to himself to have begun and to be going to end.

In the light of these remarks, we see clearly that value can only be incarnate: if indeed it is reduced to an abstract definition we fall back once more into our game and consequently into falsehood, for here the game does not know itself to be a game. The truth is that we do not consent to die for beauty in general, or even for liberty in general: all that means absolutely nothing. We accept death in order to save our country, or perhaps more truly for our enslaved brothers. Again, it would be as well to ask ourselves exactly what we mean by *dying for*. Death must be an act, it must be felt as a positive mode of sharing in a certain good which is itself bound up with history. From this point of view it seems likely that it would be absurd to say that anyone died for an idea, because an idea has no need of such a death, it cannot even know about it, it is self-sufficient. On the other hand, my brothers do need me, and it is very possible that I cannot answer their call to me except by consenting to die. Here, to be sure, the consent is everything, but on condition that it is not abstractly isolated from the extremity, the limit to which it obliges us.

It seems probable then that a fundamental relationship is established between value and courage by the facts these reflections have disclosed and by the mediation of sacrifice. We find here transposed on to a different plane the implication of the terminology in use in the seventeenth century.

The conclusion seems, I admit, to conflict with the realism concerning values that a great many contemporary thinkers have claimed to establish. Furthermore, it is somewhat difficult to see how it can be applied to purely *æsthetic* values. Is not gracefulness a value for instance? And what relationship could ever be discovered between gracefulness and courage? Perhaps the answer is that we establish a category of the graceful and then set it up as a value by virtue of an illusion. What really exist are graceful human beings, there are also works of art that are graceful, and besides these there is a spiritual attitude to which these beings and works correspond. This attitude, however, cannot be considered by itself either as a value or as something creative of value. Must we not then in some way identify value and merit, in other words must we localise the value in the effort at the price of which the work of art was achieved? This interpretation is obviously absurd. All that we have to remember from our foregoing analyses is that there can certainly be no value in the precise meaning of the word without vigilance on the part of a consciousness exposed to the temptation of surrendering to a facile and complacent system which is springing up around us. Only it is quite clear that we have so far only

succeeded in formulating a quite negative condition which cannot
be conceived of without an opposite – and perhaps this opposite is
not absolutely definable. I am inclined to think that it can only
become clear by a consideration of the working consciousness *(conscience œuvrante)*.

There is no doubt that we must proceed *a contrario* here, that is
to say we must get to the root of the nature of unemployment.
Unemployment is first seen from outside as a fact. It tends to
become boredom or tedium as it becomes more conscious. The
unemployed appears to himself to be unattached and even cast
away by what is real, as it were on some desert shore; it seems to
him that life has no more use for him. He tries to invent interests for
himself; to form habits, but he does not manage to dupe himself
with them. The wife of the man on the retired list busies herself in
punctuating his life, in making sure that he has regular amusements, which means in reality that she creates different forms of
slavery for him, but the result of it all is only to provide a very
imperfect disguise for his unemployment. What eats into him is the
more or less distinct sense of life's almost inconceivable cruelty.
Why should it persist within him, since he has no further interest in
anything, since no one needs him any more? The only unknown
element he can still look for is that of sickness and death. All this, of
course, only applies to the lonely unemployed, or the one who has
felt the loosening of the vital bonds which united him to his friends
and relations. Here unemployment borders on despair; despair is
nothing but unemployment which has attained the most acute self-
consciousness, or again, to put it rather bluntly, it is the breaking of
an engagement, the desertion of a conscience which has no further
part in reality.

To be at work, on the other hand, is to be possessed by the real
in such a way that we no longer know exactly whether it is we who
are fashioning it, or it which fashions us. In any case, difficult as it
is to form a perfectly intelligible idea of this operation, we can say
that it involves the reciprocal movement by which man and reality
embrace each other, which is none the less effective in the artist and
the scholar than in the artisan, for instance, or the labourer. All that
varies is the manner in which the real is present to man or, correlatively, the manner by which man is present to the real. One thing

becomes apparent in all cases – to the confusion of a superficial logic which only applies to the world of things and Having (here these terms are synonymous) – it is that wherever the operating consciousness is effectively at work, a mysterious inversion takes place and in the end an identification is established between giving and receiving. It is not, indeed, enough to say that we receive in proportion to what we give; the truth is far more paradoxical and more subtle: we receive in giving, or to put it still better, giving is already a way of receiving. The unemployed or the man without hope of whom I spoke just now is not only someone who no longer gives anything, he is someone who has lost the power of animating the world into which he feels he has been thrown, and where he is superfluous. But this animating power should not be understood in a purely subjectivistic sense, like the faculty of making fantastic shadows move across a lifeless screen: the power of animating is the power of using to the full, or, to go more deeply, of lending ourselves, that is to say of allowing ourselves to be used to the full, of offering ourselves in some way to those *kairoi*, or life-giving opportunities which the being, who is really available *(disponible)*, discovers all around him like so many switches controlling the inexhaustible current flowing through our universe.

And yet is there not something deep down in us which protests against this optimism? Not by an abstract opposition or a sneering denial drawn from our pride: no: but does not the spirit of truth itself force us to face those extreme cases – those cases where all sources of help seem really to have dried up, where everything seems to have failed – the case of the prisoner, alone in the depths of his cell, of the exile, lost in a strange land, or, finally, of the incurable invalid who day by day feels the flickering flame die down and remains helpless while life, continuing its relentless and purposeless game, slowly deserts him.

It seems to me that a philosopher worthy of the name can never consider these extreme cases with too great anxiety and insistence, and it is indeed the spirit of truth that requires him not to turn away from them in order to establish some well-adjusted, harmonious, soothing system where they are all omitted. We are here at the exact point where honest thought changes into a *De profundis* and by the very fact of so doing opens to transcendence. I am speaking of the one authentic transcendence and ask you to be good enough to ignore or rather to refuse to accept the often vague and most certainly injudicious use which so many contemporary thinkers, for the most part existentialists, have made of this word.

Yes, it is indeed here that invocation arises, that an appeal for help to the absolute Thou is articulated. I have never ceased repeating this many and many a time. But I should like to be much more explicit on a point which, to tell the truth, has always seemed to me essential and upon which there should be no possible uncertainty. The spirit of truth bears another name which is even more revealing; it is also the spirit of fidelity, and I am more and more convinced that what this spirit demands of us is an explicit refusal, a definite negation of death. The death here in question is neither death in general, which is only a fiction, nor my own death in so far as it is mine, as Mr. Brunschvicg admitted in the course of the debate which brought us to grips at the *Congas Descartes;* it is the death of those we love. They alone in fact are within reach of our spiritual sight, it is they only whom it is given us to apprehend and to long for as beings, even if our religion, in the widest sense of the word, not only allows us but even encourages us and enjoins us to extrapolate and proclaim that light is everywhere, that love is everywhere, that Being is everywhere. "To love a being," says one of my characters, "is to say you, you in particular, will never die." For me this is not merely a sentence in a play, it is an affirmation which it is not given to us to transcend. To consent to the death of a being is in a sense to give him up to death. Moreover, I should like to be able to show that again here it is the spirit of truth which forbids us to make this surrender, this betrayal.

Yet nothing could at first sight seem more arbitrary or even more iniquitous than to compare what appears to be the pure and simple recognition of a fact to a betrayal. Is it not, on the contrary, unreasonable and almost blameworthy to refuse to accept this fact, and ought we not to say that those who, silencing their longings and even their aspirations, admit and proclaim it, are the more truly courageous? Is it not the unbeliever who refuses all fallacious consolation who is the real representative of the spirit of truth? In addition, it might be asked what does this active negation of death amount to? Is it anything but a purely verbal negation, the refusal made by minds all aureoled with infantile sentimentality to accept the reality which they have not the courage to face? There we have in my view one of the most important problems with which the existential philosopher has to deal, and the solution which I am inclined to propose is in direct opposition to the positions adopted in our own time by such men as Heidegger and Jaspers.

It seems to me that we should begin by observing that there can be no question of treating the absolute cessation of consciousness as a fact, and this is a sufficient answer to the supposed objectivity on which he who is hardened in his denial prides himself. In the first place, in fact, we have no sort of possibility or right to speak of a consciousness in the same way as we speak of an object which can be defined as "this particular thing," which first appeared at a given moment of time and will come to an end (will break, for instance, or dissolve) at another equally fixed moment. I should also be quite ready to say that consciousness cannot be defined ostensively; what can be designated is never it itself, it is something (the particular body) which perhaps keeps up and doubtless tends to impair a whole set of relationships with it, which are inextricable to the point of contradicting themselves as relations. Moreover, we must remark that if we admit that consciousness is a manifestation there can be no question of observing anything but the more or less prolonged eclipses of consciousness. We are, however, unable to go to the extreme limit and to speak of a final eclipse or an absolute disappearance, for unless we fall into an indefensible materialism, we can neither apprehend nor even imagine the principle of which consciousness is the manifestation. From this point of view we might say very simply that if death is a silence we cannot mark its boundaries, for we neither know what it is veiling, what it is protecting, nor what it is preparing. The fallacy, the treason, consists in interpreting this silence as nonexistence, as a decline into non-being.

Perhaps it may be objected that such considerations do not take us beyond an agnosticism which many of the poets of the end of the nineteenth century, from Tennyson to Sully Prudhomme, expressed, with pathos, no doubt, but with very unsound philosophy. Only I do not in the least think that agnosticism is the last word here. The active negation of death, which I was advocating a moment ago, has in it both something of a challenge and of piety;

more exactly, it is piety which from our mode of insertion in the
world is bound to appear as a challenge. The world seems to assure
me cynically that this tenderly loved being no longer exists on its
lists, that he has been struck off the universal register – and I for my
part claim that he exists all the same and that he cannot help existing. I am thus caught in the toils of an agonising contradiction. Can
I free myself from it?

First, I have to remind myself that the departed being of whom
they now want me to believe that there is nothing left but a past,
who is altogether past, was at the beginning nothing but a future. A
loving conspiracy had at first to be formed around him, at a time
when nothing was as yet known of what he would or could be. The
essence of this being was still only the prophetic hopes he awakened in his relatives. And I have to ask myself in the presence of this
death, which is perhaps only a birth or an ascension, if the conspiracy is not to be reproduced on a higher plane. This time it is round
a sleep that the conspiracy must be centred – a sleep which must not
be disturbed by intruders. But against what intrusion except that of
infidelity and negation have we to guard?

There is still a serious ambiguity, however. You may say that
this infidelity is simply forgetfulness; it is a *memory* which we have
to respect, and we are guilty of a veritable paralogism in fraudu-
lently changing this *memory* into an existence, to be protected and
promoted. We have then to choose between two interpretations, the
one modest and in strict conformity with the given facts of experience, the other arbitrary and almost delirious.

But if this divergence is possible, it is because we are no longer
in the realm of practical existence, where it is always possible, at
least in theory, to investigate what we seek to verify. To return to the
simile of sleep, everything happens as though we were watching
from the other side of a transparent partition; we cannot make sure
of the exact state of the sleeper; the very meaning of the words "real
state" is no longer quite clear. The sleeper has been taken beyond
our reach, we are no longer permitted to proceed to any sort of
examination by manipulation which would give us some way of
pronouncing upon his state. If a manipulation is still possible it can
only be carried out upon a thing which, because it is a thing, is no
longer *he,* and which, moreover, is in process of disappearing. It is

required of us, whatever the circumstances, to triumph over the obsessions which cling to this thing, whether it be to preserve a memory or to dwell upon a presence.

Nevertheless, it appears upon reflection that he who limits himself to respecting a memory is at bottom still sufficiently in awe of the "thing" to consider it as the remains of what we can no longer preserve within ourselves except as an image. Moreover, this image grows fainter each day, like a badly printed photograph which we vainly keep on dusting. But would it not here be as well to destroy an illusion. Supposing that I really do cherish a materialised or purely mental image, it is not for itself that I do so, but out of love for the being this image evokes. This being himself, then, should not and cannot be created as an image, otherwise we shall fall into an absurdity, the image being referred back to another image, and so on and so on for as far as we can see. Our fidelity can only be founded on an unfailing attachment to an existence which it is impossible to relegate to the world of images. If our thought here tends to be confused, it is really because some image, rudimentary as it must be, and consequently a mere shadow, is necessary for this unfailing attachment to become conscious of itself. This shadow, which may be only a name still impregnated with affection, is the mode by which a presence makes itself known to me.

It does not seem as though all this can be seriously disputed. It may certainly be objected, however, that the existence seen through the image is only something from the past; we shall therefore speak of a "still existing" (*un exister encore*), of that which "no longer exists" (*n'existe plus*), if we want to define what we are here considering. But if we break away from this abstract jargon, we shall without a doubt be forced to recognise that the question is always and ever concerned with the image; yet it is precisely from this that we want to free ourselves, it is a non-shadow that we are striving to grasp, that is to say something indefectible. There is not and cannot be piety except where relations are maintained with what is indefectible. But we must at the same time emphasise the paradox that as a matter of fact the memories, or more exactly the images, can very well tend to stifle the indefectible essence which it is their business to evoke. There is no piety which is not in danger of degenerating into idolatry.

Let us penetrate further: indefectibility is that which cannot fail where deep-rooted fidelity is preserved, and this amounts to saying that it is a reply. Only this reply could not be automatic without fidelity becoming weakened in its very essence (for it would degenerate into a process or technique). It must therefore be well understood that the faithful soul is destined to experience darkness and that it must even be familiar with the temptation to let itself be inwardly blinded by the night through which it has to pass. Moreover, this is saying too little and the language I have used here is not courageous enough. Fidelity is not a preliminary *datum*, it is revealed and established as fidelity by this very crossing of the darkness, by this trial combined with everyday life, the experience of "day after day." So then the Indefectible is not the permanence of an essence, or, more exactly, it is not in the mode of such a permanence that it can be given to us. The essence is in fact made known to thought as it advances, by way of a law definable only in universal terms. This law is not conceivable where relations between one being and another are in question. Consequently, there is room for every sort of error, false move and deception on the side of the subject. It is through these errors and vicissitudes that we are allowed to behold the intermittent gleaming of the indefectible fire. I will not try to disguise, but emphasise rather, the contradiction which these words contain; it seems to me to be bound up with our human condition.

Such I think are the preliminary data concerning what is really somewhat improperly called the problem of personal immortality. I am actually very far from hazarding any conjectures on the mode of existence of the departed and the nature of the palingenesis for which they are no doubt destined. Moreover, it does not matter that I refuse to be interested in such speculations. It must, however, be recognised that those who do indulge in them are generally quite unprovided with any equipment for reflection, hence their theories are in danger of degenerating into pure fantasies. On the other hand, theological interdicts, of which it would be well to examine the foundations very closely, help in great measure to paralyse all independent research in this realm.

I should like now to go back briefly in order to bring out the unity, admittedly hard to grasp at first, which underlies the preceding considerations. The fundamental connection seems to me to be as follows: whatever the Stoics or idealists say (we will not here consider the less elevated doctrines), if death is the ultimate reality, value is annihilated in mere scandal, reality is pierced to the heart. This we cannot disguise from ourselves unless we enclose ourselves in a system of pleasure. Simply to admit or accept this scandal is not only to bow before an objective fact, for here we are outside the order of fact; it is rather to destroy human communion itself at its very centre. The spirit of truth here identifies itself with the spirit of fidelity and love. We should really go further: value can only be thought of as reality – and by that I mean saved from a verbalism which destroys while thinking to proclaim it – if it is related to the consciousness of an immortal destiny. We have seen clearly that it is not separated from courage and sacrifice: but whatever the being who sacrifices himself may think about himself and his metaphysical chances, reflection cannot accept this annihilation, even if he is himself resigned to it. Do not let us be the dupes of words: reflection, as an abstract entity, is nothing; what is real is I myself, meditating about the destiny of my brother.

I do not in the least disguise from myself the numberless questions which arise here – particularly concerning the part played in this realm by the appeal to absolute transcendence. Is it possible to conceive of a real personal survival independently of this transcendence? I think that my reply would be as follows: there is no human love worthy of the name which does not represent for him who exercises it both a pledge and a seed of immortality: but, on the other hand, it is really not possible to exercise this love without discovering that it cannot constitute a closed system, that it passes beyond itself in every direction, that it really demands for its complete realisation a universal communion outside which it cannot be satisfied and is destined to be corrupted and lost in the end. Moreover, this universal communion itself can only be centred upon an absolute Thou. It is time to do away once and for all with the positivist illusions on this subject.

There is another point on which I should like briefly to explain myself. What real relation can be established between value and immortality? There is, for instance, no doubt that the beautiful work of art is uncorrupted and untouched by time. "A thing of beauty is

a joy forever," as the poet says. But is it true that this is in any way
connected with what we understand by a real survival, by the
soul's or the person's actual victory over death? Perhaps we could
reply as follows: in a world of scandal where absurdity had gained
the upper hand, that is to say where what is best and highest was at
the mercy of blind forces, where "because a little piece of iron had
passed through their heads, it had become for ever impossible to
get on with people like Péguy or like Alain Fournier" (Jacques
Rivière, *A la Trace de Dieu)* – there would not perhaps be a single
value which was not in danger of appearing ludicrous and suspect.
We are thus led to wonder whether the essence of value – independently of what we have seen to be its function – is not to be found in
its translucency. This amounts to saying that value is the mirror
wherein it is given us to discern, always imperfectly and always
through a distorting mist, the real face of our destiny, the "truer
than ourselves." What it shows us certainly reaches its full development in another world – a world which it seems to be the property
of our earthly experience to open or half open to us, or in extreme
cases, to prevent us from entering.

    Thus to make the other world the axis of our life is, of course, to
take the opposite position from that of nearly all contemporary
philosophers, and I do not deny that, at the bottom of my mind,
there is an anxious voice protesting and persistently arguing in
favour of the metaphysicians of Earth. It is, however, to be wondered whether the systematic refusal to accept this other world is
not at the origin of the convulsions which have reached their paroxysm at the present time. Perhaps a stable order can only be established if man is acutely aware of his condition as a traveller, that is
to say, if he perpetually reminds himself that he is required to cut
himself a dangerous path across the unsteady blocks of a universe
which has collapsed and seems to be crumbling in every direction.
This path leads to a world more firmly established in Being, a world
whose changing and uncertain gleams are all that we can discern
here below. Does not everything happen as though this ruined universe turned relentlessly upon whomever claimed that he could set-
tle down in it to the extent of erecting a permanent dwelling there
for himself? It is not to be denied, of course, that the affirmation of
the other world entails risk, it is the "noble venture" of which the

ancient philosopher spoke, but the whole question is to know whether in refusing to make this venture we are not starting upon a road which sooner or later leads to perdition.

Paris, 1943.

To GUSTAVE THIBON

DANGEROUS SITUATION OF ETHICAL VALUES

From an abstract point of view, which has been that of most of the philosophers up till now, it may seem ridiculous to speak of a situation of values: and if values are considered as ideas there is no sense in saying they are situated. It is quite otherwise if one admits, as I do not hesitate to do, that a value is nothing if it is not incarnated. Moreover, the word incarnated must be defined. What does it mean for a value to be embodied? To simplify matters let us only consider what are properly speaking ethical values here. The property of a value, as I said recently, is to assume a certain function in relation to life and, as it were, to mark it with its seal. For that, it is still necessary for the value to be incorporated in some cause. It seems to me, in fact, that in its general lines we can adopt the theory which was presented with such force by the American philosopher, Royce, in his fine book, *Philosophy of Loyalty*. A cause is neither an individual nor a collection of individuals, nor an abstract principle. A cause is not impersonal, but rather supra-personal; it is a particular type of unity which holds together a number of persons within a life which they share. Hence a relationship of a special kind, which we can call loyalty, is established between the individual and the cause; it is not a mystical renunciation, but a fully conscious attachment which presupposes the free subordination of the self to a superior principle. "My loyalty," Royce says, "means nothing theoretically or practically if I am not the member of a community. No success I can achieve will be valid if it is not also the success of the community to which I essentially belong, in virtue of the real relations which bind me to the whole of the universe." This last detail is extremely important. If we only took the first definition we might indeed fear that it justified allegiance to a party, for instance, with all the servitudes which can go with it. But, for Royce, if loyalty is a supreme good, conflict between varying loyalties is the greatest of evils. It must be recognised that some causes are favourable and others contrary to the development of loyalty in the world. "A cause is good not only for us but for humanity – that is to say, in itself – according to the measure in which it serves the spirit of loyalty, that is to say that it helps us in our loyalty to our fellows and fosters it."[1] This amounts to saying that there is a universal cause which is that of loyalty in the world. Loyalty is infectious, it is a good which spreads wide, it is a ferment of extraordinary potency. Such is indeed the cause to which I should consecrate myself. When I speak the truth I do not only serve the supra-personal community which I form with my interlocutor, I help to make man's faith in man grow in this world, I help to strengthen the bonds which make a universal community possible.

I do not think all this can be seriously disputed, and the effort of the American philosopher to save universality without becoming separated from the realm of concrete action is to be admired. But at the same time we should most certainly be giving way to baleful illusions if we made any mistake about the opposition this idealism is bound, in fact, to meet with today, even if it obtains a theoretical and lifeless assent from many minds. And it is precisely here that we are obliged to introduce the notion of situation. It is probable that at no time the faith of man in man, not only faith in his fellows, but in himself, has been subjected to a more harsh and formidable test. What is in danger of death today is man himself in his unity, and this is just as true of the individual considered as a concrete whole as of the human race considered as the flowing out or expansion of an essence. Hence there is a great risk that Royce's idea of the spirit of loyalty will be felt as an empty aspiration, as an inconsistent dream, as a fiction.

It is evident that a metaphysic of faith can be built on the ruins of humanism: and here there develops an impassioned dialectic.

1   Royce, Philosophy of Loyalty (Macmillan), p. 118.

For if it is possible to say that the death of God in the Nietzschean sense preceded and made possible the agony of man which we are now witnessing, it is legitimate in a certain sense to say that it *is* from the ashes of man that God can and must rise again. Am I mistaken in presuming that the ideas of Barth in particular draw part of their strength from the radical pessimism to which events have brought us on the purely human level?

But here the particularly serious problem arises which I want to consider now. Have we the right, even from a strictly Christian point of view, in a certain sense to sacrifice the ethical? What in reality would such a sacrifice amount to? To put it briefly, it would consist in sanctioning an actual division which we are tending to create between those on the one hand who establish their existence on a mystical basis and those on the other who try simply to get along with as little harm as possible in this adventure, so incomprehensible and in the end so frightful, this adventure into which they have a sense of having been hurled by chance, or by inhuman and uncontrollable forces, which comes to the same thing. In thus imagining the fissure which is tending to develop at the centre of the human mass, we are however in danger of excessively over-simplifying and even of misrepresenting a situation which is infinitely more complex and which it is probably scarcely possible to schematise.

When we speak of existences seeking to base themselves on mysticism we are in great danger of letting ourselves be taken in simply by a word and of grouping realities which have nothing in common under one head. The very term of mysticism, so abused, so emptied of all value but nevertheless so difficult to avoid, calls for serious reservations. What is really in question is, on the one hand, fidelity to "God's Word" – and, from this point of view, differences of denomination should be treated as of relatively secondary importance; and on the other a phenomenon of magnetic attraction or we might say of crystallisation. The announcement of an order to be set up in accordance with what the masses are vaguely awaiting is here embodied in some leader or group of leaders. In both cases we can say with certainty that the individual is required to make the sacrifice, not only of his immediate interests but eventually even of his life, to a supra-personal end. In the first case this end is found in an eternity which envelops and transcends the present, and in the second case in a more or less near future. But between these ends which, if one may so put it, are not situated in the same metaphysical dimension, it seems to me very difficult to establish either a definite connection or a radical opposition. One point, however, is clear: in so far as the terrestrial order to be established allows the domination of some and the subjection of others, it must be stated without hesitation that it can only be set up in defiance of all the values converging towards the inaccessible centre for which we reserve the name of eternity. On the other hand, in so far as the terrestrial order is conceived of as effectively excluding all privilege and all slavery, it is just possible to see in it a symbol, imperfect, no doubt, and perhaps even inconsistent in the main, of a reality which can only be effectively established under conditions incompatible with the fragile, ephemeral and contradictory structure of our actual experience. These simple observations will be enough to show the equivocal and even dangerous character of certain momentary alliances which at a time of crisis may be entered into between Christianity or some Christian confession on the one hand and on the other the most active form of earthly mysticism – the only one which stands a real chance of still surviving tomorrow after the nameless tempest we are passing through today. On the strictly tellurian plane, that is, in an order where given concrete dynamisms are at work, it is difficult to see how anything but a more and more powerfully organised systematised plutocracy can oppose this earthly mysticism tomorrow. Such a plutocracy would, moreover, be inevitably tempted to mobilise in its service, not so much genuine spiritual forces, as some of the feeblest interpreters – those most open to suggestion and seduction – whom the spiritual forces must call upon to represent them in visible form before the eyes of the majority. Hence there will be a danger that a situation may develop which will be all the more inextricable because, in such a struggle, what might originally have still figured as mysticism will have inevitably degenerated into a pure system of spite and gratification.

Under these conditions it may seem as though the Christian were condemned simply to retire from a conflict in which the stake appears to him to be more and more futile, since this stake amounts to nothing but the possession of the world, in other words the seizure of the unseizable. At the end of this dialectic, which it would be only too easy to illustrate with concrete examples, we are apparently faced with what was already given us at the start: an irreparable rent in the very stuff of which our humanity is made.

But at the same time, as we have already suggested, it is clear that the Christian cannot rest content to observe and accept this rent without denying his own Christianity and without emptying the very notion of salvation of its substantial content.

Does this mean that in order to preserve the meaning and value of this notion, the Christian has to arrogate to himself a sort of right or duty of guardianship over the non-Christian? Briefly, must we subscribe to the establishment of a spiritual paternalism which will be both at the cost and to the advantage of the Christian? I am sure that such a position is impossible from every point of view. On the one hand, indeed, it would give the Christian an essentially pharisaical sense of superiority; on the other hand it would none the less fatally cause in the nonbeliever a sort of bitterness, or *invidia,* which is probably the root of anti-religious passion. The Christian in fact cannot in any way think of himself as possessing either a power or even an advantage which has been denied to the unbeliever. There we have one of the most paradoxical aspects of his situation, for in another sense, he is obliged to recognise that grace has been bestowed upon him. This, however, only remains true on condition that the grace should inhabit him, not only as radiance, but as humility. From the moment that he begins to be proud of it as a possession it changes its nature, and I should be tempted to say it becomes a malediction.

Philosophers as a whole have taken little trouble to scrutinise the nature of this humility. Yet it is essentially in its name that the Christian must constantly be on his guard against the temptation to paternalism. At its root there is an assurance, or I should be ready to say a knowledge that, in his quality of a Christian, he acts neither on his own account nor through the power of a virtue which is his property, or even which having been infused into him has become authentically his own. Under these conditions he cannot in any way claim to be worth more than the disinherited brother to whom he is speaking. It would moreover be unlawfully pretentious on his part should he glory in having a good leader, or a good master, whilst the unbeliever has no one, for this would mean that he was putting himself once more on the plane of Having, the plane where one boasts about what one possesses. It would not be difficult to show how this paradoxical humility tends at first to strike the unbeliever as unbearable hypocrisy. This has given rise to a tragic misunderstanding, especially as the sincere Christian can always wonder whether the humility he is practising is any better than an attitude adopted in conformity with something he has been taught.

If this is the case, to come to the help of the unbeliever spiritually can scarcely mean claiming literally to bring him something of which he has been deprived. Such a claim would in fact always be in danger of annulling or making sterile the good which we set out to do. All that we can propose to ourselves is, in the last analysis, to awaken within another the consciousness of what he is, or, more precisely, of his divine filiation; to teach him to see himself as the child of God through the love which is shown him. From this point of view, I should be rather tempted to say that, contrary to what Kierkegaard proclaimed, there is probably a Christian maieutic, of which, however, the essence is naturally very different from what we know of the Platonic maieutic. It is in treating the other as a child of God that it seems to me to be within the limits of possibility for me to awaken within him a consciousness of his divine filiation. But in reality I do not give or bring him anything. I merely direct the adoration of which God is the unique object on to the divine life as seen in this creature, who from the beginning has been unaware of his true nature and is all the more unaware of it the greater his self-complacent vanity may be.

These considerations may at first seem rather far removed from the problem we have set ourselves, but they are not really so. We shall, however, have to apply what we have been saying about any Christian, to the Christian thinker.

I am going to strive to put the question in as distinct terms as possible. We shall get a better idea of its immense range if we remember that it does not only concern the relations of the Christian with the non-Christian, but also the relations of the Christian with himself, in so far as he discovers within himself "immense regions where the Gospel has not been preached." Moreover, it is in the depths of these regions that a greater part of his existence develops; the most important part, perhaps, often the most visible and sometimes the only visible part.

In the light of the preceding remarks what would the theory of a Christian philosopher amount to if he set out to deny the specific and authentic character of the ethical values, that is in fact to say if he set out to crush them to nothing between revelation on one side and undiluted sociology on the other? Let us get away here from pure abstractions. A theory is absolutely nothing apart from the subject who propounds it, there is no affirmation without someone who affirms. But who is making an affirmation here? It is I as a philosopher, it is I, consequently, in a special definite capacity, as I address "you others," or, which comes to very much the same thing, as I take counsel with myself concerning those others on whom I am going to give judgment. From the position which I occupy, I declare that what you consider good is not truly good, or again that the reasons you think you have for adhering to it are without solidity or truth, and that, in the last analysis, you only act in conformity with impulses of which the temporal and impure origins are to be found somewhere in the social structures which control your existence. As for me, on the other hand, I claim to see the light which is actually hidden from you and which alone could illuminate the darkness in which you are groping – you who do not even know that you are surrounded with gloom, so complete is your blindness. It is only too clear that an assertion of such a kind, a judgment so summary, must be regarded as contrary to the Christian, and particularly to the Catholic tradition, which has always granted so large a place to the natural virtues.

But all these reflections are precisely concerned with the phenomenon of the eclipsing of the idea of natural virtue, and this phenomenon is itself bound up with another very genuine fact which it seems to me has been the chief feature in the evolution of western humanity for the last century and a half: the disappearance of a certain confidence which is both spontaneous and metaphysical in the order which frames our existence, or again what I have elsewhere called the severance of the nuptial bond between man and life. We shall be able to show without any difficulty, I think, that the optimistic humanism of the eighteenth century or of the middle of the nineteenth, paradoxically as it may seem, marked the first stage in this tragic disintegration. "Everything leads us to think," I said recently, "that the giving way of religious beliefs which has been going on for five hundred centuries in large sections of the civilised world has brought as its consequence a weakening of the natural foundations on which those beliefs were built. If this be so it means that what we need to reawaken within and around us is this piety, not Christian but pre-Christian, or more exactly peri-Christian. Each one of us probably knows Christians who are over super-naturalised and who have lost the sense, we will not say of nature but of the nascent grace which stirs at the heart of nature. I am strongly inclined to think that, apart from Revelation, this piety is the only true *vinculum* which can bind men together, and that all abstract universalism which claims to do without it, however upright its intention, really serves only to prepare the way for a nihilism whose devastating action we can discern on all sides."

I should express very clearly what I mean if I formed the hypothesis that the forces of destruction which are let loose everywhere around us and tend to sweep away all the embodied values, whether they are incorporated in the life of a family, a school, a hospital, a museum or a church, have only been able to develop beyond all limits because they started from a way of thinking which, if we may say so, denied the real by deconsecrating it. But of course there can be no more fatal error than to imagine that anything with which to reconsecrate it can be found in these forces themselves. There is no possible doubt that to seek to return to paganism under any form whatever, is to sink even lower into delirium and abjection. The Christian philosopher who wants to do positive work in the field of ethics today should, it seems to me, start by acquiring on his own account an increasingly concrete and extensive consciousness of the underground connections which unite the peri-Christian to what may strictly be called revelation. These connections are not of a strictly logical order, but they depend on a metaphysical anthropology of which for the last fifty years or so thinkers as different as Scheler, Peter Wust or Theodor Haecker, as Chesterton, Péguy, or today Thibon, have begun to trace the features. To undertake this, perhaps the most delicate of all tasks, requires an analytical effort of the utmost patience and severity, but also a most ardent faithfulness to the human element which is of the order of love and without which the analysis will become dry and barren. To tell the truth it is only the counterpart on the plane of intelligence or human creation of the mysterious work by which a tissue is re-formed or an organ regains its power. I do not think I can convey my thought to you more explicitly than by here introducing this reference of which the implications go far beyond those of a simple metaphor in my eyes.

I am indeed very far from under-estimating the dangers which there can be in introducing biological categories into the spiritual. And on this point it may be permissible to think that Bergson, the Bergson of *Deux Sources*, is not altogether beyond reproach. But is it not a fact that in reality the biologist as such, by a fatality of which it is not impossible to discover the principles, tends increasingly to lose all consciousness of what life is, and, I should say (though of course this does not apply to Bergson) that he does this in so far as he has managed to persuade himself that he will one day be able to produce it himself. Here again we have to recognise a sense of proportion which it is the function of humility to preserve. It seems clear that when biology claims to grant itself rights comparable with those belonging to physics and chemistry in the realm of inanimate nature, it is inevitably guilty of the disastrous intrusions that we have seen becoming widespread in our time. Actually I am quite prepared to recognise that it is difficult, and perhaps even impossible, to trace a precise line of demarcation between what is lawful and not lawful in this field; on its boundaries there are questions and species about which one can only speak with knowledge after the most minute examination of each case and all the principles which it involves. The thing, however, that we can assert – and it is what matters from the point of view I am taking – is that all demarcation disappears and man gives an irreparable opening to the Monstrous from the moment when he weakens in that piety in his relations to life which can alone guide his steps in an order where murder seems to be so easy, so indiscernible, so tempting, that it is not even recognised as such by him who accomplishes it.

A serious objection, or at the very least a delicate question, can scarcely fail to occur to our minds at the point we have now reached. If we put a sort of pre-Christian or peri-Christian piety at the basis of ethics are we not either making them depend on an irrational feeling over which we have no control, or else embarking upon the paradoxical or even hopeless undertaking of trying to resuscitate natural religion which the philosophy of enlightenment tried vainly to establish? Are we not in any case ruining the specific quality of ethical values which we meant on the contrary to safeguard?

It is certainly difficult to reply to this question in a completely satisfactory way within the limits of a brief exposition such as this. It could only be done, I think, by first of all attacking the classic and arbitrary distinction which it presupposes between feeling and reason. As an illustration of my objective at the moment, we might call to mind the beautiful analysis which Soloviev, for example, has given of modesty, pity and reverence, in his *Justification du Bien.* There we have principles expressing the human quality as such, this human quality which we mutilate and betray when we claim to reduce its essence to a mere faculty of association, a faculty, moreover, which the higher animals are far from lacking.

The real and most agonising problem seems to me much rather to concern the extent of our control of these principles. How far does it depend on us to revivify them? It is impossible to be too sceptical about the efficacy of philosophic preaching in this field – and I am not even thinking, of course, about the vulgarised expressions which such preaching is liable to adopt. As Thibon has so admirably pointed out, it is above all a question of moral renewal. It is conceivable that it will be the task of small communities coming together like swarms one after the other to form what we might call centres of example, that is to say nuclei of life around which the lacerated tissues of true moral existence can be reconstituted. It is not here a question of fleeting dreams. The most actual and immediate experience shows that men can relearn how to live, when they are placed in conditions which are real and when a light illuminates the group they form (with each other and with the things supporting them) at its summit. There is every reason to think that the guarantee of the success of such undertakings is bound up with the humility in which they originate and which shapes their first objectives. Levelling, in the ambitious forms under which it was conceived before the war, characterised by a titanism which was its original defect, has every chance of being wrecked in a nameless cataclysm. In any case, on ethical grounds it can be asserted that it is not only doomed but that it is complete nonsense.

I have no illusions about the disappointment which may accompany such a conclusion. What I really want to stress is that it is urgent in all departments to carry out clearing operations which will make it possible to find once more the lost springs for lack of whose values men would be condemned to an infra-animal existence, an existence of which our generation will have had the painful privilege of witnessing the first apocalyptic symptoms.

Paris.
December, 1943.

BEING AND NOTHINGNESS

The importance of Mr. Sartre's new book[1] is incontestable. It is to be wondered whether it is not the most important contribution yet made to general philosophy by the generation of "under-forties." Is it a perfectly original contribution? We are at first tempted to doubt it, so much do we feel on every page the influence, upon the form at least, of Martin Heidegger. We should surely be wrong, however, to stop at this first impression. The thought of Mr. Sartre diverges from the doctrine worked out in *Sein und Zeit* on some very important points, and it seems very possible that the central intuition of the young French philosopher is his own. It is this intuition that I want above all to try to bring out in the following pages without attempting to keep scrupulously to the author's own order. I may say in passing that he has himself owned that the introduction is one of the stiffest parts of this difficult book and makes it particularly hard to get into.

The fundamental principle of *L'Etre et le Néant* (Being and Nothingness) is the irreconcilable opposition which exists between the being in itself *(l'être en-soi)* and the being for itself *(l'être pour-soi)*. It is the property of *l'être en-soi* to be identically and fully what it is. "There is not in the *en-soi* the smallest particle of being which does not belong to itself without distance. There is not in the being thus conceived the slightest hint of duality. The *en-soi* fills itself and it would be impossible to imagine a more total plentitude, a more perfect co-extensiveness of content and container: there is no empty space in the being, through which nothingness could squeeze an

1   *L'Etre et le Néant*, Edition of the N.R.F.

entry" (p. 116). It may be asked what right we have to postulate the existence of this *être en-soi*. The reply is that it is of the essence of consciousness to be *conscious* of – that is to say to be aware of a reality which is properly speaking aimed at, but at the same time treated as independent and irreducible. To be conscious of something is to be confronted with a full and concrete presence other than the consciousness. "Transcendence is an essential structure of consciousness" (p. 27). For myself I should express this by saying that when I consider the consciousness which I – or anyone else – can acquire of some reality, I am irresistibly led to imagine this reality as existing in itself (*en-soi*) and as consequently being an example of that fullness of being, that self-sufficiency which logically appears to be the characteristic of the *en-soi*. It is true that we still have to find out whether what we have here is not simply a way of seeing the world which is implied in the very structure of consciousness. If this were the case the *en-soi* would in some sort destroy itself, since it would be reduced to a sort of façade or optical illusion. What has to be borne in mind for the moment is that it is in its opposition to *l'être en-soi* thus defined that we shall be able to recognise what constitutes the originality of *l'être pour-soi*.

Analysis shows, indeed, that it is impossible to define consciousness, that is to say the being *pour-soi*, as something exactly coincident with itself. I can say of this table that it is purely and simply this table. It is not thus with my belief. I should not in all honesty be able to say only that it is belief, precisely because, in so far as it is *pour-soi*, it is consciousness of belief. From the very fact that my belief is apprehended as belief, it tends in some sort to escape from its belief-being. It is disturbed belief. A belief which was purely and simply and absolutely belief would not be aware of itself, and would therefore no longer be consciousness, nor even, when all was said and done, would it be belief. Let us say then both that belief is only itself on condition that it escapes in some sort from its own identity, and, inversely, if it coincides fully with itself in the manner of the *en-soi* it will tend to do away with itself *as* belief.

These arguments which may at first seem singularly subtle and abstract, are illustrated by an admirable analysis of bad faith *(la mauvaise foi)* which forms one of the most outstanding and solid chapters of the book. The author, considering the conditions under which bad faith is possible, shows that it presupposes the existence of a being so constituted that it is not exactly or fully what it is, and this same structure is moreover implied in the ideal of sincerity set for himself by the man who proposes to be himself, to coincide with himself, that is to say, in reality, to fulfil the conditions of the being *en-soi* within the heart of the being *pour-soi*, however contradictory and hopeless such an undertaking may appear.

In the eyes of Mr. Sartre, a constant phenomenon such as bad faith can only be understood if it has been realised once and for all that negative judgment, under all its forms, supposes a previous presence of nothingness within and outside us. What does this mean? Are we not falling into the worst kind of conceptual mythology? But it is enough to reflect upon the implication of a question or interrogation of any kind. The questioner, by the very fact that he questions, admits and therefore recognises the possibility of a negative reply. Moreover, the reply, even if it is strictly positive, will contain something negative, that is to say some not-being. "What the being *will be* must necessarily be that which detaches itself from the background of what it *is not*; whatever the reply was it could be formulated thus: 'the being is that, and outside that nothing'" (p. 40). It is to be observed that the non-being always appears within the limits of a human expectation. This is undeniable; the world does not show its non-beings to anyone who has not first postulated them as possibilities. Can we, however, conclude from this that they are reducible to pure subjectivity? It must be noted that the question in a dialogue is only one form of interrogation: "If my car breaks down, it is the carburetor, the plugs, etc., that I interrogate. If my watch stops I can interrogate the watchmaker about the causes for which it stopped, but it is the different parts of the watch's mechanism that the watchmaker will question in his turn. What I am expecting from the carburetor and what the watchmaker expects from the works of the watch is not a judgment, but an *unveiling of being*, on the grounds of which a judgment can be formed. If, however, I am expecting an unveiling of being, it means that I am prepared at the same time for the possibility of the unveiling of a non-being. If I interrogate the carburetor it is because I consider it possible that there is nothing in the carburetor. Thus my question by its nature envelops a certain prejudicative comprehension of non-being . . ." (p. 42). It would be difficult to find a more complicated way of expressing a simpler idea and it is to be wondered whether the author is not unsteadily balanced here between a pure truism and a sophism which, moreover, he does not manage to formulate distinctly (perhaps because it is a kind of monster which cannot stand the fresh air of reflection and is only able to live its precarious life in some sort of twilight). This comprehension of non-being founded on being is moreover implied in all activity directed towards destruction. The examination of destructive behaviour leads to the same result as that of interrogative behaviour. All this, in short, goes to show that human reality which is at the same time "consciousness of" and *pour-soi* cannot be constituted without reference to non-being. But can we say that this non-being, this nothingness exists? Certainly not, and here the author hazards a frightful solecism: "As nothingness is not, as it has only an appearance of being, it should rather be said that it is made to be *(est été)* or else that it is made to not-be *(est néantisé)*. A being must therefore exist whose property it is to make Nothingness nothing *(néantiser le néant)* and to support it with its being . . . a being by whom Nothingness comes to things" (p. 58). Do not let us be taken in here by what is certainly very defective terminology. *Néantir* does not in any way mean to annihilate or to annul, but, to use a frequent illustration of this author, it means much more to surround the being with a casing of non-being, or, as I personally should be more ready to say, to put it into the parenthesis of non-being. Following from this the problem is to know what this power of *néantisation* is. "The Being by which Nothingness comes into the world is a being in which the question arises within its being of the nothingness of its being: the Being by which Nothingness comes into the world must be its own nothingness" (p. 49). These obscure formula which border on pure nonsense need I think to be translated into somewhat different language. The very clumsy expression, "the question arises" means seemingly that such a being keeps up a living connection with the possibility of its own nothingness: it should be added at once that this possibility, from the very fact that it is thus recognised and taken into consideration or assumed, becomes what might be called an element of being. The words *comes into the world* should also be analysed. The world here envisaged has nothing to do with the cosmos; as a matter of fact, we might wonder whether a doctrine such as the one we are studying is not at bottom acosmic in its fundamental intention. The world here is the *Umwelt* in relation to which each one of us has to take his place in order to exist and even to become conscious of himself.

From this point of view it is easy to see that the power of *néantisation* is liberty itself. What it is given to human reality to modify is its relationship with the being which is placed opposite to it. If it, as it were, switches out some particular thing which exists it is really switching itself out in relation to this thing. In this case the human reality escapes from it and is beyond its reach, the particular thing cannot act upon it; for it has retired beyond a nothingness – I should rather say it has placed itself in an insulated position. As far as human reality is concerned, to separate itself from the world (or from anything in this world) is to separate itself from itself; and it is this capacity to *prendre du champ par rapport à soi*[1] (the expression is my own invention) which constitutes liberty. The author, following Kierkegaard, recognises that "anguish" is the mode of being of liberty as a consciousness of being, "it is in anguish that liberty within its being is in question for itself" (p. 66). Here again let us translate: it is in anguish that liberty becomes aware of itself; not as an object, which would have no meaning, but as a concrete possibility not to be eluded. A fine analysis of dizziness here elucidates the author's thought. "At the very moment when I am aware of myself as being horror of the precipice I am conscious of this horror as not being determinant in relation to my possible behaviour. . . . It is of the very being of horror to appear to itself as not being the cause of the behaviour it calls for. . . . The decisive behaviour will emanate from a self which I am not yet. Thus, the self that I am depends in itself on the self that I am not yet to the exact extent that the self that I am not yet does not depend upon the self that I am. And the dizziness appears as the awareness of this dependence" (p. 69). It appears then as clearly as possible that it is of the nature of human reality to contain what we might call gaps, instead of forming like the *en-soi* a tissue so closely constituted as to have in it no empty

1   This means roughly: to stand back from oneself.

space. Hence the liberty which makes itself known to me in anguish can be characterised by the existence of this *nothing* which insinuates itself between motives and actions; and it is the structure of the motives as inefficient or as non-determinant which is the condition of my liberty. Let us say once again that consciousness is not its own motive in so far as it is empty of all content and in so far as it confronts its past and future as it confronts a self which it is in the mode of not being *(sur le mode du n'être pas).*

Here we have the point of departure for a general theory of temporality which I cannot attempt to develop within the limits of this article. What matters is the general fact that it is the property of the being *pour-soi* to be what it is not (for instance, what it has ceased to be and what it is not yet or what it would like to be) according to modes which on the contrary are excluded by the *en-soi* wherein the principle of identity triumphs. This is very strongly expressed in the following lines: "There are many ways of not being and some of them do not reach the innermost nature of the being which is not what it is not. If, for example, I say of an ink-pot that it is not a bird, the ink-pot and the bird are still untouched by the negation which is an external relation and can only be established by a human reality which is its witness. On the other hand, there is a type of negation which establishes an internal relation between what one denies, and that of which one denies it. Of all the internal negations the one which penetrates deepest into the being, the one which makes the being of that which it denies to constitute the being of that *of* which it denies it, is lack. This lack does not pertain to the nature of the *en-soi* which is all positiveness. And it only appears in the world with the arising of human reality" (p. 129). Lack makes its appearance with man and this amounts to saying that human reality itself is a lack. But let us have a good look at what that means: this lack is not discovered from outside, on the contrary it is lived from within as lack, and the author goes so far as to say that the being in question establishes itself as its own lack. Desire is not possible except as presupposing such a structure – desire, or modes of thought such as the present or past conditional, characterising regret or nostalgia. To tell the truth we are fed on a fallacious psychology which systematically eludes the antimony inherent in the fact of being what one is not, by imagining mystical realities which are *states of consciousness:* for example, a regret or a memory "which one has." Hence an entirely fictitious duality is set up between the self on one side and on the other parasitic structures which attach themselves to it or find room in it. A mode of reflection which invents these psychic objects and results in a false mechanical process which we should recognise as a veritable magic is not a pure one. For my part I admit I can only discern somewhat imperfectly what the pure reflection could be which, dissipating the clouds of the psychological and "being the simple presence of the reflective *pour-soi* to the reflected *pour-soi* is both the original form of reflection and its ideal form" (p. 201).

What is brought out much more clearly is the notion of knowing *(le connaître)* which one arrives at when one understands lack as an essential element of human existing *(exister)*. (It is tiresome to have to take a verb as a substantive, but it is perhaps the only way of avoiding the ambiguity which in French attaches to the word *être*, on account of its two-fold grammatical nature.) First of all, knowledge is a way of being. Knowing is neither a relation established after the event between two beings nor an activity of one of these beings, nor a quality, property or virtue. "It is the being itself of the *pour-soi,* in so far as it is *present to.* . . . That is to say, in so far as it has to be its own being by making itself not to be a particular being to which it is present. This means that the *pour-soi* can only be in the mode of a reflection, making itself reflected as not being a certain being" (pp. 222–3). We shall certainly need to translate this paragraph. What Mr. Sartre means, I think, is that there are no grounds for admitting the existence of a positive activity which constructs given realities as idealism would have it. All that is given is only given by the act of negation whereby I exclude it from me and at the same time establish it for myself. It can only appear within the framework of a making nothing *(néantisation)* which reveals it (p. 558). This is elucidated when we come to the explanations given by the author on the subject of the relationship which defines my place, of my "being-there" *(être-là)*. The establishment of the connection fixing my place presupposes that I am able to carry out the following operations:

1. To escape from what I am and to make it nothing in such a way that while yet being existed *(existé)* what I am can nevertheless

be seen as the term of a relation. This relation is given directly not in the simple contemplation of objects but by means of our immediate action (he is coming upon us, let us avoid him, I run after him, etc.). But at the same time it is necessary to define what I am, in starting from the *being-there (l'être là)* of other "thises" *(d'autres "ceci")*. As a *being-there, I am* one who is pursued or one who still has an hour's climb before he reaches the top of the mountain, etc. Thus, for example, when I look at the top of the mountain it involves an escape from myself accompanied by a reflux from the top of the mountain towards my being-there in order to fix my place.

2. To escape by an internal negation from the *this* in the middle of the world that I am not, and which I cause to tell me what I am.

"To discover and escape from them is the effect of one and the same negation. . . . My liberty has given me my place and fixed it as such in situating me; I can only be strictly limited to the *being-there* that I am because of my ontological structure is not to be what I am and to be what I am not" (pp. 272–3).

This passage is instructive in that it shows clearly that my place is situated, if one may so express it, at the junction of being and knowing. Moreover, Mr. Sartre rightly adds that it is in the light of the end that my place takes its significance, and is for example apprehended as a home or as a place of exile. It is in reference to the future and to non-being that its position can be – and is, in fact – understood or more exactly recognised by me. We here discern the indissoluble link between *facticité*[1] and liberty. It is liberty which in proposing its end and in choosing one that is inaccessible or difficult of access, makes it apparent that our situation is impossible, or difficult, for our plans to surmount. "Liberty is only free if it establishes *facticité* as its own restriction. It would be no use to say that I am not free to go to New York because I am an unimportant civil servant of Mont-de-Marsan. It is, on the contrary, in relation to my plan of going to New York, that I am going to *situate* myself at Mont-de-Marsan. My location in the world, the relation of Mont-de-

---

1   This word has no equivalent in English. It means the actual limitations of our condition, time of birth, place where we live, contingent possibilities, etc.

Marsan to New York and to China would be quite different if, for instance, my plan was to become a rich farmer of Mont-de-Marsan. In the first case Mont-de-Marsan appears against the background of the world systematically related to New York, Melbourne and Shanghai; in the second it emerges from an undifferentiated world background. About the real importance of my plan to go to New York it is for me alone to decide; it may just be a way of choosing to be dissatisfied with Mont-de-Marsan, and in this case everything is centred on Mont-de-Marsan, I simply feel the need perpetually to nullify *(anéantir)* my location, to live in perpetual withdrawal with regard to the city I inhabit – it can also be a plan to which I am wholly committed. In the first case, I should perceive my location as an insurmountable obstacle, and I should simply have made use of an expedient to define it indirectly in the world; in the second case, on the other hand, the obstacles would no longer exist, my location would no longer be a point of attachment but of departure . . ." (p. 576).

All this analysis can be considered as valuable. Only, perhaps, the use of the word choice might be called in question. We might ask whether I really choose to be dissatisfied with Mont-de-Marsan? This way of speaking seems to misrepresent the facts of experience. It would be no use to try to show me the advantages and pleasures of a life passed at Mont-de-Marsan, I should try in vain to let myself be persuaded. It is something I cannot help; Mont-de-Marsan disgusts me. Where is the choice here? Where is the liberty? For common sense and for a certain worldly wisdom this liberty can only consist in disregarding the dislike with which this small town where I am obliged to live fills me: let us say in the language of Sartre I have to nullify *(néantiser)* this dislike. But the point of view of our author is different. For him we are *doomed* to be free, liberty is our fate, our slavery much more than our victory. In reality it is here conceived as starting from a lack and not from a plenitude, and one is sometimes tempted to wonder if it is not a defect, if it is not our imperfection made evident. I think, at least, that in Mr. Sartre's mind there is a current flowing in this direction. But it must at once be added that another current, perhaps the main one, flows in the opposite direction. Indeed, in so far as liberty consists in assuming responsibility or taking charge, it is quite obvious that it is no longer possible to understand it by starting from lack or from a disengagement from oneself *(décollement d'avec-soi)*. To tell the truth the author would probably deny us the right to carry out this disjunction. From the point of view of the *cogito,* which he maintains to the end, lack is the consciousness of lack, and there could not be consciousness without a passing beyond, a transcendence. Let us grant this, but in that case should it still be permissible to say that we are "doomed to be free" (p. 639)? This statement only has a meaning in opposition to a situation or an ontological modality different from it, which it should at least be possible to conceive in the abstract or to imagine in some way. I do not think I am mistaken in suggesting that this modality can only be the state of the creature. At bottom, what the author strives to define as being ours is the status of a being which is at the same time finite and uncreated; does it mean that this finite being thus becomes divine? This could not be claimed. From all appearances, it is doomed to total extinction. There is consequently nothing in common between this philosophy and the pluralism of a MacTaggart. We cannot say here without the most explicit reserves that the individual being is self-caused *(par soi)*. It certainly is not given him to raise himself *ex nihilo,* which would make of him a God in miniature. For Mr. Sartre, it is the idea of God at all levels if one may so put it, which is contradictory. This stands out clearly in the remarkable development of his arguments concerning *l'être pour l'autrui* (the being for others). The most forceful of his analyses has to do with looking *(le regard).* Others exist for me as a subject from the moment when I am aware of myself as looked at.

Let us suppose that I have been led by jealousy or curiosity to put my ear to a keyhole. . . . Behind the door a scene is as though waiting to be seen, a conversation waiting to be heard. The door and the lock are at the same time obstacles and instruments for me. . . . My attitude is a pure connecting of the instrument (keyhole) with the object to be obtained (scene to be witnessed); it is "purely a way of making myself absorbed by things as ink is by blotting paper"; the end justifies or fixes the means, the whole only existing in relation to a free planning of my possibilities. I *am* my jealousy or my curiosity. I do not know them. There is a scene to behold on the other side of the door only because I am jealous, but really my jealousy is nothing if not the objective fact that there is a scene to witness behind the door. The whole of this constitutes the situation which, as we have seen, reflects both my *facticité* and my liberty. "But suddenly I hear some steps in the passage; someone is behind me; someone is looking at me. . . . Immediately shame comes over me: it is the recognition that I am really this object which others look at and judge." "I am the *self* that I am in a world which others have alienated from me; for the look of others embraces my being and correlatively the walls, the door, the lock. . . ." This world of which all the landmarks are instruments or utensils for me, arranges itself suddenly in relation to a subject that I am not, for whom I have an outside, a nature – whereas by virtue of that transcendence which is as it were the source of the *pour-soi,* I was always aware of myself as not strictly coinciding with what I am. For the others-subject *(autrui-sujet)* on the contrary, "I am sitting, like that ink-pot is on the table, I am bent towards the keyhole like that tree is bent by the wind," "My original fall is the existence of the other, and shame is, in the same way as pride, the becoming aware of myself as a nature. . . . The other is my transcendence transcended" (pp. 317, 319, etc.).

Moreover, according to Mr. Sartre, we should always distinguish between the massive certitude bearing on the existence of others in so far as they are others, and the *facticité* of others, that is to say their contingent connection with an object-being *(être-objet)* in the world. The presence of others he says is original, it is beyond the world. That means, I suppose, that reflection on certain modes of experience such as shame or pride leads us to recognise the presence of the others-subject *(autrui-sujet)* as forming part of our structure, without it being permissible in principle to attach this presence to a particular given being in the world. I own, however, that such a position seems to me singularly arbitrary, in so far as the author – quite rightly no doubt – expressly denies that *others* are a category. In reality it seems as though I can only distinguish by abstraction and in an indefensible manner between others and a particular other, who is above all *thou* for me, and through whom I come to recognise a trans-subjective reality. "I am ashamed of myself before others," Mr. Sartre says very rightly (p. 350). But should the analysis be taken further? To begin with, I am ashamed before some particular being who has prestige and influence over me; before a slave, treated as a slave, I should doubtless feel no shame. It may be claimed perhaps that if shame is lacking here it is because the slave is not really considered as another person; but exactly why is he not? He looks at me nevertheless in the same way as anyone else. Must it not be that otherness in its purity is full of a value which the analysis seems to ignore here? This *is* surely the reason why it would seem that the author has nowhere succeeded, I do not say in giving an account of love, but in conceiving it, whilst under the head of sexuality and particularly of the caress, he gives the most pertinent details. It might be said that his thought gains all the more force or body the more it itself dwells on the body.

"The body is the contingent form which the necessity for my contingency takes" (p. 371). This definition seems somewhat unintelligible at first. It simply means that it is both contingent that I should be (since I am not the foundation of my own being) and necessary that I should be under the form of *être-là*, and finally that, although it is necessary that I should be "identified with a point of view"; it is contingent that I should be thus, within this point of view to the exclusion of all others. The body is not distinguishable from the situation of the *pour-soi* (for which to exist or to be situated are the same): on the other hand, it identifies itself with the whole world "in so far as the world is the total situation of the *pour-soi* and the measure of its existence." The obscurity of this last formula is to be deplored. Have the words "total situation" a meaning? it is doubtful, for there is really nothing in the situation or situations which could be totalised. We cannot even see in the least how a situation could be added to another situation. As a matter of fact the author himself recognises it implicitly when he adds "a situation is only revealed in so far as the *pour-soi* passes beyond it towards itself." This last formula is scarcely any better than the preceding one, but Mr. Sartre is easier to understand when he says that "the body is everywhere as that which is passed beyond and only exists in so far as I escape from it in making myself nothing *(me néantisant)*." Could we not say, however, much more concretely and simply, that, as a living being, I am perpetually consumed and reborn from my ashes: that life is death and perpetual resurrection. In this sense I only cease to make myself nothing *(me néantir)* when I become a corpse. The body is then destined to be perpetually more than itself or less than itself. In no case is it identical with itself. In the language of Mr. Sartre we should have to say that it is the very opposite of the *en-soi*. It is certain that a great many questions arise here, particularly that of whether it would not be well to find out if the ontological modality of the body thus defined can really be reduced to the *pour-soi* as the author claims, and is even obliged to claim by reason of his premises.

He observes on the other hand that if the body is my contingency, if Plato had good grounds for saying that the body is that which individualises the soul, "it would be vain to suppose that the soul can tear itself from this individualisation in separating itself from the body by death or by pure thought, for the soul is the body in so far as the *pour-soi* is its own individualisation" (p. 372). Here what it is difficult not to call the crudely materialistic foundation of the doctrine appears in full daylight.

This dogmatic foundation is no less evident when the author, after having truly observed that the absence of a being is still a mode of presence, sees fit to add that this only applies to the absence of a living being. "Pierre, in London, in India, in America or on a desert island, is present with Thérèse who is still in Paris; he will only cease to be present with her at his death" (p. 338). But by what right can this be asserted? From the phenomenological point of view an experience of communion continuing between a living being and a beloved dead one is enough to take all value and all meaning from this assertion. A concrete analysis will, moreover, enable us to establish our point. Pierre, who is travelling far away, is present with Thérèse even if she is without news of him for some time; his letters no longer arrive because Pierre has fallen ill and cannot write; in the end Pierre dies of this illness. The situation of Thérèse, who knows nothing of Pierre's death and is still expecting a letter, is, however, not changed by what has happened, unless we consider it from the grossly materialistic point of view of the *en-soi*. It is a fact that, from November 24th, Thérèse is a widow; but since she does not know it, in what way is Pierre less present on the 25th than he was on the 23rd? How can we help wondering whether there has not been a disastrous confusion here between two planes which, moreover, should have been kept distinct at all costs; the planes of the *pour-soi* and the *en-soi* – and whether in the end, whatever effort the author generally makes to keep clear of it, it is not the *en-soi* which has influenced him most, not so much in his thought as in his imagination? This is actually all the more strange since the author who, I repeat, claims to found himself on the pre-reflexive *cogito,* that is to say on the immanence of the consciousness in an experience of whatever kind, applies himself with a most admirable tenacity to develop all the implications of the *pour-soi.* The most serious question which this work raises then, is really to know how it can come about that starting from premises which in another age would have been called idealistic, Mr. Sartre arrives at conclusions which a materialist would not disclaim. No doubt the author would protest, alleging the central place which liberty occupies in his doctrine. But did we not see as we went along that it is really for him only the counterpart or even the positive expression of a lack, a disengagement, an imperfection? Does not that join up in a very unexpected way with the epiphenomenist conceptions according to which consciousness is connected with an imperfect adaptation? To be sure it would be excessive and even wrong to assert this categorically. The truth seems rather, I would repeat, that this complex thought, which becomes ceaselessly encumbered in a vocabulary taken over wholesale rather than re-created, is crossed by divergent currents. It is to be thought that we might locate the principle of these contradictions in the obscure introduction to the work. I believe it is to be found in what Mr. Sartre calls by the dangerously ambiguous term of the transphenomenality of the being. Contrarily to what we might suppose, the meaning of this expression is in no way like that of the "thing in itself" of Kant. "The transphenomenal being of the phenomena . . . is the being of this table, of this packet of tobacco, of the lamp and more generally the being of the world which is implied in consciousness. It requires simply that the being of that which appears does not only exist in so far as it appears. The transphenomenal being of that which exists for consciousness, is itself *en-soi*" (p. 29). This becomes clearer or more precise further on when the author defines intuition – which he regards as the only real knowledge – as the presence of the consciousness to the thing, and introduces what he calls the phantom dyad of the reflecting reflection *(reflet reflétant),* the only purpose of the reflecting being to reflect the reflection and the reflection only being a reflection in so far as it returns to the reflecting. Here again we can wonder if we are not coming back by the most tortuous and often most badly cleared paths to a rudimentary doctrine which has, moreover, throughout the course of history been united by bonds of good neighbourliness or even of parentage with pure materialism! I mean to say a realistic attitude towards knowledge which actually tends to do away with it as a form of activity. But is not this reduction of knowledge to a reflecting reflection purely imaginary also? It is difficult to see how the transphenomenality of the being could be anything but a fiction invented by thought which has not yet fully succeeded in making itself explicit.

In his conclusion, Mr. Sartre introduces a distinction between ontology and metaphysics, destined, it seems, to calm in some measure the anxiety which all this can scarcely fail to awaken even in the most inattentive of readers. It goes without saying that ontology is understood here in a phenomenological sense, as a description bearing upon structures which reflection elucidates starting from experience. "Ontology teaches us," he says (p. 714), "(1) That if the *en-soi* is to establish itself it can only attempt to do so by making itself consciousness, that is to say, that the conception of the *causa sui* bears within itself that of the presence to-the-self, or, in other words, of the decompression of the *néantisant* being (the being which makes to be nothing). (2) That consciousness is in fact the project of establishing oneself, that is to say of attaining to the dignity of the *en-soi-pour-soi* or *en-soi-cause-of-itself*."

This project is evident in every attempt at appropriation with a view to possessing the world through a special object (p. 681): an attempt, moreover, which is doomed to failure in its very principle but which none the less constitutes the *nisus* by which the individual adventure whatever it may be is distinguished. Mr. Sartre adds that "nothing authorises us to assert on the ontological plane that the *néantisation* of the *en-soi* in the *pour-soi* signifies from the beginning, and in the very heart of the *en-soi*, the project of being its own cause. Ontology here comes up against a deep contradiction; since it is by the *pour-soi* that the possibility of a foundation comes into the world. In order to be the project of founding itself, the *en soi* would have originally to be presence to itself (*présence à-soi*), that is to say it would have to be consciousness already. Ontology therefore confines itself to declaring that everything happens as if the *en-soi* in a project of itself founding itself gave itself the modifications of the *pour-soi*. It is for metaphysics to form the hypotheses which will permit of the conception of this process as the absolute event which crowns the individual adventure of existence" (p. 715).

Let us set to work to bring out all the meaning of the avowal contained in these few lines. They seem very much like the expression of an agnosticism strangely akin to that of Spencer – or, to be more exact, it could be said that the thought here oscillates between such an agnosticism and a pure and simple materialism. We are obliged, for reasons of method still more than of doctrine, to refrain from any statement as to what the *en-soi* is. It is just possible that it may have something in it, that it may be a consciousness or a world of consciousness, but we can know nothing about it. We are obliged to treat it as pure *en-soi*, and under these conditions should we not be careful to avoid imagining it to have some sort of aspiration to become conscious of itself? By so doing should we not interfere with this very purity? Let us content ourselves with noticing once more that "everything happens as if" the *en-soi* in order to grant itself a more complete existence changed itself into *pour-soi*. But to me the expression "everything happens as though" either really implies nothing at all, or else acknowledges that perhaps everything is quite otherwise, which would seem to mean that this modification follows a sort of shock or pure cataclysm occurring at the centre of the *en-soi*. If such a hypothesis is contradictory, it is to be concluded from it either that the *en-soi* effectively wills to be *pour-soi*, however confusedly this may be possible, that is to say that the *pour-soi* itself somehow anticipates itself, or else that the whole of this so laboriously constructed edifice can only remain standing in a dream world, for an imaginative mind which does not develop its postulates. Moreover, these two possibilities seem to be in fact identical. The whole system falls if the *pour-soi* is anterior to itself, and if it is impossible for thought to place before itself the act of *néantisation* by which the *pour-soi* "would rise." It remains then to wonder if the hypothesis of a shock or cataclysm can be seriously considered. The end of non-receiving which the author opposes to creationism could very well have as counterpart the unacknowledged attachment to this strange conception which is linked with I scarcely know what pre-Socratic or even pre-Anaxagorian speculations. Only Mr. Sartre has the sincerity expressly to recognise that it is impossible for us to conceive the previous totality of the *en-soi* and of the *pour-soi*, unless in the form of a self-causative being. This is actually not possible and its concept involves a contradiction. "Can one," he asks, "postulate the spirit as the being which both together is and is not?" "The question has no sense. It supposes in fact that we are able to adopt a point of view on totality, that is to say to consider it from outside. But that is impossible for the precise reason that I exist as myself on the foundation of this totality and to the extent that I am involved in it. No consciousness, not even that of God, can see the other side, that is to say grasp totality as such. For if God is consciousness, he integrates himself in totality. If, moreover, by his nature he is a being beyond consciousness that is to say, an *en-soi* which establishes itself, totality can only appear to him as object, in which case his inner disaggregation as a subjective act of self-apprehension is lacking; or as subject, in which case as he *is not* this subject, he can only feel it without knowing it. Thus no point of view on totality is conceivable; totality has no exterior, and the very question of the meaning of its other side is without significance" (p. 363).

If, however, totality is unthinkable, the hypothesis of a shock taking place in it cannot even be entertained. Hence in every case we are driven to the unthinkable. "The total being, he whose concept would not be divided by a hiatus and who nevertheless would not exclude *l'être néantisant néantisé* (the nothing-making-being made-nothing) of the *pour-soi*, he whose existence would be a unitary synthesis of the *en-soi* and of consciousness, this ideal being would be the *en-soi* established by the *pour-soi* and identical with the *pour-soi* which establishes it, that is to say the *ens causa sui*. But precisely because we adopt the point of view of this ideal being to judge the real being which we call *holon*, we should discover that the real is an abortive effort to attain to the dignity of the self-cause. Everything happens as though man, the world and man-in-the-world, only managed to realise an abortive God. Everything happens, then, as if the *en-soi* and the *pour-soi* appeared in a state of disintegration in relation to an ideal synthesis. Not that the integration has ever taken place, but on the contrary precisely because it is always indicated and always impossible" (p. 717).

It seems to me that we are here at the very heart of absurdity. How, in fact, could there be real disintegration of a thing that had never been really integrated? The very most we can admit is that we are forced to represent to ourselves, or imagine, this disintegration, whilst at the same time acknowledging that we can neither conceive nor imagine the state of the world which preceded it. Under what conditions is this possible? Have we not reason to wonder whether the consciousness which receives this impression of a breaking up of the real is not led when it reflects upon its own state to regard *itself as degraded,* without being able, however, to think in concrete terms of the world before the Fall? This expression is foreign not only to the vocabulary of the author, but also to the universe in which he moves. But we may wonder whether in excluding it together with its implications he does not condemn himself to move in an infernal circle, a circle, moreover, wherein he has imprisoned himself of his own free will. There would indeed be scarcely any sense in alleging that it is the given facts or the structural conditions of our existence which have forced him into it. Is not the one authentic transcendence (it would no doubt be better to say the one authentic transcending), the act by which we break free from these facts and these conditions and substitute for them renewed facts and conditions? As far as we can see it would still be necessary to acknowledge that this act cannot be carried out by the mere powers of our own being, left to itself, but that it needs a help or inflowing which is nothing else but grace. From this point of view one of the merits of the work of Mr. Sartre, and not the least, consists, without any doubt, in showing clearly that a form of metaphysics which denies or refuses grace inevitably ends by setting up in front of us the image of an atrophied and contradictory world where the better part of ourselves is finally unable to recognise itself. It is, in fact, not enough to say that the world of Mr. Sartre does not seem to allow of any supernatural grafting, because the *pour-soi* has established itself there in a consciousness of its incompleteness which it even proudly claims as its privilege. Perhaps it should be added that the act by which the philosopher, be his name Nietzsche, Jaspers, or Sartre, shuts himself within the narrow circle of immanence, denying any other world or after life, appears in the last analysis much less as the expression of reason made wise by experience and ever ready to learn from it, than as the Luciferian refusal with which a rebellious individuality, intoxicated with itself, spurns the signs and calls to which Love alone could make it sensitive – on condition that this Love succeeded in getting clear from the fantasms it is reduced to when it turns back on itself instead of attaining its fulfilment.

Paris.
November, 1943.

THE REFUSAL OF SALVATION AND THE EXALTATION OF THE MAN OF ABSURDITY

The book of Mr. George Bataille, *L'Expérience Intérieure*,[1] is one of those about which it is very difficult to speak with precision and justice. In the first place this is because the thought in it is very often self-contradictory. It even tends perpetually to challenge and arraign itself, and, at the same time, paradoxical as it may seem, to identify itself with the accusation. On this account one finds if one is in good faith that one has to be on one's guard against a temptation to exploit certain extreme formulæ against the author when, after all, they only mark the acme of a particular torment. I say torment deliberately. I prefer it to the word torture which Mr. Bataille misuses in a tiresome way. It is nevertheless very difficult only to consider the book as a mere description of a fever or an agony. "I teach how to turn agony into delight," declares the author (p. 59). "To Glorify: that is all the meaning of this book." But to glorify is not to describe, it is to exalt, and *a fortiori* it is to appreciate. Furthermore, the author himself recognises that his experience in some way has need of others, if only so that it may be offered to them. "Each being is, I think, incapable of going to the end of Being by himself. If he tries he is drowned in a particular which only has meaning for him. Now, there is no meaning for one alone; the 'solitary' being would himself reject the particular if he saw it as such

1   Edition of the N.R.F. (*Nouvelle Revue Française*).

(if I want my life to have a meaning for myself, it must have one for others; no one would dare to give life a meaning which he alone recognised, which was inapplicable to the whole of life with the exception of himself)" (p. 71). Here we discern Hegelian harmonics which agree as best they can with the generally rather more Nietzschean sonority of the book. It is moreover to be observed that the word "dare" in the passage that I have just quoted is ambiguous. Does it mean: no one would have the courage or the strength to give life a meaning that none but he could perceive: or: no one would have the unreasonable *impudence* to proceed in such a way? I really incline towards the second interpretation, but without guaranteeing that it is right. It is further to be wondered whether spiritual torment does not here comprise a sort of fluctuation between judgments of contrary values. In any case, as soon as an experience offers, it calls for a judgment. Now one does not judge a fever, one verifies it, one measures its effects or some of its effects. We are then obliged to find out what there is here that is capable of taking some shape or some form of truth, if only in order to respond to the pathetic appeal made to us.

Mr. Maurice Blanchot, who is not only the friend and confidant of the author, but a remarkably penetrating interpreter of his thought, here does us the great service of formulating what he regards as the fundamental propositions of the "new theology" (*sic*). This is how he lays the foundation of all spiritual life, saying that it must:

"Have its principle and end in the absence of salvation, *in* the renunciation of all hope.

"Assert of interior experience that it is authority (but all authority pays its own penalty).

"Be at war with itself and non-knowledge" (*Faux Pas*, p. 158).

I really doubt if anyone has ever gone further in the formulation of radical nihilism. But, before examining the meaning and range of these propositions, it would be well to see precisely what Mr. Bataille and Mr. Blanchot mean by interior experience.

"I mean by interior experience that which we habitually call mystical experience" (p. 17). This is perhaps more categoric than it is distinct. Elsewhere the author will declare with some ingenuity that he has "followed the desiccating methods of St. John of the

Cross to the end." This, however, does not prevent him from condemning asceticism for reasons to which I shall return later. "That an atom life, bloodless and without laughter, avoiding all excess of joy, lacking in liberty, should attain or claim to have *attained the extremity*, this is a snare and a delusion. We reach the extremity through a plenitude of means; beings full to overflowing are needed, capable of every kind of audacity. I oppose asceticism on the principle that access to the extremity is gained through excess not lack. . . ." The extremity, to attain the extremity, what does this mean? and how can we help asking whether or not this ascetic who is compared to a mirthless atom, deprived of all liberty, etc., is or is not St. John of the Cross?

"I call experience a journey to the end of what is possible to man. Each one is able not to take this journey, but if he does take it, it follows that the existing authorities and values which limit the possible are denied. Because it is a negation of other values, other authorities, experience, having positive existence, itself becomes value and authority positively" (p. 22). This does not yet enlighten us much on what the extremity or the end of the possible can be. "By definition the extremity of the possible is the point at which, in spite of what to him is his unintelligible position in Being, man, ridding himself of all enticements and all fear, advances so far that no one can conceive a possibility of going further" (p. 66). We do not yet get away from tautology: the extreme is the *ne plus ultra;* all that we learn is that one only reaches it by means of a complete self-stripping. "If one renounces the average man for the extreme, one is throwing down the challenge to a fallen humanity, cut off from the Golden Age, and to avarice and lying. One repudiates at the same time that which is not the desert where the extreme is found, the desert where the saturnalias of solitaries are unrestrained. . . . The being is a point there, or a wave, but it would seem that he is the only point, the only wave; the solitary is in no way separated from the other, but the other is not there" (p. 200). "We are only totally laid bare when we are going without any trickery to the unknown. It is the share of unknown which gives the experience of God, or of the poetic realm, their great authority. But in the end the unknown demands an undivided empire" (p. 20).

There are numerous things to say about these passages. This

extreme "takes place" only so far as it is itself experience – experience of God, for instance; but such experience only has authority where it is not perfect, for if it were perfect it would make emptiness around itself; there would therefore no longer be any thing or person it could command, and under these conditions it would cease to be authority. The author owns, moreover, that "experience ends by achieving the fusion of object and subject, being as subject not knowing and as object the unknown" (p. 25). And he says besides that "when the extremity is there, the means of attaining it are there no longer" (p. 82). But this is to say too little: it is quite clear that the extremity immediately disproves itself as such; for it only appears as extremity because it is the end of the perspective we see before us; once we have followed our path to its end the appearance has altered, the end is no longer there. Would Mr. Bataille say that we attain to non-knowing? The answer would have to be that this non-knowing only retains a reality, a value as non-knowing, on condition that in spite of everything it is still apprehended as such, which supposes a minimum of survival of the subject, or else (to use language whose extreme subtlety I beg you to excuse) a minimum of knowledge of non-knowing. The use which is here made of the word *unknown* also calls for serious reservations. It seems, indeed, that, in using it, there is a somewhat illegitimate speculation on the uneasy curiosity which the prospect of knowing something unknown arouses in us; but there cannot be anything left of this curiosity where there is precisely nothing to know any more. Further, we must denounce the perpetual deception of enshrining amongst the adornments of verbal gems what is perhaps a mere void of experience, pompously baptised as experience of God. Actually the author himself shows great reserve about the question of knowing whether he has attained the extremity, whether indeed he can ever envisage its attainment. "One can, I suppose, only touch the extremity in repetition, because never is one sure of having attained it and never will one be sure. And even supposing the extremity to be attained, it would not yet be the extremity if one went to sleep. The extremity implies 'there must be no sleeping during that time' until the moment of dying. But Pascal accepted not to sleep in view of the beatitude to come (he gave himself this reason at least): I refuse to be happy (to be saved)" (pp. 71–2).

Here again there are a thousand comments to be made. The chief one seems to be the following: the injunction "there must be no sleeping during that time" only has any meaning if it refers to an expected visitation, awaited either with hope or fear. I should add that from the point of view of an eventual visitation the word *unknown* would once more have a positive value. It is, however, just such expectation or hope that it is claimed we are forbidden; or, more exactly, to this hope, suggested and scorned, is opposed an unreceptive attitude which is final. It should perhaps be added that what one is never sure of attaining or of having attained is an aim: now an aim involves some action or project. The author, however, here tells us distinctly that "interior experience is the contrary of action which is itself entirely subordinated to the project." Besides, and this is weighty, discursive thought itself is involved in the mode of existence of the project. (Here the author uses language characteristic of Heidegger.) ". . . The project is not only the mode of existence implied by action and necessary to action, it is a way of being paradoxical in the time order: *it is putting existence off till later on (c'est la remise de l'existence à plus tard).* . . . To speak, to think, unless one is joking or . . . this is to conjure away existence; it is not to die, but to be dead. This is to go into the extinct and motionless world where we drag about habitually; everything there is suspended, life is put off till later on, over and over again . . ." (pp. 76–7). An accusation is next brought against Descartes. "According to Descartes, the world we are in is the world of progress, that is to say with a project in view . . . interior experience denounces all intermission, it is Being without a break." And here, of course, we recognise a metaphysic of the instant which is directly derived from Kierkegaard. It is well, however, not to be intimidated by such neighbours and to fix upon a formula such as: To have a project is to put off existence till later: or again: to think is to conjure existence away.

It is impossible for me not to see in all this the exaggerated and affected expression of truths which are as it were taken out of their orbit. It is merely untrue to say that to form a project is to put off existence till later; it is only true when the project in some way consumes the existence which its function is to direct, when a being forms projects instead of living. To condemn the formation of a project is simply to condemn man; and, be it understood, this is exactly the proposal, the *project* of Mr. Bataille. The author, who is certainly not without mental agility, is aware of this contradiction, but see how he tries to get over it: "Interior experience always consists of planning, whatever the desired goal may be. This is because man is entirely so constituted by language, which, if we make exception of its poetic perversion, is essentially purposeful. But the project in this case is no longer the positive one of salvation, it is the negative one of abolishing the power of words and hence of the forming of projects" (p. 45). Since asceticism is out of the question, because it is the sacrifice of only one part of the self which is lost with a view to saving the other – since it is a question of losing the whole of the self, it is "by starting from a bacchanalian movement," and in no sense of the word coldly, that this loss is to be achieved. It is quite evident that it is the Nietzschean or pseudo-Nietzschean, the Dionysian or pseudo-Dionysian aspect of Mr. Bataille's thought that comes out here. Actually some of the best pages of the book are coloured by the feeling expressed in this passage. The author vigorously attacks everything which savours of satisfaction and sufficiency. But it is alarming to see how quickly the steadiest thought can immemediately drift into grandiloquent nonsense. "To seek for sufficiency," Mr. Bataille stoutly asserts, "is the same mistake as to shut the being up in some point: we cannot shut anything up, we only find insufficiency" (p. 138). He repeatedly gives expression to similar ideas when he speaks of the necessary renunciation which consists of *"Ceasing from wanting to be everything."* But all at once the thought becomes clouded over or engulfed, whichever you prefer to say. "We try to put ourselves in the presence of God, but God, living in us, immediately demands to die. We can only grasp him by killing. (Incessant sacrifice necessary for survival, we have crucified once and for all, and yet each time we crucify anew. God himself crucifies)" (p. 138).

It will be necessary to come back to this idea of sacrifice which is essential in Mr. Bataille's thought. I only want to point out the confusion, not involuntary, but on the contrary deliberate, here surrounding the relations of God and the self. This literally invalidates his thought which is unable to dissociate a superficial need for severity from a fundamental need for lyrical exaltation, a need which cannot and should not be developed on the same plane. The author is expressing something both profound and true when he says that "the *ipse*, seeking to become the all is only tragic at the highest point for itself," but that it is "laughable when its power-lessness is openly exhibited (in this case it cannot suffer itself; if it became conscious of its powerlessness, it would give up its preten-sion, leaving it to someone stronger than itself, which is only possi-ble at the highest point)" (p. 140). Mr. Bataille is also right in saying that "Laughter is born of a change of level of depressions brought about suddenly . . ." that it is often, perhaps essentially, combined with an overturning strikingly illustrated by the Saturnalia. He has equally good grounds for maintaining that laughter, like poetry or ecstasy, is not the *means* to anything else and does not give satisfac-tion (p. 172). But we cannot regard with too great a caution the Dionysian corollaries into which he allows himself to be enticed when he declares "that the intoxicated existence in me addresses the intoxicated existence in others . . . ," that "I cannot be my own *ipse* without having thrown out a cry to them" (p. 180). Still more brutally he asserts "that excesses are suddenly substantiated signs from what is supremely the world" (p. 186). And it is indeed here that we catch a glimpse of the nature of that bacchanalian move-ment by which the utter loss of ourselves can be brought about. Here we have the most challenging self-accusation of the tendency which brings extremity and excess so near as almost to identify them with each other. Would not the author himself declare that the extremity is not to be attained by renunciation but by excess? But the poverty of such thought shows up at once in the clearest possi-ble light, for, after all, what is the excess and what the renunciation in question? Mr. Bataille seems scarcely to suspect that what we are considering is Love and that it can be nothing else. But not only has this Love nothing in common with the excesses, erotic or otherwise, which are forbidden by the "laughterless atom," etc., but it repudi-ates and excommunicates whoever indulges in them. For it cannot but be reverent, and just as the raising up of a range of mountains cannot take place without corresponding depressions being hol-lowed out, such a love is surrounded with abysmal zones of sacri-lege such as those in which the author seems often enough inclined to set up his abode. "In sleep, although mute, God addresses himself to me; insinuating his meaning in a whisper as in love: Oh, my father, thou who are on earth, the evil that is in thee delivers me. I am temptation, into which thou art the fall. Insult me as I insult those who love me. Give me each day the bread of bitterness. My will is absent in heaven as on earth. I am bound in impotence. My name is insipid. Hesitant and troubled in mind I reply: `Amen'" (p. 201). And a little further on: "I rely upon God to deny his own existence, to execrate himself, to repudiate what he dares, what he is, in absence and in death. When I am God, I deny him to the deepest limit of negation. If I am only myself, I do not know him" (p. 202).

"When I am God" . . . "if I am only myself" – such are the limits of the dialectic keyboard on which it seems to me that something much less like a bacchanal than the mournful pacing of a prisoner in his cell is being marked out. Moreover, it may easily come about that this prisoner cuts a few capers in his attempt to forget his boredom. But (starting with himself) who could be taken in by such gymnastics? I imagine that we might give the author some satisfaction by telling him that we felt asphyxiated by some of the pages of his book, but that would only be due to a misunderstanding. It is not the intoxicating, rare atmosphere of the heights to be inhaled at the summit of Nietzsche's work which we are breathing, but rather the stifling air of the basement. Why is this so? Before tackling the question directly, I should like to say a few words about Mr. Bataille's conception of sacrifice and about his refusal to entertain any idea of salvation.

"The forces which are working for our destruction find tendencies within us which co-operate with them so willingly and sometimes so violently that we cannot just simply turn from them as it is in our interest to do. We are led on to play with fire . . . without going so far as to surrender ourselves we can surrender a part of ourselves: we sacrifice some goods belonging to us, or – and this binds us by many a bond which we discern so very indistinctly – our fellow. Surely this word 'sacrifice' means: *that men, of their own will, place some goods in a dangerous region where destructive forces are rampant*" (p. 151). In its most extreme form there is "the bare sacrifice without a ram and without Isaac. Sacrifice is madness, renunciation of all knowledge, falling into the abyss, and nothing is revealed either in the falling or in the abyss, for the revelation of the

abyss is only a way of falling further into the void" (p. 85). It must
then be recognised that sacrifice is the contrary of project-forming.
"If it falls into the pattern of a project it is only by accident or in so
far as it is decadent. . . . Sacrifice is amoral like poetry, since the
moral plane is the plane of project-making and, for the matter of
that, speech-making" (pp. 209–10). It is even added in a note that
"the sacrifice of the Mass is in its essence the greatest of all crimes"
(p. 310). "The meaning of sacrifice is to keep a life, which necessary
avarice is ceaselessly leading back to death, alive and tolerable"
(p. 207). We must note well what precautions have had to be taken
here in the choice of words. If by an unlucky chance we had happened to say that the *end* or *function* of sacrifice is to keep a life, etc.,
we should have immediately changed its nature in reducing it to a
project.

And now, what is to be our judgment of such a conception? The
words of abuse and confusion are those which suggest themselves
most naturally, and perhaps it will be possible to define what constitutes this abuse and this confusion. Beyond all doubt there is a
folly of the Cross. If then we look at things entirely from outside, the
author might be able to produce positive evidence to support his
allegations. It is however to be feared that such an analogy would
be found most superficial and misleading. When Mr. Bataille
asserts, for instance, that "if one renounces the average man for the
extreme, one is throwing down the challenge to a fallen humanity,
cut off from the Golden Age and to avarice and lying," it is quite
evident that what he means by extreme is, as we already know, an
experience at its highest limit, which is to be chosen for its own
sake, which is its own justification (in so far as this word has any
meaning here). It is an experience, moreover, which *is* fleeting, as
we know only too well, and tends to vanish in the very act by which
it is fulfilled. But this consecration of the experience, as such, can
appear on good grounds as the deliberate negation of Love and
consequently of martyrdom, in so far as the latter is a creative attes-
tation stretching towards a transcendence, a transcendence in no
way to be swallowed up in the inward dynamism which it moves
and directs. Moreover, we cannot declare ourselves too definitely to
be against the method which isolates that part of the great mystics'
experience considered suitable for exploitation, independently of

all Christian teaching or even against the fundamental positions of any Christian confession, and attributes the orthodox pronouncements of these same mystics to a prudent or self-interested conformity or a childish misunderstanding of themselves. Those following such a method would say, for instance, that "if St. John of the Cross had had more courage or if he had thoroughly understood himself" or "if he had lived in a more enlightened age," he would not have confessed the Catholic faith; "it is however quite possible to forgive him because," etc. I am persuaded that we must denounce as literally unbearable this commonly met-with modern pretension to put such a one as St. John of the Cross in his place, to understand him, for that matter, better than he understood himself, to go to the very end where he stopped half-way, etc. Mr. Bataille, as I said, has made a remarkable analysis of laughableness, but if he had gone more deeply into the nature of self-complacency he would have seen clearly that his book affords a very significant illustration of it in some places. If we would do full justice to the pretentiousness which aims at making a clean sweep of salvation, and in a more general fashion of hope itself, we must view it from the same angle.

"There is no longer any question of salvation: it is the most hateful of all subterfuges" (p. 29). "It is doubtful in every case," we read elsewhere, "whether salvation is the object of genuine faith or whether it is not a mere convenience enabling spiritual life to be presented in the form of a project (ecstasy is not sought for the sake of the experience itself, it is the way leading to a deliverance, it is a means). Salvation is not exactly that value which the end of suffering represents for the Buddhists, and God for the Christians, the Mohammedans and the non-Buddhist Hindus. It is the perspective of value from the point of view of personal life. Moreover, in both cases the value is totality, completion; and salvation for the believer is 'to become all', divinity directly attained for the majority, non-individuality for the Buddhists (suffering according to Buddha means the individual). The project of salvation once formed, asceticism is possible. Let us now imagine a different, even an opposite will, where the will to become all would be regarded as a stumbling of the will to lose oneself (to escape from isolation, from self-compression), where to become all would be held to be the sin not only

of man, but of all possible things, even of God himself. To lose oneself in this case would really be to lose oneself and not in any way
to be saved" (p. 44).

It is regrettable to find once again how easily the author slips
from an idea of truth to a paradox in which we have the impression
that he is draping himself with the most terrestrial ostentation.
"Salvation," he says, "means for the believer, to become all." What
exactly do these words mean? We can admit – and I have already
admitted it just now – that natural man has within him an uncon-
trolled desire to possess the world, to let nothing remain beyond his
grasp. The great conqueror would not occupy the place he does in
recorded history if in some confused way everyone did not see in
him the immeasurably enlarged likeness of what he himself aspired
to become. But how is it possible not to recognise that spiritual life
is found in the renunciation of ambition? The "becoming all" which
is condemned here is of the order of a plethora: to put it in other
words, it comes from the will to power. The aspiration to salvation
is seen to be all the more different in character because in its principle it is not and cannot be a will, and it thus escapes from the world
of the project which the author never tires of excommunicating.
Salvation can only be deliverance, but deliverance from what, if not
from the prison of the egoistical self ruled over by avarice? It
remains to be seen how this deliverance is possible and whether it
really comes about, as Mr. Bataille seems to think, in ecstasy – but
why not just as well by opium or hashish, or by cunningly elaborated erotic practices? "Why not indeed?" The author repeats, unhin-
dered by any ethical prejudice in his course of total sincerity, which
for that matter, costs him very little. At the very most he proposes
in the name of acquired experience to establish a hierarchy among
these different processes arranged according to their respective
degrees of efficacy. But the faithful will declare outright that this
hierarchy cannot bring anything like the deliverance he aspires to,
a deliverance separated by a fathomless abyss from those releases
which inferior Magi, at best nothing but magicians, have to offer.
The faithful – what a fullness of meaning there is in that word! It is
not only faithfulness to Christ, the Head of the Church, which it
evokes, but simply all that fidelity to one's neighbours which for a
way of thought such as the one we are considering is swallowed up

in nothingness. How could we so much as conceive of fidelity in an inner world of which such a description as the following is offered to us: "What you are is the result of the activity which binds the countless elements composing you, of the intense inter-communication of these elements . . . where you would seize the timeless substance, you will only meet with a slipping away, only those of your perishable elements which are badly co-ordinated . . . the lasting vortex which constitutes you comes up against other vortices with which it forms a vast animated figure in rhythmic movement. Now, to live means for you not only the waves of light which are unified in you, but the passing of warmth or light from one being to another. We are nothing, neither you, nor I, beside the burning words which could go from me to you, printed on these leaves, for I should only have lived to write them, and if it is true that they are addressed to you, you will live from having had the strength to hear them. I am and you are only a stopping place from which to rebound in the vast flux of things. . . ." And, finally, this, which is strangely charged with meaning: "The stabilised order of isolated appearances is necessary for the agonised consciousness of the torrential floods which sweep it away" (pp. 147–9).

This last sentence makes it as clear as possible that agonised consciousness is itself the central value. At bottom it is to a regular cultivation of anguish that we are invited. But how is it possible to avoid seeing that from this point of view all the structural relations which constitute the framework, not only of a community but of a human life worthy of the name, are at once depreciated and evaded? Here pure and simple conjuring away of values is beyond all measure. No doubt with such a one as Nietzsche, the prophet of the new age, we have to recognise a genuine vocation for solitude: but what a difference! Nietzsche most certainly did not evade anything: we cannot for a second doubt the seriousness of his mission, even if one is inclined to think that this mission was bound in the end to further the process of destruction which is taking place before our eyes. But it must be admitted that in a case like the one we are concerned with, it is just this very seriousness and authenticity which we cannot but call in question, and the fact that the author himself constantly talks of conflict, or experience which conflicts with itself, does not make this searching question any less acute.

Is the interior experience genuine? And admitting that it is, is it exemplary? This is what we now have to decide.

First of all, is it genuine? Has the author really had the experience which he describes with precision almost worthy of Proust ("I felt the softness of the sky present within my head like a vaporous shimmering," etc.)? Here there is and can be no good reason for doubting it. On the other hand, when he declares: "I perceived that the state of felicity into which I had fallen was not entirely different from mystical states," it is necessary to correct it and to say: was not entirely different from *the idea* that I had formed of mystical states. He adds, moreover, sincerely, that this experience was partly spoilt, and tries to explain how, without transition, he passed from a zealous clasping to complete dispossession (p. 194). All that we can but accept. I wish only to point out that in such a realm the idea of authenticity loses much of its value and weight. When I wonder if a document is authentic I ask myself a perfectly definite question to which theoretically the reply should be a categorical yes or no. Watteau really did or did not paint this picture; Pascal really did or did not write this letter. The reply to the question changes something in the way we imagine Watteau or Pascal and consequently the world. It is to be feared, on the other hand, that where we are dealing with experiences occurring on the fringe of what it is possible to put into words or describe, the question loses much of its meaning and it is no longer possible to reply by a yes or no; this is all the more so since, in his effort to communicate his experience, the witness or subject, however sincere he may be, is inevitably led to introduce conceptual determinants, of which it could not strictly be said either that they were or that they were not involved in the experience as such. This brings us to a fact which, though negative, is well worth noticing; it is that we are here in a region where no criterion can be set up or indeed conceived. When someone describes an experience of pure ecstasy to me, I neither have nor can have any way of telling whether his account is accurate or not; and that is because in the last analysis the word accuracy is not applicable here. In the case we are considering I am morally convinced that the author is doing his best to relate what it was actually given him to live through. It is impossible to go further, and it must be understood that if ever one of his friends or relations came to me saying,

"Be careful, he is a humbug," I should have no conceivable possibility of contradicting the accuser. I must own that, as far as I am concerned, remarks of this kind tend appreciably to diminish the interest I am able to take and the importance I am able to attach to such accounts. It would be quite otherwise, of course, if the experiences took place within the context of what you must allow me to call an exemplary life – that of a saint or someone of great spirituality, whose testimony would have the more value the more any kind of exhibitionism was foreign to his nature, and the more he visibly bore that aureole of humility which seems to me to be one of the most unmistakable signs of the true mystic. Could it not be affirmed that in principle "a mystical experience" (I put these words in inverted commas) which has not first gained the victory over all self-complacency, must be regarded as negligible, at any rate in the spiritual realm, that is to say in the order where judgments of value can be made with a minimum of justification? Now, it seems evident to me that Mr. Bataille's book is dripping with self-complacency – a complacency which can in certain places affect the superficially misleading impression of the condemnation of self. I recall in support of this assertion not only the sentence about St. John of the Cross "whose method of desiccation" the author has "followed to the end," but all he says about asceticism, and the strangely irresponsible way he expresses himself concerning the spiritual life of the Hindus as well as that of the Christians – who have the unforgivable weakness of troubling themselves over their salvation. Like a pedal persistently held down from the beginning to the end, we discern throughout the book, with increasing impatience, the aggressive attitude of a "we the élite," of a "we the true, the pure, the liberated, the tormented," and this is enough, at least in my eyes, to throw the greatest suspicion upon the message "these others" seek to convey.

But at this point I think that we should be able to give our opinion as to the claim put forward by such experience to "set up an authority." In the first place, we do not see any way in which it can be established as primitive in the sense of the German word *ursprünglich*. What we really have before us is a sequel and a hybrid sequel: the sequel of Hegel, of Kierkegaard and of Nietzsche: and who would dare to claim that a lasting agreement could be

established between the residual elements of such divergent
philosophies? I am well aware that the author would deny that he
had put forward anything at all resembling a system, that he would
if need be make a counter-attack, and would have no difficulty in
showing in high relief the reasons we have today for being on our
guard against all attempts at philosophic systematisation. It is none
the less true that a book like *L'Expérience Intérieure* conveys dogma
– dogma in reverse, if you like, but dogma all the same. Let us, in
fact, recall the first proposition, stated by Mr. Blanchot in full agreement with the author: "spiritual life can only have its principle and
its end in the absence of salvation, in the renunciation of all hope."
Can it be said that this is only a deliberately chosen attitude
towards reality? We must go further, I think: what is here defined is
an irrevocably set opinion which bears on the apprehension of this
very reality itself; *I want reality to be of such sort that it gives me no*
grounds for expecting any salvation or cherishing any hope; I hold out
the hand of brotherhood to all those who have their souls well
enough tempered to sustain the same exigency: as for the others,
can I feel anything but disdain for them? It is quite clear that this
way, not only of facing destiny but of shaping it from within and
wanting it to be as hard as possible, is altogether in line with
Nietzsche: but, I repeat, we have only a sequel of Nietzsche there.
Whatever we may think of Nietzsche in the last analysis, his own
destiny always has an exemplary character for us. Why? Because
Nietzsche, if one may say so, went through with his adventure to
the very depths, to madness and to death, and, moreover, because
he was himself, the first to face such a trial. Who could dream of
denying that he had in him that *Ursprünglichkeit* which we cannot
in any way recognise in his modern disciples? Of course, this would
not in any way be a reason for adopting the theories of Nietzsche,
supposing that they could be regarded as forming a coherent and
organic whole, but it would at least be a reason for honouring the
enduring greatness of Nietzsche, and no doubt for seeing in him the
involuntary witness of a truth, still declared through the negations
and sometimes the blasphemies by which he claims to oppose it.
Whatever consideration one may have for Mr. Bataille and his
friends, it is difficult to see them as witnesses in this secondary, yet
grandiose sense. The verb "to pretend" is one which I should never

allow myself to use in speaking of Nietzsche, so burning is his passion for sincerity: it comes naturally, however, when one is writing of these other authors. One feels pretty sure that with them the adopted attitude controls every sentence, even if, as is more or less certain, they have become so far its prisoners as no longer to feel it as an attitude.

Perhaps some of their friends may protest that this is a biased judgment. But what is really in question here? What they bring us cannot be presented by way of a demonstration or even a formal argument, and we can only adopt it, or oppose it by our refusal. "Very well," they may reply, "but in refusing you are judging yourself." It is well here, I think, to denounce what is really an imposture, I mean to say a kind of patent of superiority which they claim to grant themselves when they declare that spiritual life can only be founded on an absence of salvation, etc. I mean by this that it is a little too easy to claim to place oneself beyond the limits which the great spiritual giants of humanity have reached at the price of the most severe asceticism, and to rest one's claims merely on phrases ("words, words!"). No, they cannot install themselves thus in an authentic world beyond, they merely limit themselves to playing a game of which the inspiration is boundless pride merging into a will to intimidate, and our wisest course is probably to reply with a smile and a slight shrug of the shoulders.

Nevertheless, if I confined myself to this, I think there would be good grounds for accusing me of bad faith and for insisting that I was simply evading the real problem, perhaps because it was awkward and to some extent insoluble. At the root of Mr. Bataille's book, and those of many others, there is what one might call a general declaration of absurdity. Perhaps, however, this formula itself needs to be amended. Mr. Albert Camus, whose talent cannot be disputed, particularises further in the following very able passage: "I said that the world was absurd and I was going too fast: the world in itself is not reasonable – that is all that can be said. But what is absurd is the comparison of this irrationality with that desperate yearning for light, a light which man craves for from the very depths of his nature. Absurdity comes as much from man as from the world. It is the only link between them at the moment. It fastens them to each other as only hate can rivet beings. This is all that I can discern clearly in this measureless adventure where my own adventure takes its way" (*Le Mythe de Sisyphe*, p. 37). This may at first seem utterly confusing: is not absurdity pure negation, discordance admitted to be impossible to harmonise? How, under these conditions, can the author speak of "this absurdity which controls my relations with my life"? It is because at bottom, from the moment that it is recognised, *absurdity is a passion, the most heart-rending of all passions*" (p. 38). Elsewhere we are told that the notion of absurdity is essential and that it can figure as "the first of my truths" (p. 49). These formulæ are not very easy to reconcile. Everything becomes clear, however, when Mr. Camus tells us that absurdity, the sin without God, is a state in which life has to be lived. "I know what it is founded upon: it is this spirit and this world buttressed one against the other without being able to embrace each other. I ask for the rule of life in this state, and what is suggested to me neglects the foundation, denies one of the terms of the painful opposition, orders me to resign. I ask what the condition I recognise as my own brings with it, I know that it involves darkness and ignorance, and I am told that this ignorance explains everything, and that this darkness is my light. But no one replies to what I mean, and this intoxicating lyricism does not hide the paradox from me. . . . To seek the truth is not to seek what is desirable. If we have to feed on illusion, like donkeys, in order to escape from the question of the meaning of life, the absurd spirit prefers to adopt Kierkegaard's answer of despair, rather than resign itself to falsehood. All things well considered, a resolute soul will always manage somehow" (p. 61).

How can we help, at first, admiring this desire for lucidity at any price? Let us be very careful, however. Have we here an example of the stoical pessimism adopted by the great souls at the end of last century – Thomas Hardy, for instance, or Mme. Ackermann – souls for whom in a last analysis truth always remains as the supreme and sometimes the only value? Apart from the fact that the word "absurd" is not generally found in the vocabulary of these pessimists, it would not have occurred to any of them to speak of absurdity as a passion, "the most heartrending of all the passions." If, as Mr. Camus writes somewhere, absurdity were simply enlightened reason becoming aware of its own limits, it would be impossible to understand how absurdity could be a passion. Let us, however, penetrate further and we shall see more clearly.

It is in my nature not to form part of the world in which I am involved in some way, if not in every way; I am opposed to this world by my whole consciousness and by all my need for the familiar. . . . "And there is nothing at the bottom of this conflict between the world and my spirit but my own consciousness of it. If then I want to keep it up" – we shall come back to this sentence – "it must be by continuous consciousness, constantly renewed and always tense. That is what I have to remember for the moment. At this moment absurdity, so obvious and at the same time so difficult to conquer, enters a man's life and finds it is at home. . . . All problems again become acute. Abstract evidence disappears before the lyricism of forms and colours. Spiritual conflicts become incarnate and once more take a miserable yet magnificent refuge in the heart of man. Not one of them is settled. Nevertheless, all of them are transfigured. Are we to die, to make our escape by a leap, to reconstruct a dwelling-place of ideas and forms to fit us? Or are we, on the contrary, to take up *the heartrending and marvellous wager of absurdity?* Let us make a last effort with regard to this and accept all the consequences. The body, affection, creation, action, human nobility will all fall into place then. Man will at last find there the wine of absurdity and the bread of indifference on which he feeds his grandeur" (pp. 74–5).

This passage is not without beauty; yet, though this is hard to express, it seems to me that a critical ear can detect beneath the self-confidence of the words an indefinable element of discord which at once arouses suspicion. The author had begun by wondering whether life should have a meaning in order to be lived. Here, on the contrary, it appears that it can be lived all the better for having no meaning. To live through an experience or fulfil a destiny is to accept it fully. Now, we could not fulfil this destiny, knowing it to be absurd, if we did not do everything to keep before ourselves this absurdity brought into the full light of day by consciousness. . . . "To live is to make absurdity live. To make it live is first of all to look at it. Unlike Eurydice, absurdity only dies when one turns one's back on it" (p. 76). "Revolt is man's constant awareness of himself. It is not aspiration, it knows no hope. This revolt is the certainty of a crushing destiny without the resignation which should accompany it" (p. 77). Suicide is thus condemned, since it resolves the absurdity, whereas, in order to be kept up, absurdity cannot be resolved. "The opposite of suicide is the state of the man condemned to death" (p. 78).

This last sentence throws a blinding light on the end of Mr. Camus's novel, *L'Etranger,* a remarkable work on which I should have liked to dwell at greater length. I should then have been able to quote in full the scene which takes place between the man condemned to death and the chaplain who comes to visit him in prison. The novel is contrived in such a way that if the man did indeed commit the act of which he is accused, he did it under such conditions that none the less he is really the victim of a misunderstanding which is absurd yet impossible to remove. This is because poor human logic obstinately insists on explaining this act and on creating an imaginary chain of circumstances to account for it. "I will pray for you," the chaplain has just said. Then the condemned man explodes. "He, the chaplain, was not even sure of being alive, since he lived like a dead man. As for me, I appeared to be empty-handed. Nevertheless, I was sure of myself, sure of everything, more sure than he was, sure of my life and of this death which was to come. Yes, that was all I had. But, at least, I held this truth as firmly as it held me. . . . It was as though I had waited all the time for this instant and for that other brief little one when I should be justified: nothing, nothing at all, had any importance, and I knew quite well why. He knew why, too. From the bottom of my future, during all this life of absurdity which I had led, an obscure breath had been rising up towards me across years not yet come, and this breath as it passed made equal everything they were proposing to me then, in the no more real years which I was living through. . . . Did he understand, could he understand? Everybody was privileged, there were none but privileged people" (*L'Etranger,* p. 157).

What does this mean? "Privilege," writes Mr. Blanchot (*Faux Pas,* p. 260), "expresses the final justification which puts each one in harmony with what he has done, which rewards him for having evaded nothing and kept nothing back for later on, which makes him aware of his kinship with the unknowable world." I do not care much for this last extract. It seems to me to be likely to mislead the reader. Mr. Camus himself, in an important article on Franz Kafka, expresses himself more crudely, but also more forcefully: "In a world where everything is given and nothing explained, the fruitfulness of a value or of any attempt at metaphysics is a meaningless notion."

Obviously, the last assertion could be disputed from beginning to end. First, is there any sense in speaking of a world where everything is given and nothing explained? Is it not evident that *in any kind of world* explanation's special property is precisely not to be given, but only to be discovered, so that the author is contrasting with this world of ours not another as yet unrealised world, but something which is not a world at all? But this is not all; we cannot see why positive values cannot be established within an irrational world. Nietzsche would certainly not have subscribed to Mr. Camus' formula. It will be well, however, to make a still more direct attack upon the position which is here defended with something more than talent – with a kind of harsh exaltation which could scarcely fail to intimidate the unprepared or unprotected mind, or even to make breaches in the consciences of those who have not fully reflected upon the convictions which they imagine they live by.

Revolt as it has been defined for us "gives life its worth. . . . Absurdity is man's most extreme tension which constantly upholds him by his solitary effort, for he knows that in this consciousness and in this day-today revolt he is witnessing to *his one and only truth which is defiance*" (p. 78). "From the moment when I met with absurdity I have been cured of believing in my own liberty wherein I appeared as the prisoner of the aims I set myself in daily life" – that is to say the project, to use Mr. Bataille's term. "Thus I have gained access to true liberty – the liberty of absurdity."

"And here we find the divine readiness of the man condemned to death, the man whose prison doors will open before him one early dawn, this unbelievable disinterestedness about everything except the pure flame of his life; we feel it, death and absurdity are here the principles of the only reasonable liberty: the liberty that a human heart can feel and live. . . . The man of absurdity thus catches a glimpse of a universe burning and frozen, transparent and limited, where nothing is possible and everything is given, past which there is downfall and nothingness. Then he can decide to agree to live in such a universe and to draw his strength from it, his refusal to hope is the persistent evidence of a life without consolation" (pp. 83–4).

"What does life stand for in such a universe? Nothing for the moment but indifference to the future and a passion to exhaust everything that is given. . . . To know if one can live a life without appeal is all that interests me" (p. 84). "The thing that matters is not to live as well as possible but to live as much as possible" (p. 84).

Let us notice at once the ambiguity of these last words. To feel life, one's revolt, one's liberty, and to do so "as much as possible." It seems then that the word "much" here applies to the intensity of an awareness or an enlightenment. But a little further on we are told that "in the eyes of the man of absurdity, no depth, no emotion, no passion and no sacrifice can make a life of conscious awareness of forty years (even should he desire it) equal to sixty years of lucidity" (p. 87). And here it seems to be an extendible quantity which is in question. What appears quite clearly is that Mr. Camus first gives us the witness of a generation on whom a sentence of death had been pronounced, and for whom to live is, in fact, only to benefit by a reprieve liable to expire tomorrow or this evening. Such is the setting, given as the drama opens, for it is indeed a drama. We now have to see what attitude consciousness is going to adopt in such a situation. It refuses to imagine a metaphysical background from which some light might shine forth to transfigure the scene. It refuses, out of honesty in the first place, but also out of pride, and we have there two states of mind so closely interconnected that we cannot think of separating them. But there cannot be any question either of consciousness giving in to its fate, for that would still be to lower itself. Only one course remains: it is not only to proclaim the nameless absurdity of such a situation, but to become so rooted in it as to make it one's own, to assume and in a sense exalt it. Is not this the only way, not to test, but to prove oneself? Here we see outlined in an almost total darkness a sort of proof by absurdity which could serve as an inverted or inarticulate answer to the Cartesian *cogito*, in tune with Pascal or Kierkegaard if it were possible to imagine one or other of them as having no faith, but on the contrary bearing the sign of the most stubborn refusal it is possible to oppose to religious certainty. To be sure, the terms of 'defiance', 'challenge', 'wager', which I emphasised in passing, take on their full meaning here. There can be no question at all of a statement. But can there be a challenge or a wager without any value? "Without any fruitful value; yes," the author would surely reply. In other terms, we are concerned with an attitude which is not expected to bear fruit for anybody. "In the world of absurdity," declares Mr. Camus, "the value of an action or a life is measured by its unfruitfulness" (p. 96). This can only mean that here we are in a world closely and hermetically sealed up in itself. How great then is the inconsequence of the author when he speaks elsewhere "of the only luxury, that of human relationships . . . of the strong and chaste friendship of one man for another," etc. (p. 121)? How does he not see that a friendship or a love of any kind creates a world around it in which this formula no longer has any meaning, unless we are most unpardonably to confuse fecundity with usefulness? The truth is that there has never been so radical a monadism as that of Mr. Camus. There is no longer any question of an orgy, or of the passage of light and heat from one being to another. There is no longer either light or heat; and if for a moment the author seems to forget it, he only does so in faithlessness to the principle he himself has laid down.

It is only too evident that a rebel in the style of Mr. Camus challenges in advance, with the greatest possible scorn, the judgment we might be tempted to bring against his revolt. Much more: he can only reject the very compassion we might at some times be tempted to show him. In these conditions, at the end of a development like his, there is room for nothing but non-communication or contagion. It is necessary to insist on this last word. We see only too clearly how seductive such an attitude can be. Here as before, only in a still more perceptible way, a veritable intimidation is at work, particularly on the consciousness of adolescents. Why, in a sudden access of pride, should they not set to work on their account to embrace this world of absurdity which is suggested to them, or to brandish the torch of revolt in their turn?

The task which here devolves upon the critic is thus a thankless one. He must know that he runs the risk of being accused of cowardice, of bad faith or of stupidity and probably of all these things at once. It must be added that such a position appears to be impregnable in principle. For if we warn the author that in the end he will himself feel suffocated and will be forced to break a window-pane in order to breathe, he can always reply that this is only so because he has proved to be too weak to fulfil his wager to the end. He may even go so far perhaps as to admit or concede that no one is strong enough to endure such a trial: but what does that prove if not that man's condition is seen to be inhuman as soon as it is thoroughly thought out: he has never claimed anything else.

Henceforward what means have we at our disposal for attacking this stronghold? We shall no doubt have to make a very important distinction here.

First, it is to be wondered whether there is any way of convincing our adversary, and on that point I am as pessimistic as possible. I do not think that there is any form of argument, or that any can be invented, which would be able to triumph over such a narrow and such a hardened will. Arguments do not, and cannot, act like a magical charm. They require a certain receptive power, an open-mindedness which cannot but be lacking in this case. We must have the courage to acknowledge that only grace can have any effect here, it being well understood that *a priori* the hardened denier can only have a very inadequate idea of its action which he accordingly challenges. By definition, the hardened denier cannot imagine the ontological change which grace is able to bring about within him; we therefore have good grounds for saying that when he thinks he is refusing it, he is really refusing something else, a shadow or mirage.

The other question, which seems to me much more important, is that of knowing how we can both protect ourselves and put the defenceless on their guard against the contagion of which I spoke just now.

There are, I think, three main ways by which this evil thing can reach us. I say it is an evil thing. I do not, indeed, hesitate for a second in considering as an evil thing the process at the end of which our life is felt to be a prison – a prison in the midst of a world destitute of all the attributes which by common consent were formerly regarded as its glory. This will instantly be disputed. I shall be told that it cannot be an evil thing to see our situation as it really is, to face the truth. But it will be well to denounce an error – which is surely a sophism. The situation in question cannot be separated from the preconceived opinion of those who fix and define it, and, in spite of appearances, this opinion is in no way that of a scholar in search of pure objectivity. As I have already said incidentally: we have here, first and foremost, the claim not to allow oneself to be consoled: this claim implies a pride quite foreign to the pure scholar as such. This accounts for the refusal to consider the signs, numerous enough for whoever takes the trouble to notice them, of a supernatural intervention which is regarded as being lowering for those who accept it or adapt their lives in accordance with it. This is the first way of infiltration. There is a temptation, specially for the adolescent, to perch on the top of a tower, or to view scornfully from behind the bars of his cell, the vacillating, grovelling crowd. I am inclined to think that great experience of life makes one almost totally immune from this temptation. But how difficult it is to make someone, who not only lacks but challenges such experience, profit by it! In such cases exhortations are in vain and arguments have no effect; we have already seen why. We can only count on chance meetings, on all the opportunities scattered throughout life like pollen in the summer air.

There is another way of infiltration by which evil can reach our very foundations. The events which assail us can at any moment devastate our existence in such a way that we no longer see anything stretching around us but the undefined no man's land of universal inanity. Each of us can quite easily imagine some actual situation in which he might suddenly find himself as a result of passing events, and where he would be in danger of sinking into absolute nihilism. We can go further: that other beings, not even personally known to us, should be plunged into inescapable despair, is enough for the question inevitably to arise in our minds as to the meaning or absurdity of life. But the problem is always the same, and I maintain that it is not and cannot be a problem of truths. Is there really a superior kind of ethics which forbids us to seek a refuge beyond the shimmering lagoon which perpetually sends us back the reflection of our own dereliction? I find it hard not to believe that we are really considering a delusion which is perhaps a dramatised form of vertigo. I knew two people, actually as different from each other as possible, who at a definite moment of their adolescence worried over the idea that they would be too cowardly to dare to steal a little cake at the pastry-cook's – so much so that they ended by committing this petty theft in order to discomfit the sarcastic tempter who questioned their courage. Should we say that they were acting in the name of a superior code of ethics? I should take good care not to. The illusion here seems to consist in giving an intrinsic value to courage, or in another case to sincerity, whereas courage and sincerity, which are *essential conditions of value,* only become true values when they are in conjunction with other constituted values. There is a serious temptation to take courage or sincerity out of their orbit, that is to say to detach them artificially from a certain spiritual *organon,* in which each of them has its particular function. If, for instance, I make it my business to erect around myself a life-décor of the most desolate and depressing style and to prove that I can live in the midst of such surroundings, what is the spiritual value of such an attempt? It seems very much as if its inspiration is my desire to please myself. And the fact that I come to need this décor, that something within me demands it and refuses to do without it, proves that this is no longer a question of stoical resignation. In a world which was not absurd, in a world which had meaning in itself – and a transcendent meaning in relation to my personal aims – I should have no occasion to test myself and to establish myself as a central focus of values. In other words, I should feel I had come down in class, that I was depreciated, and that is really what I do not want to feel. Where the agnostic pessimist of the end of last century found it impossible to accept the existence of a providential order in which he would have liked to believe, the nihilist of today repudiates any idea of such an order; it would be no exaggeration to say that he congratulates himself upon finding that this order cannot be accepted, so that he reaches the point of offering an apologetic in reverse, an apologetic of absurdity for which total absence of value becomes the supreme value.

But if without any bias we come to consider the process expressed by this apologetic in reverse, I think it is difficult not to see in it a flowing back of life – should we say from the centre to the furthest extremities or from the extremities to the centre? The point is precisely to know which is the centre and which the extremity. Solipsistic idealism, exaggerating and distorting certain time-honoured formulæ, has come to consider the *ego* as the one and only centre; it is then necessary to speak of the reflux towards the centre from the circumference. But is it not precisely that which constitutes not merely the archetypal error, but in a certain manner the unforgivable sin – intellectual sin, metaphysical sin? Is not secular ontology founded on the assertion, too often repeated and moreover in terms which are inadequate and somewhat unconvincing, that the true centre is actual being itself and not in any degree the subject which asserts its being, especially if this assertion is shown as a projection or as the act of constructive thought. Ontology has always maintained that the *ego* itself can only assume an appearance of substance or content in so far as it is the image of, that is to say that it bears a likeness to, a plenitude which is beyond all possible representation. If this is so, we have on the other hand been witnessing a reflux towards the extremities for the last three centuries, as though, while the heart no longer carried out its regular function, the blood flowed to the surface and there became stagnant and hardened or else spurted out in a mortal hæmorrhage. . . .

It is not without a motive that, at the end of this long account, I have made use of a physiological comparison which must be seen as more than a simple metaphor. The third way of infiltration to which I have alluded is the *tedium vita,* the boredom and disgust with living, which claims as its victims hundreds of thousands of human beings who do not ever know how to recognise the disease which is attacking them; we must not forget that many of the most incurable ailments to which man is subject are painless and not easy to detect for a long time. But this *tedium vitæ* encouraged by inhuman conditions, as much among the idle rich as among the disinherited working classes, is only made possible by the rupture, or more exactly the loosening, of the ontological bond which unites each particular being to Being in its fullness. It seems to me that psychiatry or psycho-analysis will not get beyond the most superficial stratification of human reality and human ills, so long as they are not able to diagnose this functional lesion, or if you like, this ontological traumatisation, however hard it may be to formulate.

Still, however – and this is the essential point upon which I would like to insist in conclusion – still it is necessary that the traumatisation should be recognised as a traumatisation, that the anomaly should be seen to be an anomaly. In order to fulfil this

condition the notion of the human order should first be safeguarded, and it is precisely this notion which is attacked from all
sides today. No doubt man's essence has, in a sense, the power to
call itself in question; this is, at the most, scarcely more than the
spiritual or ideal parallel of what the permanent possibility of suicide stands for on the plane of physical life. Has Mr. Camus any suspicion that the spiritual attitude he advocates is at bottom only a
more subtly destructive equivalent of the suicide against which he
has taken up his position? In reality what is prescribed for us is the
restoration of dogmatics of which all the foundations have been
systematically undermined. It seems, however, that we have here a
vicious circle. If these dogmatics are to be reconstituted, do they not
presuppose the conviction of which they are to be the justification?
The problem, stated in purely intellectual terms, is insoluble, but
that is because anything in the way of definition is quite inadequate. The problem arises for living beings – for beings engaged in
a strange destiny which they have to face squarely and to understand. Perhaps we have grounds for thinking that it is by becoming
conscious of the destruction and chaos which all nihilism inevitably
engenders that the human being can awaken, or rather reawaken,
to consciousness of Being in its fullness.

To sum up, I should say that the mode of thought of which I
have tried today to analyse two particularly significant manifestations, can be conceived either as a perverse but fascinating game,
or at a deeper level and more truly, as the end of a process of auto-
destruction which is going on within a doomed society, within a
humanity which has broken, or thinks it has broken, its ontological
moorings. However this may be, it is nothing but a pure and simple imposture to claim to hold up as some unheard-of metaphysical
promotion or as a triumph of pure lucidity the really blinding gesture by which all that humanity has ever acquired is swept away
and we are thrust headlong into the dungeon, itself a sham, of a
Narcissism of nothingness, where we are left with no other resource
but to wonder tirelessly at our courage, our pride and our stubborn-
ness in denying both God and the being full of weakness and hope
which in spite of everything and for ever – we are.

Paris.
December, 1943.

RILKE: A WITNESS TO THE SPIRITUAL: PART I[1]

The title under which these two lectures have been announced I consider to be justified first of all in a negative way. For reasons which will soon appear, I did not feel it was possible to speak either of Rilke's mysticism, of his religion or even of his spirituality; this last word itself has a sound which strikes me as not strictly Rilkian.

But what exactly does "Witness to the Spiritual" mean here? In using such an expression I am referring to the notion of creative testimony to which my reflections during the last ten years have led me to give an increasingly important place. The witness, of course, is not just he who observes or makes a statement; that is not what he really is, but he is one who testifies and his testimony is not a mere echo, it is a participation and a confirmation; to bear witness is to contribute to the growth or coming of that for which one testifies. But what does the spiritual mean for Rilke? I fear that we cannot risk offering a definition of it yet. We shall have to work out the elements of this definition by degrees, and I do not in any way guarantee that we shall be able to weld them into a formula. I will simply quote as an epigraph the first verse of the Twelfth Sonnet to Orpheus (first series):

> Heil dem Geist der uns verbinden mag;
> denn wir leben wahrhaft in Figuren.
> Und mit kleinen Schritten gehen die Uhren
> neben unserm eigentlichen Tag.

1 Lectures given in January and February, 1944, at the *Centre de Recherches Philosophiques et Religieuses.*

(Hail, the spirit able to unite!
For we truly live our lives in symbol,
and with tiny paces move our nimble
clocks side by side with our true day.)[2]

Here the close relationship appears which unites the Spirit to the Symbols, to the images in which it clothes itself. We shall have to come back to this. A difficulty arises immediately, however; should we not regard Rilke as a pure artist whose only concern really was to gain an ever fuller and more distinct consciousness of the mission of his art? This is roughly the theory which the most recent of Rilke's interpreters, Werner Günther, defends with great talent in his book, *Weltinnenraum, die Dichtung R. M. Rilkes*, to which I shall often have to refer in the course of these lectures. "Rilke wants to be a poet, nothing but a poet. His religious position, his wisdom, are bound up with the particular nature of his poetry, they are indeed only side-issues and, as it were, marginal problems which suggest themselves to his artist's nature" (*loc. cit.*, p. 41). We shall see, for example, that for Günther the *Book of Hours*, which at first appears to be an almost mystical work, can only be correctly understood if it is considered from this particular æsthetic angle. There is here, I think, an element of truth which, however, presented without any precautions could quite easily give rise to a misinterpretation. The declaration: "Rilke is an artist, nothing but an artist; a poet, nothing but a poet" – seems to support a limitative conception of the poet and the artist, which would separate them from the common run of mankind, even though it be by relegating them to a sort of sanctuary where the common folk have no access. I do not know whether I am mistaken, but I feel that this conception, which was Mallarmé's for instance, is utterly foreign to such as Rilke. Rilke has a sense of the poet and his vocation which is both too human and too cosmic for anyone to have the right to introduce such a dissociation – a dissociation which, while claiming to purify the vocation, impoverishes and even mutilates the very idea we should form of it. I am sure that Rilke would have subscribed from the very depth of his heart to these lines of Charles du Bois: "The valley where souls are

---

2   *Sonnets to Orpheus*, translated by J. B. Leishman, p. 57 (Hogarth Press, 1946).

fashioned, wherein intelligence is put to the test and made into a soul." (We recognise here the celebrated words of Keats.) "That is actually life – and literature is nothing but such life itself when it reaches its fullest expression in the soul of a man of genius. Life and literature, far from opposing and contradicting each other, are bound together by the closest and most intimate of ties. Literature would have no content were it not for life; but were it not for literature, life would be but a waterfall, that ceaseless waterfall in which so many of us are submerged, a waterfall without meaning, which we merely accept, which we are incapable of interpreting; and literature carries out the functions of a hydraulic belt with regard to this waterfall, catching, collecting and raising its water" (*Approximations*, VII, pp. 320–1). If Rilke's message was really only addressed to artists, his poems and above all his correspondence would not ring with the marvellously fraternal understanding which souls cruelly wounded in life's journey find in them; there would not flow from them those emanations for which I do not believe we could ever discover a parallel: I doubt indeed whether we could find anything comparable, even in the letters of Katherine Mansfield, which have awakened such eager echoes everywhere.

To sum up, I should say that it would be quite ridiculous to try to find in Rilke anything like a philosophy in the traditional and systematic sense of the word; but, on the other hand, existential philosophy, as we are coming to conceive of it today, tends more and more to be identified with an experience which not only elaborates its own development but defines its allusion, one might even say its adherence, to a reality apprehended more and more intimately as a network of protective or hostile influences. I should not hesitate to assert from this point of view that the work of Rilke helps me, in my own studies, for example, infinitely more than some system drawn up by a specialist and based on personal grounds, which are at times quite obviously defective. Here, on the contrary the grounds are imposing, almost inexplorable and at the same time the implications of the affirmation reach beyond all the limits we might at first have fixed. I think it would be wise to point out before we go any further the limitless or even vague and hence ambiguous quality which we find in the conclusions Rilke reaches – I do this in order to avoid any disappointment. Moreover, the word "conclusions" is in this case the most unsuitable we could have found. The process which takes place in Rilke is not in the least comparable with a discursive development, but rather with a progressive transformation of vision – not only of interior vision, but just vision in the ordinary sense of the word – which takes place side by side with the perfecting of his poetic technique. I shall, of course, say nothing about the latter here; I shall have quite enough to do in pointing out certain characteristics of this vision, one of the most unusual possible, and in trying to evoke this Rilkian atmosphere, seemingly so well suited at the present time to many souls which Christianity has so far failed to hold.

It will be as well to say once and for all that we should be giving a completely false idea of Rilke's thought if we did not make it quite plain that there is in him an increasing opposition to the religion of Christ. Angelloz wonders whether the origin of this disaffection is not to be traced to a feeling of bitterness for Him who having taught him resignation and compunction gave him up in advance to the humiliating sarcasm of his comrades at the Cadet School. The incident he relates in a letter to his fiancée, Fraülein von David Rhonfeld, might indeed have produced a traumatism in him with far-reaching effects; but I think it would be rash to exaggerate its importance. Rilke's opposition to Christianity has other and deeper roots. This extract from his diary of October 4th, 1900, seems to me particularly significant: "For young people . . . Christ presents a serious danger; he it is who is too close, who hides God. We get used to seeking the divine by human methods. We get into soft and easy habits with all this human element, and later on we shall be frozen by the keen air of the heights, the air of eternity. We drift between Christ, the two Maries and the Saints. We are lost among forms and voices. We are deceived over and over again by this half-familiar element which causes neither surprise nor fear and does not tear us from our everyday outlook. We get accustomed to this, but there can be no getting accustomed to finding God." It seems as though a retrospective confession is discernible in these few lines which enlighten us concerning the conditions under which Rilke broke away from Christianity very early, probably only a short time after he left Sankt Pölten (in 1891, when he came away from the Cadet School, he was sixteen years old). Certainly the passage I have just quoted shows an indisputable craving for transcendence. Let us remember all the same that it is never very wise to make use of a technical vocabulary only suited to professional philosophers when we are speaking of Rilke. What at the very least we do detect in these few lines is a horror of anything confined, and also of a certain promiscuity; this corresponds with the love of the poet of the *Elegies* for solitude, and also with his passion for space on which Rudolph Kassner has insisted with such good reason. These two points deserve our attention.

Let us recall what he wrote in the *Letters to a Young Poet:* "Only one thing is necessary: solitude. The immense inward solitude. To withdraw into oneself and not to meet anyone for hours – that is what we must arrive at. To be alone, like a child is alone when grown-ups come and go." This solitude, as Günther says very aptly, does not consist in shutting ourselves away from people, but in practising recollection, in gathering our faculties together under a law which is genuinely our own. Rilke himself said quite early that we cannot be alone, except within the heart of the All. It is impossible to have a more acute consciousness of the tension which connects solitude and immensity with each other. And here what I have just now called his passion for space shows itself. But, of course, this kind of space is not that of everyday life, nor that of science and nature; it is the space of the visionary, "the space wherein God has established all things with his creative hands, the mystical space of metamorphoses, that which was at one and the same time the world, the world of God and of Childhood" (Kassner, *Buch der Erinnerung,* p. 306).

I do not think that we can separate the deep and lasting impression which his journey to Russia in 1899 must have left with him from this passion for distance and for spaces, but it must immediately be added that in his case this passion itself is joined with his devotion to intimacy. Only, just like the word "space" which we used just now, this word "intimacy" has to be defined and purified. There is a stifling intimacy which prevents the soul not only from opening out, but from breathing: he would not have been able to endure such an intimacy as that for a moment. Perhaps we could say without any paradox that, for him, intimacy did not exclude distance, but demanded it. *Abstand, Entfernung, Ferne* – these words are essentially Rilkian. And surely it is not by chance if we feel that it is in his correspondence that he is closest, most immediately present, to those whom he seeks, for instance, to stimulate or console. However tempted we may be to evoke Kierkegaard, of whom Rilke knew and admired at least some writings, though of course not the entire works, I think we should be very careful: the note he strikes seems to us to be really as different as possible. The very idea of paradox, central as it is with the Danish philosopher, I feel to be completely foreign to our poet; it suggests a mood which is not and never will be his. The truth is that with Kierkegaard we discern a smirk, we feel at times that he is grimacing; the fictitious characters he chooses as a disguise do not mind assuming a falsetto voice, and can even be suspected sometimes of ventriloquism. There is nothing like that here – happily! How much more even, more musical or just more human is the voice of this poet!

"It was in Russia," says Angelloz, "that Rilke had the revelation of a world wherein God creates himself" (*Rilke*, p. 122). This is probably quite true. "Russia," Rilke was to write later to Ellen Key, "was reality, with at the same time the deep daily intuition that reality is something far away, coming with infinite slowness to those who have patience. Russia, the country where men are solitary beings, where each bears a world within him, where each is full of gloom like a mountain, where each is deep in his humility, is not afraid of abasing himself, and for that very reason is a being full of piety. Men full of far distance, of uncertainty and hope, beings who are always growing spiritually. And over all a God who has never been defined, who eternally changes and who eternally grows." Already on July 6th, 1898, on the eve of his journey to Russia, he evoked the solitary of the future, of whom all creators are the ancestors. "There will be nothing outside him, trees and mountains, clouds and waves will have been but the symbols of those realities which are found in him. Everything has flown together in him. . . . He no longer prays, he is. . . . And each God is the whole past of a world, its ultimate meaning, the unified expression, and at the same time the possibility of a new life. . . . So then I feel it, we are the ancestors of a God and by our deepest solitudes we plunge into the centuries to come till we reach his beginning." This passage clearly goes to support the interpretation suggested by Günther. I refuse, however, to believe that Rilke's God in process of being, or to come, can be thought of purely and simply as a masterpiece or genius of the future. "I was speaking of him in a low voice," Rilke tells us in a diary fragment of which I have already quoted a few lines. It is God of whom he is writing here. "I was saying that his lacunæ, his injustice, the inadequacy of his powers were due to the degree of his development. That he was not yet completed. When will he have been able to develop? Man has so urgent a need of him that from the beginning he feels him and sees him as though he were already there. Man needed him to be finished, and he said: God is. Now he has to catch up with this anticipated becoming and it is for us to help him. It is with us that he becomes, he grows with our joys, and our sorrows throw shadows across his face. We can do nothing which does not affect him once we have found ourselves. And you must not think of him as above the multitude. He did not wish for the *multitude;* it is by a multiplicity of *individuals* that he wished to be carried. In the multitude each one is so small that he cannot put his hand to God's edifice. But the individual who places himself opposite him looks at him and is sure to reach him as high up as his shoulders. And he has power over him. And he matters to God. And thence comes my best courage in life: I have to be great in order to be the auxiliary of his greatness, I must be simple so as not to throw him into confusion, and my gravity should somewhere meet with his. . . . But while I express these thoughts, I feel that I am not simply in living contact with him, just because I am speaking about him. Those who pray to him do not speak about him. Perhaps I may be more than a simple worshipper. Perhaps a sort of ordination has been conferred upon me, perhaps others having become strangers to me, it has befallen me sometimes to approach a man with solemnity, as though I had access to him by a golden gate. But then they will always be the only ones to see me, those who dwell beside golden gates" *(Briefe und Tagebücher,* 1899–1902, p. 369–70). Here already we find the idea which he was to formulate in a letter of October, 1907, in which he said that he had never been able to receive God simply, but that he always had "to fit himself to him productively." There is a deep experience here which we must extricate from the abundant and contradictory images which as we shall see, swarm around it in the *Stundenbuch.* What we can most certainly affirm is that there is nothing in this evocation of a God in process of becoming which can be compared with the ideas familiar to the readers of the later Renan. We are not here in line with the thought of Hegel; perhaps the fact that the God of Rilke is not the God of the multitude, but of individuals who are all creative in their way, would be enough to prove it. The only thing which I think we should add is that, as we shall see more clearly later on, this creation need not take shape in a work of art. A great love is a creation as well as a poem or a statue; a great love is creative participation in what, in order to simplify, I shall call, in scarcely Rilkian language, the divine life.

It seems to me important, at the point we have reached, before embarking on the *Stundenbuch,* to quote a part at least of the admirable passage from the diary (December 19th, 1900), which refers to Gerhardt Hauptmann's *Michael Kramer.* This drama, the Silesian writer's masterpiece and, to my way of thinking, one of the masterpieces of the modern theatre, had made a deep impression on Rilke. I will very briefly remind you of the subject. A painter, Michael Kramer, who has the highest and most exacting sense of his art, but to whom it has not as yet been given to realise his ideal fully, had at first transferred the centre of his ambitions to his son, Arnold, who is exceptionally gifted. But Arnold is physically tainted, being a hunchback, irresistibly attracted by less reputable pursuits: drink, gambling, sexual indulgences. He arouses aversion and sarcasm everywhere; he falls in love with a barmaid who spurns him; after a frightful scene, which his pride makes it impossible for him to survive, he commits suicide. The last act is a *tête-à-tête* between the father and the dead son. . . . The corpse has been brought into Michael's studio; he has been watching beside it all night. "And now the day breaks when the great sorrow, which has been seated voicelessly beside him, takes him in its hands and we see how he is transformed by those hands of sorrow. His words are not words but the features of an austere countenance which light up and attain completion and nobility. The old man does not speak, he becomes great, and we hear, as it were, the imperceptible murmuring of growth. He finds he is, as it were, infinitely confirmed. Death has raised the treasure he could not lift and placed it where it belongs. On Arnold's face ugliness was only a reflection. Death has torn away all masks, opened the shutters and revealed everything. And Michael knows that he has not been mistaken: his son was indeed there; he is there. It was not an empty casket which in former days he carried to the temple when he presented the newborn child to Eternity. They were inestimable treasures which he bore in his trembling arms, and life has not touched them, life has not opened the casket – it has spent nothing out of these riches, it has not discovered them. For life is blind and makes no demands. But death has opened everything out, like someone rich and powerful who knows where his gold lies, even when it is most hidden and deeply buried. 'Death, the most merciful form of life.' The infinite justice which raises and protects has recognised him whom life never understood; the unfortunate being, hounded by everyone, has been received by equitable death as a prince is received. Death is above life, as love is above life, and it is still greater than love, since love left the hunted child without help. And so it is revealed to the father that this death – the shameful death – of the only and beloved son is not a simple 'decease', as all those might think who view it from outside with a heart dulled by custom. He feels that it is something great which has fallen to his lot, an experience which dilates his life, a sorrow which changes all the proportions of what he feels. So strong is the sense of being, of truth and of reality which takes possession of him at this moment of death that it is as though God had affirmed his existence before Michael's very eyes. For there, on the pillow, the face of his child lies in respose, like an open book where the confirmation of reality can be read word for word; this he no longer desires for himself but it is something he has to know in advance, for the sake of him who is one day to come in order to apprehend it. What is time? Who would lose patience in the presence of Infinitude? What does it matter if certain mute presences to whom treason is unknown transmit the sacred deposit after an interval of one, or even several, centuries, and if no one sees it or guesses it is there. Now for an instant, on this face of the dead, what should be is exhibited. And that exists. All is well, that exists. And we should go on our way resolutely with calm dignity, we the forerunners of him who is to come and who will not come in vain, of him he who will dig up and discover the treasure. Amen."

I have made a point of giving some sort of a translation of this

magnificent passage because in it we find united in a rare harmon-
ic fullness a sense of God and of death; we see clearly here how in
Rilke the ideas of being and becoming are closely interwoven. The
revelation which comes to Michael Kramer really bears on being; it
is something of eternity which is freed for him at the sight of the
face made peaceful and transfigured by death; but at the same time
it is an annunciation, it is an anticipated testimony to what will
come to pass one day, what will one day be revealed.

And now we come to the *Stundenbuch*. It was from 1899 to 1901
that Rilke composed the first two books: the Book of the Monastic
Life and the Book of Pilgrimage. The third, the Book of Poverty and
Death, was composed in 1903 after the Book of Images, and after he
had made the discovery of Paris, that is to say, of the great modern
city and of the nameless trial which it involves not only for an artist
but a man.

What then is the God of the *Stundenbuch*? To avoid certain misunderstandings we must always bear in mind what Rilke himself
said later on: "God is a direction of the heart." This sentence is
found in a letter of a much later date written to Ilse Blumenthal-
Weiss from Muzot, December 28th, 1921.[3]

"Faith! There is no such thing, I had almost said. There is only
– Love. This forcing of the heart to regard this and that as true,
which is ordinarily called Faith, has no sense. First you must find
God somewhere, experience him as infinitely, prodigiously, stu-
pendously present, – then whether it be fear or astonishment or
breathlessness, whether it be, in the end, Love with which you
comprehend him, it hardly matters at all, – but faith, this compul-
sion towards God, there is no place for it once you have begun
your discovery of God, a discovery in which there is no more
stopping, no matter in what place you have begun. And you, as a
Jewess, with so much immediate knowledge of God, with such
ancient Fear of God in your blood, ought not to have to worry
about 'faith' at all. . . . I have an indescribable trust in those peoples who have come up against God NOT through faith, but who
experienced God through their own nationhood, in their own
tribal sources (*Volkstum*). Like the Jews, the Arabs and to a certain

---

3   *Selected Letters*, translated by R. F. C. Hall (Macmillan), pp. 33–57.

extent the Orthodox Russians – and then, in a different way, the peoples of the East and of ancient Mexico. For them God is Origin and hence also Future. For the others he is a derivative, something they struggle away from or struggle towards as though he were a stranger or had become estranged, – and so they are in perpetual need of the Mediator, the truth, someone who translates their blood, the idiom of their blood, into the language of Godhead."

It would be as well to notice here how ambiguous and uncertain the thought of Rilke is on this point, and how badly the idea he has formed of faith corresponds with what a truly lived faith really is. It is to be wondered if he is not going entirely by what he remembers of a devitalised religious instruction through which he had been unable to make any contact with true Christianity.

"Religion is something infinitely simple, simple-souled. It is not knowledge, not the content of feeling (for every kind of content is admitted at the outset when a man enters into collusion with life), it is not duty and not renunciation, it is not a limitation: but within the perfect amplitudes of the universe it is – a direction of the heart. Just as a man can go and wander off to the left or right, and bang himself and fall and get up again, and do wrong here and suffer wrong there, and here be maltreated and there harbour evil in himself and maltreat and misunderstand; so all this passes over into the great religions and preserves and enriches in them the God that is their centre. And Man, who lives at the outermost periphery of such a circle *belongs* to this mighty Centre, even though he has only once, perhaps, at dying, turned his face towards it. When the Arab turns at certain hours towards the East and casts himself down, that *is* religion. It is hardly 'faith'. It has no opposite. It is a natural animation within a being through whom the Wind of God blows three times a day, as a consequence of which we are at least – supple."[4]

Now, with your permission I am going to quote some fairly long passages from the *Stundenbuch*, though I cannot disguise from myself the imperfections of my attempted translation.

Thy mouth, of which I am the breath, is all dark
and Thy hands are of ebony.

4   *Selected Letters*, pp. 336-7.

Thou art so great that I cease to exist
as soon as I even approach Thee.
Thou art so dark; my little light
has no meaning at Thy boundary.
Thy will moves like a wave
and each day is drowned therein . . .

Thou, darkness whence I issue,
I love Thee more than the flame
which limits the world
shining
for a circle
outside which no being knows it.
But darkness holds everything to itself,
forms and flames, and animals and me,
as it takes possession
of men and powers.
And it is possible that a mighty force
is moving in my neighbourhood,
I believe in nights

I believe in everything that has never been said.
I wish to set free my most pious feelings.
That which none has yet dared to wish
I shall one day not be able to help wishing.
If that is presumption, God forgive me. . . .

I am too alone in the world, and yet not alone enough
to consecrate each hour.
I am too puny in the world, and yet not small enough
to be in Thy presence like a thing,
dark and gifted with wisdom. . . .

Thou art the forest of contradictions.
I can rock Thee like a child,
and yet Thy curses, which lie terrible over the nations,
are fulfilled. . . .

I know; Thou art the Mysterious One
round whom time stopped hesitant.
How beautiful Thou wert as I created Thee

In a tense hour,
with an arrogant gesture of my hand. . . .

Thou, God my neighbour, when sometimes
during a long night I disturb Thee with hard knocking,
it is because I rarely hear Thy breath
and know Thou art alone in the hall.
And shouldst Thou need something no one is there
to place refreshment in Thy groping hand.
I listen always. Give some slight sign.
I am quite close.

Nothing but a thin partition divides us.
This is but chance; for it could be that at a
call from Thy lips or from mine
it would be rent
without any sound or noise.

It is formed of pictures of Thee.

And Thy pictures stand, before Thee like names,
And when the light in me
by which my depths know Thee blazes up
it wastes itself in glitter about the periphery,
and my perceptions, which quickly flag,
are left homeless and are parted from Thee.

We see how difficult, even impossible, it is to gain anything in
the way of a notion of God from such poems; on the contrary, Rilke
purposely destroys the images which he has just called up and sub-
stitutes others which seem to be their opposite. "God," Rilke himself said, "is a direction given to love." A direction, not an object.

And here is the *Book of Pilgrimage*.

The influence of Russia is clearly discernible in it.

Here we find him singing of the Son of Man, which is partly
explained by the fact that he was going to be a father; but this son
of man is not Jesus here.

I was a house after a fire
in which only murderers sometimes sleep
before their gnawing punishments

drive them further into the country;
I was like a town beside the sea
where a plague raged,
which hung heavy like a corpse
upon the hands of the children.

I was a stranger as anyone might be;
and all I knew about him
was that once he hurt my mother
while she was bearing me
and that her heart, her constricted heart,
beat very painfully against my embryo. . . .

I am effete like an old man
who no longer understands his big son
and knows little of the new things
upon which the will of his seed is set.
I tremble at times for thy deep happiness
which travels in so many strange vessels;
I wish sometimes to have thee back inside me,
back in the dark which nourished thee.
When I am too much absorbed in time,
I fear sometimes that thou art no more.
Then I read about thee. The evangelist
everywhere proclaims thy eternity.

I am the father; yet the son is more,
is all the father was, and there grows in him
the being that his father did not become;
he is the future and the return of the past,
he is the womb, he is the sea. . . .

Does one love a father? Does one not leave him,
as thou leftest me, with hardness on thy countenance,
tearing oneself away from his empty, powerless hands?
Does one not put his faded words
into old books which one seldom reads?
Does one not flow like water from a water-shed
from his heart towards pleasure and pain?
Does not father mean to us the past,

years dead and gone, which we think of as strange,
out-dated manners, dead fashions,
withered hands and faded hair?
Though in his own time he was a hero,
he is the leaf which falls as we grow. . . .

That is what father means to us. And I. . . am I
to call thee father?
That would mean parting myself from thee a thousand times.
Thou art my son. I shall recognise thee
as one recognises one's only beloved son, even when
he has become a man, an old man.

Put out my eyes; I can see thee;
stop up my ears; I can hear thee;
and without feet I can go to thee,
and without a mouth I can still call upon thee.
Tear off my arms, and I shall yet seize thee
with my heart as with a hand;
stop my heart, my brain will go on beating;
and if thou settest fire to my brain
I shall still bear thee in my blood. . . .

Thou art the heir.
Sons are heirs,
for fathers die;
sons stand erect and flourish.
Thou art the heir.

And thou inheritest the green
of past years' gardens and the calm blue
of crumbled skies;
the dew of thousands of days,
the many summers which declare the sun,
and innumerable springs with their sparkle and grief,
like the letters of a young wife. . . .

Thou shalst inherit Venice and Kazan and Rome,
Florence shall be thine, the cathedral of Pisa.
The Troitska Lavra and the Monastery,

which below the gardens of Kiev
forms a dark, tortuous labyrinth;
Moscow with its bells as memories;
music also shall be thine; violins, horns and tongues;
and each song sung deep enough
shall sparkle on thee like a jewel.

For thee only do poets shut themselves in
and gather rich and intoxicating images
and emerge and ripen by their metaphors
and remain so solitary all their lives. . . .
And painters paint their pictures only
to enable thee to recover in imperishable form
that Nature which thou didst create ephemeral. . . .

Those who create are like thee.
They wish for eternity. They say: Stone,
be eternal; which means: Be thine!

And those who love come together for thee;
they are the poets of a brief hour.
On an expressionless mouth they kiss
a smile, as if to make it more beautiful. . . .

They pile mystery on mystery and die
as animals die, without understanding. . . .
But perhaps they will have grandsons
in whom their green existence will ripen;
through them shalst thou inherit the love
which they give each other blindly, and as if asleep.
Thus the overflow of things flows towards thee. . . .

As I understand it everything is made clear by the sentence I
have already referred to, which occurs in a letter of May 16th, 1911,
to the Princess of Thurn and Taxis: "I cannot understand religious
natures, which receive and feel God as that which is given, without
fitting themselves to him productively *(ohne sich an ihm productiv zu
versuchen)*" (p. 131).

But here are some other themes, some other motifs, which
together with this last one make up an extraordinary symphony, a

symphony which as a whole could never be contained within the
limits of an intelligible formula.

> . . . No one lives his life.
> Men are chances, voices, fragments,
> commonplaces, fears, many small happinesses,
> disguised, dressed up, since childhood;
> it is their mask which talks; their face is silent.

> I often think there must be treasure-houses
> where all these many lives lie
> like armour, sedan-chairs or cradles
> which no one real ever occupied,
> just like garments which are incapable of
> standing upright unsupported, but flop
> against strong walls of vaulted stone.
> Whenever I would walk abroad in the evening
> out of my garden in which I am tired,
> I know that all paths lead
> to the arsenal of things in which there has been no life. . .
> And yet, though everyone tries to escape from himself
> as from a prison which hates and confines him,
> there is a great miracle in the world.
> I feel that all life is lived.
> Who then lives it? Those things which
> stand upright in the evening as in a harp,
> like an unplayed melody?
> Is it the winds blowing upon the waters,
> the branches signalling to each other,
> the flowers weaving perfumes,
> or the long, ageing avenues?
> Is it the warm-blooded animals, moving hither and thither,
> or those strangers, the flying birds?
> Who lives this life? Is it Thou who livest it, God?

> Thou art the old man whose hair
> is ashes. . . .

> Thou art the smith, the song of the years,
> who has always stood at the anvil. . . .

There are rumours abroad that cast doubt on Thee,
and doubts which obliterate Thee.
The indolent and the dreamers
mistrust their own fervour
and want the mountains to bleed;
otherwise they will not believe.
But Thou lowerest thy countenance.
Thou couldst cut open the arteries of the mountains
as the sign for a Last Judgment;
but thou carest nothing for
the heathen.

Thou dost not wish to fight with every sort of wile
Nor to seek the love of the light,
for thou carest nothing for
Christians.

Thou carest nothing for him who questions.
With a gentle countenance
Thou lookest upon those who bear burdens.

Here to sing of God is to sing of humility and law:

Thy meaning is humility; countenances
sunk in quiet understanding of Thee.
So do young poets walk in remote avenues at evening;
so do peasants stand around the dead body
of a child. . . .

He who for the first time has Thee in his keeping
is disturbed by his neighbour, or his watch;
he walks bent over Thy footprints,
as if laden and burdened with years.
Only later does he draw near to nature,
becomes aware of the winds and the far distances,
hears Thy whisper in the meadow,
worships Thee in song from the stars,
and can never again unlearn Thee,
for everything is but Thy mantle.

For him Thou art new and near and good

and marvellous as a journey
which he makes in silently moving ships
on a great river.

And everything which follows recalls navigation on the Volga:

Sometimes the boat steers to places
which lie alone, apart from village or town,
waiting for something on the waters,
waiting for him who has no home. . . .
For him small carriages are waiting
(each drawn by three horses)
which plunge breathless into the evening
along a road which loses itself.

The last house in this village is
as lonely as the last house in the world.
The road, which the little village does not bring to an end,
goes slowly on into the night.
The little village is only an uneasy stage, full of foreboding,

between two great expanses. . . .

Sometimes a man gets up from his evening meal
and walks out, and walks and walks and walks –
because of a church standing somewhere in the east.
And his children bless him as though he were dead.
And he who dies in his house
still lives in it, lives in furniture and crockery,
and his children go out into the world
towards the church which he forgot.

The theme of a pilgrimage is now to take on increasing importance:

Oh God, I should like to be a crowd of pilgrims,
to be able to approach Thee in a long procession,
and to be a great piece of Thee,
Thou garden with living walks.
If I walk alone, solitary as I am,
who notices it? Who sees me approaching Thee?

Finally, the theme of non-possession is introduced:

Thou must not fear, oh God. They call mine
All things which are patient.
They are like the wind which strokes the branches
and says: My tree. . . .

They say: My life, my wife,
my dog, my child, and yet they well know
that everything – life, wife, dog and child –
are alien creatures, against which they blindly
knock their outstretched hands.
True, this is only known to the great ones
who aspire to have eyes. For the others
do not want to hear that their poor wandering
has no connection with anything,
and that, repulsed by their own possessions,
they are denied by that which is theirs,
and that they no more possess their wives than they possess
    a flower,
which lives a life of its own alien to all men.

Oh God, do not lose Thy balance.
Even he who loves Thee, and recognises Thy countenance
in the dark, when it flickers like a light
in Thy breath, does not possess Thee.
Even when someone seizes Thee in the night
making Thee enter into his prayer,
Thou are the guest
who later goes on his way.

Must we really accept the interpretation Günther offers us,
according to which God is nothing but the symbol of the poet's
soul? In that case the text as a whole would only take on its full
meaning for a reader who knows how to discern a continuous reference to the creative artist beneath all the diversity of the symbols.
The Son, or the Heir, would only be the work of art in process of
growth, never finished, always present. The tender affection which
is poured out upon him would be that which the creator dedicates
to his work. Again when writing about Book III, the Book of
Poverty and Death, Günther says that if God is poverty at its height,
it is still in so far as he is the symbol of the creative artist.

Du aber bist der tiefste Mittellose,
Der Bettler mit verborgenem Gesicht,
Du bist der Armut grosse Rose,
Die Ewige Metamorphose
Des Goldes in das Sonnenlicht.

(But thou art the most profoundly needy,
the beggar with concealed face.
Thou art the great rose of poverty,
the eternal transformation
of gold into sunlight.)

To tell the truth, it seems to me, as I said before, that Günther's interpretation can neither be unquestioningly adopted, nor yet categorically rejected. I repeat once more that it is of the essence of Rilke's vision, or again of the power of vibration at the heart of his work, not to isolate the artist from creation in general. Perhaps in a certain sense the poet for Rilke is the very life-centre of creation, but this amounts to saying symmetrically that the rest of creation participates in its own order and according to its particular rhythm in the cosmic order which is the poet's. The Hymn to Death and to Poverty which is the peak of Book III seems to me to lose the best part of its pathos and meaning if it is robbed of its universally human character.

There men live, their lives are wretched and hard. . . .

They go about degraded by care. . . .

Their clothes sag on them
and their beautiful hands soon grow old. . . .

And behind misery, there is death, but it is an anonymous, impersonal death, it is not our death – the one to which each of us has a right and which should ripen with his life:

O Lord, give each one his own particular death,
the death stemming from his own life
in which he had love and awareness and distress.

For we are but the peel and the leaf.
The great death which each man bears within himself
is the fruit around which everything gravitates. . . .

For what makes death abhorrent and hard to bear
is that it is not *our* death. . . .
. . . What we give birth to – is
an abortion of our death,
a twisted and anxious embryo. . . .
With the marks on his puckered brow of
the fear of all that he did not suffer. . . .

There is invocation that God will send the predestined man who in a night of universal blossoming will rediscover his child-hood:

the unknown and the wonderful
and the endless, dark cycle of rich legend
belonging to his prescient first years. . . .

Let him await his hour – and he will give birth to death, the Lord. Give us –

the austere motherhood of man . . .
him who gives birth to death. . . .

In the land of those who laugh, he will be an object of ridicule, –
        for
He will be called a dreamer, for he who watches
Is always a dreamer in the land of carousal.

Establish him in thy grace. . . .
and make me the minstrel, the baptist of this new
messiahship . . .

a singer with two voices;

One to prepare the distant things,
the other to be the countenance and beatitude,
the angel of my solitude. . . .

We have the hymn to true poverty; may God restore poverty to the poor:

They are not poor. They are only the not-rich,
who are without will and without a world;
marked with the sign of the last agonies,

and everywhere leafless and deformed.
The dust of the towns presses upon them. . . .

Yet they are purer than pure stones,
and like the blind, animal which has scarcely begun,
and full of simplicity and infinitely Thine;
they wish for nothing, and need only one thing,
the right to be as poor as they really are.
For poverty is a great inner light. . . .

Thou too art poor: like spring rain
that falls like a blessing on the roofs of the town;
and like a wish nursed by prisoners
in a cell eternally deprived of the world.
And like the sick who change their position in bed
and are happy; like the flowers along the railway line
so grievously poor in the mad wind of journeys;
and as poor as the hand into which we weep . . .

The poor man's house is like an altar-shrine
in which the eternal is transformed into bread;
when evening comes it softly returns
in a wide circle to itself
and re-enters into itself leaving many echoes. . . .

The poor man's house is like the earth;
the chip of a future crystal,
now light, now dark in its chance flight;
poor as the warm poverty of a stable.
Yet there are evenings when it is everything,
and all the stars emerge from it.

And so the poem finishes by the evocation of St. Francis of Assisi, who is not, however, named; a St. Francis who might also be Orpheus:

When he died, so light as to be nameless,
he was scattered; his seed flowed
in the brooks and sang in the trees
and gazed at him calmly from the flowers.
He lay and sang. And when the sisters came
they wept for their beloved spouse.

Oh! where has the clear echo of him gone to?
Why do the poor who wait not feel
from afar his presence, his rejoicing and his youth?
Why do they not see rising in the east
· the great evening star of poverty?

This hymn cannot be separated from the confession which is
given to us in the *Notebook of Malte Laurid Brigge,* although the latter
was only written at a rather later date, between 1904 and 1908. But,
I repeat, Rilke had already had the terrible and mortal experience of
a great city and the *Notebook* originated from this experience and
this revelation.

"The *Notebook*," Angelloz admits, "is still and will perhaps
always remain a problematical book, against which Rilke himself
on several occasions warned his friends." Everything in the book is
at the bottom paradoxical. The *Notebook* is not novel, it is not an
autobiography, he expressly said so although he does not even
seem to have made Malte go through "a single development or
express an opinion which he had not had himself." (Kippenberg's,
R. M. Rilke, p. 59). He wrote to Lou Andreas Salome on December
28th, 1911 (XII, p. 247). "No one but you, dear Lou can distinguish
between them" (Malte and himself) "and show whether and to
what extent he looks like me. Whether he, who is in part com-
pounded of my own dangers, perishes in order to keep *me*, as it
were, from perishing; or whether I have only now, with these notes,
really got into the current that will sweep me and dash me to
pieces."[6] We have here a very strange phenomenon, a deeply
ambiguous relation between the creator and his creation. He told
M. Edmond Jaloux that one day, to see clearly into himself, he imagined a conversation between a young man and a girl at a watering
place. The young man began to speak about a Danish friend, Malte
Laurids Brigge, who died and left him his papers! This figure
became a centre of inner crystallisation. Malte thus was for him
both himself and someone else, in relation to whom later on he
would appear to himself, as a survivor without resources or occupation. A paradoxical situation this, of a being wearing mourning
for himself; and I dare suggest the hypothesis that if Rilke stressed

5   *Selected Letters,* p. 184.

the deep identity of life and death more and more strongly, it was because after finishing Malte he had felt as it were a death at the heart of life.

The fundamental word for whoever wants to penetrate the extremely complex and polyphonic meaning of the Notebook is the word "experience."

"No, no," we read in the Notebook (p. 220), "there is nothing in the world which can be *represented* by the slightest thing. Everything is composed of such and such unique details which cannot be thought of abstractly *(absehen)*. In imagining, we pass rapidly over it and do not see that they are lacking. But *realities are slow and indescribably detached.*"

It must be added that the limits of this experience have been thrust back far beyond what is usual. "Artistic vision should first of all go beyond itself; to the point of seeing right into the Terrible *(das Schreckliche)*, and into what seems to us merely repulsive, which exists and which counts in the same way as all the rest." This word *schrecklich*, terrible, takes on its full value here: the war, of which Rilke felt the utter horror, only served to illustrate on a gigantic scale a fundamental intuition which found expression from the first pages of the Notebook and which we can trace back to the Cadet School and to his experience of the misery of the life of the crowds in Paris. "Distress and disaster," he writes from Munich on November 6th, 1914, "are perhaps no more prevalent than before, only more tangible, more active, more visible. For the misery in which mankind has lived daily since the beginning of time cannot really be increased by any contingency. But there may still be an increase in our understanding of the unspeakable misery of being human, and perhaps all this is leading us towards it"[6] (XIII, p. 26).

But it is important to recognise that he has owned himself that if we must be mindful of life's weight it does not mean in the slightest degree a denial or giving up of the struggle (XIV, p. 131). To give life weight is to weigh things according to the carat measure of the heart, not of suspicion or chance. There must be no denial; quite the reverse, there must be an infinite adherence to *that which exists (Zustimmunz zum Du-Sein)*. It is scarcely necessary to draw

6   To Karl and Elizabeth von der Heydt, *Selected Letters*, p. 249.

attention to the almost Nietzschean, – or more exactly Beethovian – tone of such a *sursum corda*. But it is in relation to this profession of faith that we can understand what Rilke means when he says in one of his letters that the *Notebook* should be read against the current (XII, p. 197). This is elucidated by the following passage which I am borrowing from a letter addressed to L.H., November 8th, 1915: "What is expressed in the *Notebook of Malte Laurid Brigge* is simply this; how is it possible to live when the fundamentals of this life are so completely incomprehensible? When we are always inadequate in love, wavering in our determination and impotent in the face of death, how is it possible to exist *(dazusein)?"* Rilke declares that he has been unable to express in this book the greatness of the surprise which he feels at the discovery that although man has had contact with life for thousands of years he is still such a novice, so torn between fright and an attitude of complete inward evasion when he faces his great obligations. It fills him with a sort of terror, but behind it something is hiding (I will translate literally), "close, more than close, so intense that he cannot decide in the name of feeling whether it is burning or icy." He once said that the book appeared to him himself like a hollow form, like a negative whose every depression and recess would be sorrowful intuition, inconsolable suffering, but of which the positive counterpart, like a figure poured into a mould, would perhaps be happiness, assent – a state of blessed assurance, "Who knows, I wonder, whether we do not take the gods the wrong way about? (Perhaps it is only by ourselves that we are separated from their august and glorious countenance.) Who knows whether we are not very near to seeing the expression that we aspire to contemplate, only we are at the back? – and is not the only explanation this – that our faces and the divine eyes are turned in the same direction and only make one? How under these conditions could we come towards him from the depths of the space which is before him?" This passage, which may at first seem confusing is, I believe, extraordinarily significant in reality; it marks with extreme clearness why in Rilke's poetry there can be no objective meeting between man and God; and all the rest of this letter helps us to catch a glimpse of what is to be understood by that. Ever since his remotest origin, man has imagined gods in whom the forces of anger, threat and terror, gathered into a composite whole, were concentrated. One might say that this whole was alien to man, yet at the same time man only became conscious of it and could only recognise it by virtue of a certain mysterious kinship between the alien and himself. Man was this element also, but it incarnated that part of his own experience which was beyond his grasp and with which therefore he could have no dealings. Rilke asks whether we could not consider the history of God as an unapproached part of the human soul, kept in reserve for the future, but not to be forced down with impunity by man? In the same way with death, and here I will translate as literally as possible: "Familiar, and yet in its reality unfathomable for us, knowing us through and through, and yet not truly recognised by us, mortifying and surpassing the meaning of life from its very origin – death also we have, as it were, rejected, in order to stop it from continually interrupting us in the discovery of this meaning; death which is probably so close to us that we cannot fix any interval between it and the very heart of our life; it has become an outsider, kept at a distance, watching somewhere in the void, fixing its malevolent choice on this one or that and then pouncing down upon him. . . ." Thus God and death became the Other which our life has to face, our life made human, it would seem, by this very separation, and hence familiar, possible, practicable, ours in fact in a restrictive sense. The consequence of this kind of exclusion was that life began to turn more and more quickly in a circle that was narrower and narrower, and, moreover, increasingly artificial, for nature knows nothing of this separation, and when a tree grows, death grows in it just as life does. Love recks not of our subdivisions either; it sweeps us trembling into the infinite consciousness of the All. Lovers do not really draw the elements of their life from the separated world of here-below: "God is truly present to them" and "death has no hold on them"; "for they are full of death in that they are full of life."

RILKE: A WITNESS TO THE SPIRITUAL: PART II

If you will allow me, I am going to begin this second and last talk on Rilke by giving you part of a letter to Ilse Jahr of February 22nd, 1923, in which Rilke discusses his inner evolution. This essentially important letter gives us in advance a valuable commentary on the *Duino Elegies* and the *Sonnets to Orpheus* with which this lecture is almost exclusively concerned:

"I began with *things*, which had been the veritable familiars of my lonely childhood, and it was indeed something that I was able without outside help, to get as far as animals. But then Russia opened out for me and gave me the brotherliness and darkness of God, in whom alone there is fellowship. That was how I named him then, the God who has dawned upon me, and I lived long in the antechamber of his name, on my knees. . . . Now, you would hardly ever hear me name him, there is an indescribable discretion between us, and where closeness and penetration once were, new distances stretch out as in the atom which the new science also conceives as a universe in little. The Tangible slips away, changes; instead of possession one learns the relativity of things, and there arises a namelessness that must begin again with God if it is to become perfect and without deceit. Sensuous experience retires behind an infinite longing for the perceptible world; God, now become unutterable, is stripped of all attributes, and these fall back into creation, into love and death . . . perhaps this is what was accomplished over and over again in the *Stundenbuch*, this ascent of God from the breathing heart, covering the whole heavens and descending as rain. But any open avowal of this would be too much. Less and less can the Christian experience be considered; the primordial Godhead outweighs it infinitely. The notion of being sinful and then needing redemption as a pre-condition of God is more and more repugnant to a heart that has understood the earth. It is not sinfulness and error in things earthly but, on the contrary, the pure nature of the earth that will lead to the most essential consciousness; sin is certainly the most wonderful roundabout way to God, – but why should those go a-travelling who have never left him? The strong, inward, vibrating bridge of the Mediator has meaning only when the abyss between God and ourselves is admitted, – but even this abyss is full of the darkness of God, and if ever anyone feels it, let him go down into it and howl there (this is more necessary than crossing over it). Only for him to whom even the abyss was a dwelling place will the paradise we have sent on ahead of us be retrieved, and everything deeply and passionately *here*, which the Church has pirated and pawned to a Beyond, come back once more; then all angels will decide to sing the praises of the earth."[1]

I should like to go back a little now and to glance briefly at an aspect of the creation of Rilke that we have not yet approached. What I have specially in mind here is all that Rilke learned from his prolonged intercourse with Rodin; teaching which appears to have played a large part in making it possible for him to write the *Neue Gedichte*.

In quite a general sense it would be possible to say that Rodin taught him the meaning of work with all its implications. "How should we live? Your answer to me was: by working" (Letter to Rodin, p. 16). Patience, humility in the presence of the object, in the presence of truth, but also the joy which is born in the presence of the object, of the two-fold act by which the artist opens up to it and by which it opens up to the artist. There, I think, we have what Rilke gained through contact with Rodin. Mme. Kippenberg in her book on Rilke goes so far as to say that Rodin is the only man who ever had a deep influence on him and who gave a new direction to his creative effort. It is because Rodin was more than a master for him;

1   *Selected Letters*, pp. 373-4.

he was an example, a lighthouse in the Baudelairean sense, or as he
said himself, "a marvel, visible from afar." "What he contemplates
exists for him to the exclusion of all the rest, it is the world where
everything is happening; when he carves out a hand, this hand is
alone in space, there is nothing else. In six days God only made a
hand, he spread the seas around it, above it he stretched the sky; he
rested upon it when all was accomplished" (quoted by Lou
Andréas Salomé, p. 36). This was the way by which Rilke was initi-
ated into the experience of what I should be inclined to call creative
absorption.

Rilke's love, his reverence for *things*, is already clearly visible in
the *Book of Images* and even in the earlier poems. "I want to love
things as persons." It is a great pity that we have not two words for
thing as they have in German: *Ding* and *Sache*. Of course, it is *Ding*
which we are concerned with here, *Sache* being the humanised, and
thus in a certain sense despiritualised thing. In a fragment written
in April, 1900, he speaks of the lizards that look at us through the
cracks in the little stone walls separating the vineyards; "A thousand lizards saw me, and do you know what I think? All walls are
like that, and not only walls; all things – " The eye of the lizard, as
Günther says, becomes a symbol of things – real living cosmic
things. And more and more the poet becomes conscious of his mission which consists of *saying* these *things*. "To recreate a thing, that
meant having been everywhere, having kept nothing back, left
nothing out, betrayed nothing; it meant knowing the hundreds of
profiles, all the aspects, all the different sections. Only then was a
thing there, as an island cut off on all sides from the continent of
not-knowing." These words which refer to the art of Rodin are what
he tried to justify or illustrate in his poet's world, the world of his
own. And little by little the thing, becoming animated from within
when viewed with the ardent attention the poet dedicates to it,
becomes *Gestalt*, that is to say, a living structure; we could even say
that it is by starting from the thing thus recreated and by making it
in a sense his model, that he was to bring Alcestis or Eurydice to life
on his *Neue Gedichte*. It is as well to insist upon this in order to show
to what a point Rilke saw the spiritual, not as cut off but as being
involved in things themselves by the ever closer pact which the
poet makes with them, for they only give themselves to him in

response to an ardent precision practically unknown to the romantics.

It has been very rightly pointed out that there is a close connection between the *Neue Gedichte* and the *Notebook;* but Malte, as Günther says so well, is only an antenna, nothing but an antenna, a trebling antenna, feeling its way amid the experience which surges upon it from all sides; in the *Neue Gedichte* this experience is transformed into verse, becomes *thing* and from this very fact loses its insidious and destructive character.

Once these works were finished a period of waiting and suspense began. Rilke seems at this time to have become acutely conscious of his isolation; "when all is said and done," he said, "I have no window opening upon man." During this period he travelled widely, he translated certain works which specially appealed to him: *Le Centaure,* by Maurice de Guérin, a sermon sometimes attributed to Bossuet concerning the love of Magdalene, the Letters of a Portuguese Nun, *Le Retour de l'Enfant Prodigue,* by André Gide. But above all, he composed the first two of the *Duino Elegies* in 1912 at the house of the Princess von Thurn and Taxis. The other eight were not written until nearly ten years later when he was at Muzot in the Valais, and they were produced in an extraordinary fever of inspiration. The period of the war came in between.

As Angelloz says very well, during these years he did not find that he was above the fray but that he was on both sides at once. He was not to take an active part in the conflict and suffered deeply from this inaction, and yet it seems to me that strictly speaking he could not be said to have regretted not taking any part in a massacre which he abhorred. "During these years," he wrote later, "my only occupation was not understanding." "This period," we read in a letter of May 18th, 1917, "with all the restrictions it necessitates and the terrible destruction it causes, weighs upon me like lead; I can no longer make any movement outwardly or even inwardly, or at least I cannot bury myself more deeply within myself. And if even at the roots of my being there is still a little life, I am too obtuse and opaque to feel or recognise myself there." Elsewhere he speaks of the monstrous and incomprehensible state of the world which is frustrating nearly all the tenderness of his nature. He has come to envy "those who died earlier, so that they did not have to experience it from here; for somewhere in space there must be places from which this enormity appears only as Nature, as one of the rhythmic convulsions of a universe which is sure of its existence even if we perish. And, of course, we perish into it . . . "[2] (*Letters Written During the War*, p. 55). Is it possible not to be moved when we read the following lines today: "What can be written when everything that you touch is unutterable, unrecognisable, when nothing belongs to you any more; no feeling, no hope, where terrible reserves of pain, despair, sacrifice and distress reach their fulfilment – all this in a general way, as though the mass went on existing still, but no longer the individual; nothing is measured in terms of the individual heart any more, and yet it was the unit of heaven and earth, of all spaces and all depths." "Whatever comes," he wrote to the Princess von Thurn and Taxis on August 2nd, 1915, "the worst is that a certain innocence of life in which we grew up will never again be there for any of us. . . ." "Even if no one likes to admit it out loud," he says again, "consolations are needed, the great inexhaustible consolations whose possibility I have often felt in the depths of my heart, and have been almost afraid to contain them, boundless as they are, in so restricted a vessel. Certain it is that the divinest comfort is lodged in what is itself human, for what could we do with the consolations of a God? But our eyes would have to be a shade more seeing, our ears more receptive, the flavour of fruit would have to penetrate us more perfectly, we should have to be more acutely sensitive to smell, and to be more present in spirit when we touch and are touched and less forgetful, before we could extract from our most immediate experience those consolations which are more compelling, more overmastering, and more true than all the suffering that can ever shake us." And I will end these extracts with this simple question which has never sounded with greater pathos than it does today: "Would a God ever have enough consolation to heal the enormous wound which the whole of Europe has now become?"

I may say in passing that I believe if we adopted the general view of Günther, we should almost inevitably be led unjustifiably to underestimate these wartime letters in which for my own part I

2   To Helene von Nostitz, *Selected Letters*, pp. 247–8.

see one of the finest evidences of humanity in existence. Here it is not the artist who is trying to understand and is tormenting himself; it is the man; or rather we are on one of the summits here, where man and artist are no longer in any way separable – summits to which men of the greatest genius we know, such as Beethoven or Tolstoy, have risen. This observation and the extracts which preceded it seem to me indispensable if we are to penetrate the meaning of the Elegies. Unlike Mallarmé's *Herodiade* for instance or the *Jeune Parque*, these poems really contain a message for all men; and it is upon this message, which as a matter of fact can only be deciphered very imperfectly, that we now have to concentrate our attention.

The figure of the Angel dominates the whole of the *Duino Elegies*, we might almost say that at this time the artist sees God in the form of the Angel. We must neither think of the angels of Scripture nor those of Milton or Klopstock. "The angels of the Elegies," says Romano Guardini, "are not the messengers of the living God, they are new gods. It might be stated quite generally that the intuition of the Angel must have meant liberation for Rilke." "Angels," Günther says very truly, "are focuses, radiating concentrations of being, essences of beauty, power and duration which are at home in the two-fold kingdoms of life and death." For my part, I should say we must not ask if Rilke *believes* in angels. Indeed, if you remember, in his letter to Ilse Blumenthal-Weiss which I quoted earlier, Rilke definitely takes up his position against faith. Perhaps we should be right to say that his is the realm of *Schauen*, not that of *Glauben*; it is actually to be wondered if this is not always true of the pure poet. Romano Guardini has brought out admirably the central importance of the image with Rilke; and the Angel is precisely the image which in some sort liberates inexhaustible creative forces. Guardini's commentary is of such importance here that I think it should be quoted as it stands: "Perhaps," he says, "one might describe the particular impression made upon us by the culture which existed before the irruption of technics if we said that in those days images were charged with power. This power grows as we go further back into past ages; it grows and it is surrounded with mystery up to the point when it breaks forth into magic or mysticism. Those who are attracted by ancient culture often only dwell upon antiquities and the æsthetic element, but there are also times when they give proof of genuine feeling, they feel that ancient culture is guided by something which has essential value, but which is destined to dissolve, something canonical which not only has value for thought or taste, but for the emotions, for life, for the most intimate ordering of things. From this point of view it is a real disaster when an ancient city dies or when deeply rooted customs fall into disuse. Whenever this happens something of value is lost to us, something of which very little if anything is contained in what is new: this something is precisely, images. What then are these images? Perhaps they are related to what Plato meant by the term "ideas." . . . Perhaps images are for the heart *(Gemüth)* what ideas are for knowledge: presuppositions and at the same time the final content of vital achievement; the conditions of a good life and at the same time the visible effect of a well-ordered one; the means of mastering life's irreducible enemies, chaos, devastation and madness – and the fruit of this mastery. Ideas and images are perhaps one and the same reality viewed from different realms of existence, that above or that within. They are, as it were, radiated by the Logos who creates and regulates all finite things through them; from above by the clarity of consciousness, from within by the deepening of life." This masterly passage is, I think, the best introduction to a study of the texts which we are to consider. I am, however, in some difficulty about how to present these to you. There can be no question of reading the poems in translation, and I greatly dislike cutting off, as I am obliged to do, a few selected passages, always seriously weakened and even misrepresented by translation. Again, I can scarcely dream of giving you a summary of them, for poetry cannot be summarised. I must therefore content myself with a rough-and-ready compromise consisting of developing a few central themes which I will illustrate to the best of my power. I shall, of course, make ample use of Angelloz's admirable commentaries.

The Elegies centre on the mystery of man's condition and destiny in the cosmos. I am using these words, which may seem relatively vague, on purpose. It is, in fact, evident that there is no question here of a soluble problem which the poet is setting out to tackle. We should be guilty of a misinterpretation verging on absurdity if we tried to draw the elements of a metaphysical or theological treatise from the Elegies and the Sonnets. There is nothing here in any way connected with didactic or gnomic poetry – unless one takes this last adjective in a wide enough sense to include the *Vers Dorés* of Gérard de Nerval, which I should place among the rare specimens of poetry akin to that of Rilke to be found in French literature. There is nothing in the way of demonstration or even exposition here; it is all questioning, invocation and also evocation, it is the inward debate of a soul which in a sense acknowledges the charge of the universe and, as it were, the mission of making it grow or even of repeopling it. And this is why all that I shall be able to say about the Elegies and the Sonnets is bound to be no more than an essentially unfaithful exegesis.

What is man? What can he accomplish? If a task is specially allotted to him, how does it come about that sometimes he evades it? How could he, or how will he, be able to achieve it? Such are perhaps the principal questions which beset the mind of the poet. It is immediately made known to us that man can become conscious of his deficiencies when he sees himself contrasted with the radiantly terrible figure of the Angel; and perhaps we should be more or less right in saying that the idea or image of the Angel here acts as a revealer. I will first give a few passages from the Second Elegy, together with a translation which differs in points of detail from the Angelloz version:

Frühe Geglückte, ihr Verwöhnten der Schöpfung,
Höhenzüge, morgenrötliche Grate
aller Erschffung – Pollen der blühenden Gottheit,
Gelenke des Lichtes, Gänge, Treppen, Trone,
Räume aus Wesen, Schilde aus Wonne, Tumulte,
stürmisch entzückten Gefühls und plötzlich, einzeln,
Spiegel: die die enströmte eigene Schönheit
wiederschopfen zurück in das eigene Antlitz.
Denn wir, wo wir fühlen, verflüchtigen; ach wir
atmen uns aus und dahin; von Holzglut zu Holzglut
geben wir schwächern Geruch. Da sagt uns wohl einer:

jä, du gehst mir ins Blut, dieses Zimmer, der Frühling
füllt sich mit dir. . . . Was hilfts, er kann uns nicht halten,
wir schwinden in ihm und um ihn. Und, jene, die schön sind,
o wer hält sie zurück? Unaufhörlich steht Anschein
auf in ihrem Gesicht und geht fort.

Early successes, Creation's pampered darlings,
ranges, summits, dawn-red ridges
of all beginning, – pollen of blossoming godhead,
hinges of light, corridors, stairways, thrones.
spaces of being, shields of felicity, tumults
of eternity, rapturous feeling and suddenly separate
mirrors, drawing up their own
outstreamed beauty into their foils again.
For we, when we feel evaporate; Oh, we
breathe ourselves out and away; from ember to ember,
yielding a fainter scent. True, someone may tell us;
"You've got in my blood, the room, the spring's
growing full of you" . . . what's the use? He cannot retain us.
We vanish within and around him. And those who have
beauty,
Oh, who shall hold them back? Incessant appearance
comes and goes in their faces."[3]

And in a movement which seems already to herald in the celebrated verses of the *Cimetière Marin* which Rilke was to translate
later, he wonders where the fleeting essence of ourselves goes to
and if there is any principle powerful enough to incorporate it into
itself. To tell the truth, love seems to be self-sufficient and self-contained. Does it not give us an example and a pledge of a survival to
be granted to the best part of ourselves? No: love itself waxes and
wanes, love has a history.

Erstaunte euch nicht auf attischen Stelen die Vorsicht
menschlicher Geste? war nicht Liebe and Abschied
so leicht auf die Schultern gelegt, als wär es aus anderm
Stoffe gemacht als bei uns?

3   Translation by J. B. Leishman and Stephen Spender (Hogarth Press, 1948).

On Attic stelae, did not the circumspection
of human gesture amaze you? Were not love and farewell
so lightly laid upon shoulders,
they seemed to be made of other stuff than with us?[4]

Elsewhere, in the Third Elegy, he shows that the beloved maiden awakens a world of movement in her lover wherein all our past is fermenting:

Eines ist, die Geliebte zu singen. Ein andres, wehe,
jenen verborgenen schuldigen Fluss-Gott des Bluts.
... O Mädchen,
dies: dass wir liebten in uns, nicht Eines,
                    ein künftiges, sondern
das zahllos Brauende; nicht ein einzelnes Kind,
sondern die Väter, die wie Trümmer Gebirgs
uns im Grunde beruhn; sondern das trockene Flussbett,
einstiger Mütter – ; sondern die ganze
lautlose Landschaft unter dem wolkigen oder
reinen Verhängnis – : dies kam dir, Mädchen, zuvor.

One thing to sing the beloved, another alas!
that hidden guilty river-God of the blood,
... oh, maid,
this: that we've loved, *within* us, not one, still to come, but all
the innumerable fermentation: not just a single child,
but the fathers, resting like mountain-ruins
within our depths; – but the dry river-bed
of former mothers; – yes, and the whole of that
soundless landscape under the cloudy or
cloudless destiny; – *this* got the start of you, maid.[5]

It must then be recognised that if the Angel is always self-contained, man never ceases to run to waste, nothing holds or can hold him back. And even childhood is without salvation, for it is perverted by the adult; the child seems to be condemned to turn its back on life and to consider only forms and never the open world where the

4   Translation as above, p. 37.
5   Translation as above, pp. 41, 45.

animal has its being. Here, indeed, we have the paradox that in the eyes of Rilke men are, in a certain sense, at an ontological disadvantage compared with the animals. It is, as Guardini saw very truly, that animals are apprehended here as pure existence, still rejoicing in a liberty or more exactly an integrity which is of paradise. An animal lives directly, future does not exist for it, therefore it is pure from hope or apprehension. In passing it may be noticed here that Rilke seems very much as though he accepts on his own account the strict opposition established quite wrongly by Spinoza between hope and fear. Animals have their place in what Rilke calls "the open"; and we must try to define the meaning of this enigmatical word which masks one of the central intuitions of the Elegies:

> Mit allen Augen sieht die Kreatur
> das Offene. Nur unsre Augen sind
> wie umgekeht und ganz um sie gestellt
> Als Fallen, rings um ihren freien Ausgang.

> With all its eyes the creature world beholds
> the open. But our eyes, as though reversed
> encircle it on every side, like traps
> set round its unobstructed path to freedom.[6]

(Beginning of the Eighth Elegy.)

Here again I will refer to Romano Guardini's commentary to try to clarify what is to be understood by this perplexing expression "the open."

The open is that which surrounds created things – not however in the manner of empty space or a fluid in which they are bathed; it is the fact that the creature is finite, that it has a limit, or, more exactly, it is the alternative aspect, complementary to the aspect of its limitation. We are not, then, concerned with the relative limit of a being, that is to say with all that is adjacent, but with its absolute limit, with the Other, purely and simply, with the Other in its utter otherness, that is to say with God, with the creative power of God. This is elucidated from the psychological point of view if one thinks that there are acts which are shaped by the object: the fact of considering a

---

6   Translation as above, p. 77.

thing, of experiencing it, of fashioning it, etc.; but there are also others which strictly speaking have no object, consisting either of penetrating within being and exploring its depths or of radiating beyond and above as though to soar over it. In both these cases the limit is passed, but not in the sense of crossing over to what is beside us; it is passed absolutely. This absolutely *(Überhaupt)* is in the one case the mystery of inwardness, in the other that of transcendence *(Enthoberheit)*, and of absolute space *(absolute Weite)*. In either case man leaves himself behind, in so far as he is a particular being who observes, judges, covets, etc. And in so doing he fulfils his being as a pure creature. The being swells, begins to flower and thus becomes itself. The open is the direction in which this comes about. In our last paper we saw that, for Rilke, religion or God himself is a direction of the heart. We see here that the open can be conceived of in terms of height and breadth yet also in the perspective of inward hiddenness. But, adds Guardini, what the Christian thinks of as the space where God reigns according to the testimony of his Revelation, is for Rilke merely the other side of the finite or the state to which man has access when he is able to step beyond the confines of the self. Much light is thrown on this by the Elegies themselves, but above all by the celebrated letter to Witold von Hulewicz, which constitutes their indispensable commentary: "Affirmation of life as well as of death prove themselves one in the Elegies. To admit the one without the other would, it is here realised, with exultance, be a limitation which would ultimately exclude everything infinite. Death is the side of life that is turned away from, and unillumined by us; we must try to achieve the greatest possible consciousness of our being, which is at home in both these immeasurable realms and is nourished inexhaustibly by both. The true pattern of life extends through both domains, the blood with the greatest circuit runs through both; there is neither a This-side nor a That-side, but a single great unity in which the beings who transcend us, the angels, have their habitation"[7] (Letter from Muzot, pp. 371–2).

I do not by any means claim that this passage and all those that support it are perfectly clear. Nevertheless, I think we can say this: if animals have the advantage over men in that they live in the

7   *Translated Letters*, pp. 392–3.

open, it is because the fear of death cannot touch them, because as
we have seen the future does not exist for them. Now it is precisely
this fear, with all the secondary emotions it arouses, that sets up a
barrier of unreality between the two Kingdoms, thus destroying the
great unity at the heart of which the angels have their habitation.
But perhaps, to avoid the danger of ambiguity, it would be as well
to add that animals are on this side of the barrier which is erected
and that the problem for man, guided by the poet, is on the contrary
to establish himself on the other side; that is to say to break down
the barrier without by so doing falling back into the preconscious-
ness of animals. To be quite frank, I must own that I am not
absolutely sure that a certain ambiguity does not exist here in
Rilke's own thought. He says somewhere that when we are near to
death we no longer see it, and our own gaze is fixed ahead like that
of the animals. Might one not almost wonder whether such a statement did not purposely give rise to an uncertainty in our minds?
Does it refer to a senile and strictly retrogressive state or a prescience of heaven which, like a grace, can sometimes illumine the
evening of a consecrated existence? I have used this term "prescience of heaven," and I cannot help wondering whether in the
end the open is not for Rilke a sort of de-Christianised and infinitely precarious substitute for the heaven he aspires to, and will not
accept.

What I think has a positive value is the idea which is ever present with Rilke and founded on immediate and painful experience,
the idea of a mortifying subjection which the fact of existing opposite another being and of having this being as it were over the way
(gegenüber) demands of consciousness; hence the tragic destiny
which weighs upon mutual love, or rather the need for love to be
returned. Here we have the key to one of Rilke's paradoxes: the
exaltation of one-sided love. I may say in passing that I should not
be surprised if the separation of Rilke and Clara Westhoff, following so few years after their marriage, is not precisely to be explained
by this strange need for aeration: a need comparable to the nostalgia which is seen in certain untameable animals whose gentleness
long misleads those who try to domesticate them. Did Rilke realise
that this was a personal idiosyncrasy of his own and in fact somewhat exceptional? We should be tempted to doubt it when we find

him considering our incapacity for detaching and releasing ourselves – which as we know means to go towards the open – as fatally bound up with our nature.

> *Wer hat uns also umgedreht, dass wir,*
> *was wir auch tun, in jener Haltung sind*
> *von einem, welcher fortgeht? Wie er auf*
> *dem letzten Hügel, der ihm ganz sein Tal*
> *noch einmal zeigt, sich wendet, anhält, weilt –*
> *so leben wir und nehmen immer Abschied.*

Who's turned us round like this, so that we always,
do what we may, retain the attitude
of someone who's departing? Just as he,
on the last hill that shows him all his valley
for the last time, will turn and stop and linger,
we live our lives, for ever taking leave.

(Eighth Elegy.)[8]

We must not, however, be misled about the meaning of this statement and the blame or regret it implies. There is no question in Rilke's mind of advocating a sort of liberation through oblivion – quite the reverse. What he deplores is that the fascination which the other, or the past, or perhaps the things among which we live, have for us by making us cling to them and immobilise them, immobilises us ourselves and paralyses our inward growth. This seems to be the point of view from which Rilke's condemnation of the contemporary world and its inner degradation must be understood. Here we have to refer both to the Seventh and Ninth Elegies, and to the unfailing letter to Witold von Hulewicz, in order to recapture the intuition which pervades these writings with an almost superhuman beauty.

Here the question becomes more definite and urgent. When we could have passed through this brief period of leave – existence like a plant, a bay tree, why do we have to live it as men? It is certainly not to secure a hazardous well-being which can only count on inevitable and speedy destruction, but because we have to reply to a particular call meant for us. I will read a passage from the Ninth Elegy where this is expressed with unusual pathos:

8   Translation as above, p. 88.

Aber weil Hiersein viel ist, und weil uns scheinbar
Alles das Hiesige braucht, dieses Schwindende, das
Seltsam uns angeht, Uns, die Schwindendsten. Einmal
jades, nur einmal. Einmal und nichtmehr. Und wir auch einmal.
Nie wieder. Aber dieses
einmal gewesen zu sein, scheint nicht widerrufbar.

But because being here amounts to so much, because all
This Here and Now so fleeting seems to require us and
    strangely
concerns us. Us the most fleeting of all. Just once,
Everything, only for once. Once and no more. And we, too,
once. And never again. But this
having been once, though only once,
having been once on earth – can it ever be cancelled?[9]

"Einmal . . . nur einmal." These words ring out like a funeral
gong. We are reminded of the "never more" of Edgar Allan Poe.
And so an appeal is thrown out to us from the world in which we
are involved; how are we to respond to this appeal? A task has been
entrusted to us; how are we to fulfil it?

We have an essence to safeguard or to make effective, we try to
contain it within our own hands, to fix it by our satiated gaze, to fill
our hearts with it; this is still to say too little; is not the essence really
something we have to become? But to whom are we to give what we
have thus made our own? Can we take this nameless treasure with
us into the other world? It is neither the vision nor the fact itself
which lends itself to this mysterious transfer, but perhaps only pain,
the weight of experience and of love – and all this is inexpressible.
Are we perhaps in the world in order to utter the primitive words
which clothe earthly experience with a body; house, bridge, water-
spring, orchard, window and again pillar or tower, but also to translate that intimate inward being of which things in themselves are
unconscious? Has not the silent earth found a way of self-expression,
by constraining lovers to ravish and transmute all things into their
own impressions? The praise which should rise from the depths of
ourselves towards the angelic presences, is that which exalts simple

9   Translation as above, p. 83.

inexpressible things, things which have taken form from generation to generation and live in our life, within reach of our hands and in the field of our vision. All these things, for which life is only a perpetual decline, understand that we celebrate them; perishable in themselves, they grant the power to save them to us, to us who are even more perishable than they are. They want us to take them into our invisible heart, whatever our being and our ultimate destiny may be.

> *Erde, ist es nicht dies, was du willst; unsichtbar*
> *in uns erstehn? – Ist es dein Traum nicht,*
> *einmal unsichtbar zu sein? – Erde! unsichtbar!*
> *Was, wenn Verwandlung nicht, ist dein drängender Auftrag?*
> *Erde, du liebe, ich will. Oh glaub, es bedürfte*
> *nicht deiner Frülinge mehr, mich dir zu gewinnen, einer,*
> *ach, ein einziger ist schon dem Blute zu viel.*
> *Namenlos bin ich zu dir entschlossen, von weit her.*
> *Immer warst du im Recht, und dein heiliger Einfall*
> *ist der vertrauliche Tod.*
> *Siehe, ich lebe. Woraus? Weder Kindheit noch Zukunft*
> *werden weniger. . . . Uberzähliges Dasein*
> *entspringt mir im Herzen.*

Earth, is it not just this that you want: to arise
invisibly in us? Is not your dream
to be one day invisible? Earth! Invisible!
What is your urgent command, if not transformation?
Earth, you darling, I will! Oh, believe me, you need
no more of your spring-times to win me over; a single one,
ah one, is already more than my blood can endure.
Beyond all names I am yours, and have been for ages.
You were always right, and your holiest inspiration
is Death, that friendly Death.
Look, I am living. On what? Neither childhood nor future
are growing less . . . supernumerous existence
wells up in my heart.[10]

And Rilke himself comments thus: in his letter to Hulewicz: "We are the bees of the invisible. *Nous butinons éperdument le mile du*

---

10   Translation as above, Ninth Elegy, pp. 87–8.

visible, pour l'accumuler dans la grande ruche de d'or de l'invisible.[11] And this activity is sustained and accelerated by the increasingly rapid disappearance today of so much of the visible which we cannot replace. Even for our grandfathers a house, a fountain, a familiar tower, their very clothes, their coat, was more, infinitely more intimate; almost every object a vessel in which they found something human, or added their morsel of humanity. Now, from America, empty indifferent things crowd over to us, counterfeit things, the veriest dummies. A house in the American sense, an American apple, or one of the vines of that country has *nothing* in common with the house, the fruit, the grape into which we have entered the hope and meditation of our forefathers. The lived and living things, the things that share our thought, these are on the decline and can no more be replaced. We are perhaps the last to have known such things. The responsibility rests with us not only to keep remembrance of them (that would be but a trifle and unreliable), but also their human or laric value (`laric' in the sense of household gods). . . . The Angel of the Elegies is that Being in whom the transmutation of the visible into the invisible, which we seek to achieve, is consummated. For the Angel of the Elegies all the towers and palaces of this Past are existent *because* they have long been invisible, and the still existing towers and bridges of our world *already* invisible, although still materially enduring for us. The Angel of the Elegies is that Being who stands for the recognition in the Invisible of a higher degree of reality."[12]

There would certainly be grounds for grafting into this commentary another more hypothetical one of which I can only sketch the outlines here. Once more it might seem as though Rilke was only thinking of the artist – particularly the poet, but perhaps also the painter whose mission consists of raising the visible on to a higher plane of reality. We must not forget what the discovery of Cezanne meant for him. But here again the artist's vocation is taken to be but the vocation of man himself when he has reached his highest degree of enlightenment. This appears all the more clearly

11   We madly gather the honey of the visible to store it in the great golden hive
      of the invisible.
12   *Selected Letters*, pp. 394–5.

as we become more aware of the insufficiency of a purely utilitarian theory of expression. Expression is not a simple method of intercourse in view of some ends we have before us, it is of intrinsic value, one can even claim that it is itself the greatest of all ends, where it attains complete realisation. To be sure, no one would dispute that there is a degraded and exclusively pragmatic use made of language; but such usage is precisely the sign of a human deterioration which it is the business of poets and philosophers to denounce; and it is to be wondered if this degradation of language is not connected with a loss of frankness and purity of eye, a perversion of the being which comes about as soon as man establishes his universe as an enclosed world instead of turning towards the open. (I am not sure that the expression *le large* would not be preferable at least in French, to that of "the open" which seems very difficult to acclimatise to our language.) It appears that when the philosopher Heidegger came to know the Elegies he declared that Rilke had expressed the same ideas in poetry as he had in his great work *Sein und Zeit*. Perhaps this assertion, at first rather surprising, becomes clearer up to a certain point if we consider that the enclosed world tends to become that of chattering *(Gerede)*, that of the everyday, or I should prefer to say the bad kind of everyday. But then was Heidegger aware that there could be a good or a bad everyday as there can be a good or a bad infinity? It would, however, still be debatable whether there is not an essential opposition between the *Weltanschauung* of the poet and that of the philosopher. As de Waelhens says very truly in his fine book on Heidegger's philosophy, liberty in face of death *(Freiheit zum Tode)* comes very near to the *amor fati* of Nietzsche. At bottom it is a question of fundamental readiness in relation to death. "To understand that we are dying," says de Waelhens, "is the true attitude of genuine existence in face of death. This means that at every moment of reality, all our possibilities should be projected on the screen of death." Genuine awareness of ourselves is, indissolubly, linked with the anguish of death. *"Das Sein zum Tode ist wesenhaft Angst."* This formula seems to me as un-Rilkean as possible, although in other places we trace striking analogies between the texts where death seems to be conceived by both alike as a personal completion. But we could say that for Heidegger man always has his death before

him because he bears it within him. (I am tempted to recall some
verses by Valéry here, particularly in the *Ebauche du Serpent.*) The
idea of a *Doppelbereich*, of a double kingdom, and an angelic super-
consciousness which transcends this duality and reabsorbs it into a
higher unity, seems to me contrary to both this letter and to the
spirit of Heidegger. It may be objected that we are here concerned
with what is purely mythical and that it would be unreasonable to
seek to transcribe a myth into technical language suitable for bringing out the opposition I have in mind at the moment. I agree. The
myth here is untranscribable when all is said and done.
Nevertheless, it collects and concentrates the quintessence of a particular experience; this experience is what matters here, and I
scarcely think that it can be reduced to that which is reflected in the
philosophy of Heidegger. Either the *Elegies* and the *Sonnets to
Orpheus* must after all be considered as mere exercises, in Valéry's
sense of the word, or as digressions – and this interpretation is all
the more difficult to accept since the correspondence is there to
explain the meaning of these poems in detail, and to accentuate
their parenetic significance – or else we must recognise that for
Rilke there is a Beyond not indeed to be confused with the
Christian beyond but none the less, for us unenlightened beings,
another aspect of the world to which we belong; that is to say a
kingdom of the dead where that metamorphosis takes place which
we have not so much to endure as to undertake; for it is precisely
of man's essence to have to consent to it and perhaps to prepare it:

> *Wolle die Wandlüng. O sei fur die flamme begeistert*
> *drin sich ein Ding dir entzieht, das mit Verwandlungen prunkt.*

> Choose to be changed. With the flame be enraptured,
> where from within you a thing changefully – splendid
>   escapes.[13]

So we read in the *Sonnets to Orpheus*. All this Twelfth Sonnet of
the second series should be read and studied.

> *Was sich ins Bleiben verschliesst schon ist das Erstarrte;*
> *wähnt es sich sicher im Schutz des unscheinbaren Gran's?*

13 *Sonnets to Orpheus*, translation by J. B. Leishman (Hogarth Press), p. 110.

Warte, ein Hartestes warnt aus der Ferne das Harte
Wehe – : abwesender Hammer holt aus!

That which would stay what it is renounces existence;
Does it feel safe in its shelter of lustreless grey?
Wait, a hardest is warning the hard from a distance,
heaved is a hammer from far away.[14]

To be sure, such strains awaken within us memories of the great themes of Nietzsche: consent, clinging to earth, desire for metamorphosis . . . and yet it is to be wondered if the analogy is not superficial after all. The sense of the words is quite different. I have specially in mind the desire for metamorphosis: There is nothing here which could be compared with the *Uebergang* of Nietzsche, that is to say with the development of the superman; the myth of the superman is of a kind that cannot become acclimatised in the universe of Rilke. And here it will be necessary to be as explicit as possible, even should we be obliged to go a little beyond the literal reading of the text. Without perhaps going as far as Angelloz, I should be quite ready to subscribe in a general way to his theory concerning the value of suffering, very distinctly set forth in his large work on Rilke. "Rilke," he says, "seems to us to have adopted the theosophical doctrine on this point; man is made to raise himself by means of his suffering to a higher degree, earthly existence only represents a stage in the evolution which leads him onwards from a mysterious origin to a total vanishing away. . . . By death we regain contact with pure suffering in view of an after life" (*loc. cit.*, p. 339). And he adds in a note that Rilke never spoke of reincarnation, to be sure, but that if he had not accepted it, it would be useless trying to understand him. In another place he recalls that very characteristic passage in Rilke's correspondence where, speaking about the man who commits suicide, that is to say who deliberately anticipates his own destiny, Rilke says that perhaps by such action he may incur terrible obligations for his future existence. We must also here insist deliberately on the part which the occult played for Rilke, particularly the spiritualistic experiments made at Duino when he was the guest of Princess Marie von Thurn and

14 Translation as above, p. 110.

Taxis. I am thinking above all of the séance where something describing itself as "the Unknown" was manifested through the medium of a planchette and asked to converse with the poet. "A long conversation followed; although the questions were carefully concealed, the answers were nearly always intelligible: Rilke was interested and intrigued to a very high degree." It was the answers of "the Unknown" which seem to have decided him to go out to Spain and particularly to Toledo, which, as a matter of fact had been attracting him for a long time. The town was described by "the Unknown" with such precision that a few months later he was able to find his way about in it from the first day as though he had already lived there.

But to know what he finally thought about phenomena of this description, it seems that we should refer to a letter written some twelve years later to Nora Purtscher-Wydenbruck ". . . I am convinced that these phenomena, if we accept them without seeking refuge there, and if we remain willing to incorporate them in the totality of our being – which, indeed, is full of no less miraculous secrets in all its workings – I am, I say, convinced that these phenomena do not testify to a false curiosity on our part but actually concern us to an indescribable degree, and, were we to exclude them, would always be capable of making themselves felt at one point or another. Why should they not, like everything else unknown or absolutely unknowable, be an object of our endeavour, our wonder, our awe and veneration?

"For a while I was inclined, as you yourself seem to be now, to take the existence of 'external' influences for granted in these experiments; I no longer do to the same degree. However extensive the external world may be, with all its sideral distances it hardly bears comparison with the dimensions, the *depth-dimensions,* of our inner being, which has no need even of the vastness of the universe to be itself all but illimitable. When, therefore, the dead or the unborn need a resting place, what refuge could be more agreeable or more appropriate to them than this imaginary space? It seems to be more and more as though our ordinary consciousness dwelt on the summit of a pyramid whose base broadens out in us and beneath us so much that the more deeply we see ourselves able to penetrate into it the more boundlessly do we seem implicated in those factors of

our earthly, and in the widest sense, *worldly* being which are independent of space and time. Since my earliest youth I have entertained the idea (and have also, when I was adequate to it, lived
accordingly), that if a cross-section were made lower down through
this pyramid of consciousness, Being, in its simplest form, would
become 'eventual' in us, the inviolable presence and simultaneity of
all that we, on the upper 'normal' apex of consciousness, are only
permitted to experience as flux (*Ablauf*)."[15]

He adds that if he accepts these spiritualistic occurrences obedi-
ently, reverently and sincerely, a curious instinct impels him to call
up counter-balances to them in his own consciousness as soon as
they pass over and into him: "To my mind nothing would be more
alien than a world in which these powers and intrusive elements
had the upper hand. And the strange thing is: the more I act in this
way (after each nocturnal seance trying, for instance, to see that the
spectacle of the starry silent night is equally marvellous and true),
the more I believe myself in harmony with the essence of those
occurrences. They want, it seems to me, rather to be suffered than
acknowledged, rather not repudiated than revoked; rather consent-
ed to and loved than questioned and made use of. I am, fortunate-
ly, completely unserviceable as a medium, but I do not doubt for
one moment that, in my own way, I keep myself open to the influence of those often homeless powers, and that I never cease to enjoy
or sustain their companionship. How many words, how many decisions or hesitations may not be ascribed to their working! For the
rest, it belongs to the original tendencies of my nature to accept the
Mysterious *as such*, not as something to be exposed, but as the
Mystery that *is* mysterious to its very depths and is so everywhere,
just as a lump of sugar is sugar in every part. . . . I am (and this
might in the end be the only place in me from which a slow wisdom
could sprout) completely without curiosity concerning life, my own
future and the gods. . . . What do we know of the seasons of eternity and whether it will be harvest-time yet!"[16]

I have no hesitation in saying that this letter, of which I have
only been able to quote the principal passages here, is one of the

15 *Selected Letters*, translation as above, p. 385.
16 *Selected Letters*, pp. 387–8.

most important documents that exist for an understanding of the attitude of Rilke. You may perhaps have noticed that the last lines are very reminiscent of the beautiful letter on Michael Kramer which I read you the other day. Supreme patience, supreme humility in view of the Eternal is overwhelming here. I should be strongly tempted to speak also of hope. That is perhaps the reason for disagreeing in spite of everything with Angelloz's sentence about successive lives; re-incarnation can only be a matter of belief, a hypothesis. But there is no longer any question of adopting a belief or a hypothesis when such a height of patience has been reached, for this involves a perfect accord with Being. What Rilke teaches us better than anyone, and what I think such writers as Nietzsche or Kierkegaard have generally either never known or in the end forgotten, is that there exists a receptivity which is really creation itself under another name. The most genuinely receptive being is at the same time the most essentially creative. Our own poet, Valéry, has at least had a presentiment of this:

> *Patience, patience,*
> *Patience dans l'azur!*
> *Chaque atome de silence*
> *Est la chance d'un fruit mur!*
> *Viendra l'heureuse surprise;*
> *Une colombe la brise,*
> *L'ébrantement le plus doux,*
> *Une femme qui s'appuie,*
> *Feront tomber cette pluie*
> *Où l'on se jette à genoux.*[17]

17   Patience, patience,
      Patience in the blue sky!
      Each atom of silence
      is the chance of a ripe fruit!
      The glad surprise will come;
      A dove, a stirring of the breeze,
      The gentlest shaking,
      A woman's touch will bring this rain
      When we shall fall on our knees.

But just because he was gifted to a supreme degree with this creative receptivity and because he was, moreover, capable of thinking about it and measuring its advantages, Rilke is one of the only geniuses of the first order to have adopted a spiritually sane attitude with regard to metaphysical realities: that is to say as far removed from systematic negation which is insane, as it is from crazy infatuation which is fatal and absurd.

But to my mind nothing shows more clearly the profound differences which separate Rilke from existentialist philosophers such as Heidegger or Jaspers who, whether explicitly or not, deny the reality of the *jenseits* or the Beyond, than this *disponibilité* (availability) in relation to the occult. It may be objected that the declaration of faithfulness to the earth found, for instance, in the Ninth Elegy seems to suggest as its counterpart a similar denial of the other world. But we must be careful not to be misled by formulæ here. On the one hand, the earth is essentially opposed in this case to the Christian heaven, and on the other it is evident that nowhere in Rilke can the earth be conceived of in a positivist way. We must remember that there is one side of the world which is not turned towards us, that there is accordingly, as the Romantics guessed, a nocturnal world which is precisely where the metamorphosis is carried out. It seems to me to go without saying that this metamorphosis cannot be simply transformation of the organic elements of our being as conceived by materialistic pantheism. The Tenth Elegy, which describes in an almost Egyptian manner the stages of the journey which each one of us will have to accomplish, would become incomprehensible if we considered it from this point of view. To be sure, the Tenth Elegy can be interpreted as a funeral song, celebrating "the majesty of human suffering"; but that does not take into account the fact that there seems to be for Rilke a trajectory of the dead as there is a trajectory of the stars which is finally lost to view in the distance. Moreover, at the end of this song of sombre grandeur there shines as a light or promise the humble image of the catkin hanging from the bare hazel tree which seems to bring tidings of the hidden kingdom of the earth in spring . . . the *Vorfrühling* that Rilke loved so dearly.

I can only say a few words before ending about the Sonnets to Orpheus which Rilke dedicated to the memory of Vera Ouckama

Knoop, the young dancer whose life was cut short by an untimely death. In the sonnets Paul Valéry's influence is apparent at any rate from the technical point of view – and in this connection it is to be wondered exactly how much Rilke owed to the author of the *Cimetière Marin,* whose poems we know that he translated. Actually, I cannot dream of replying to this question which falls outside the subject I set out to consider here. What must be brought out here in connection with the Sonnets is that in them Orpheus tends to take the place which was that of the Angel in the Elegies and of God in the earlier poems. From this we can say not only that Rilke is ever moving further and further away from the strictly Christian world, but that he finally succeeds in freeing his thought from the ambiguities which were still encumbering it. "In the person of Orpheus," says Günther, "the poet confidently celebrates the transformer-God. Beyond our divided evidence, after the flowering, the fruit, as it shrivels, liberates the seeds of resurrection. Orpheus is alive everywhere. He is in each rose that flowers as in everything which fades into the Invisible.

> *Ist er ein Hiesiger? Nein, aus beiden*
> *Reichen erwuchs seine werte Natur.*

(I, 6).

(Does he belong here? No, his spreading
nature from either domain has sprung.)[18]

From Christianity to Orphis: perhaps that is how we could best define this strange journey which from so many points of view is like a return through the ages towards mysterious ancestors and towards our origins – so that we might sometimes be tempted to speak of Rilke as a prophet of the past. And no doubt there is a sense in which his evolution can be considered disappointing and may appear as a sort of retrogression. I believe, however, that to think of it in this way is to misunderstand the deep lesson which is to be gathered from his work and personality. In reality the hackneyed and confused term of pantheism gives no indication of the true character of the Sonnets to Orpheus, by which I mean not only their originality and their solidly nutritive quality. The intercon-

18   Translation by J. G. Leishman, p. 45.

nected consciousness of death and resurrection which pervades them like a breath of air from another world is the principle of a pious reverence for souls and things of which the secret has to be rediscovered today. Shall I say what I really think? I believe this to be true of most Christians, even those who have been genuinely touched by grace. For to tell the truth we are all to some extent infected by the baleful influence of the world in which we are, as it were, immersed. Perhaps it should also be added that the Christian of today is very often tempted to over-accentuate the misery and degradation of the world left to itself, the better to emphasise the redemptive value of the supernatural forces which work upon it both from above and from the depths of the soul. But in this way the spirit is in danger of being led to judge things in a way which is perhaps sacrilegious in its principle and which, moreover, contributes effectually to a progressive unhallowing of the human world – of all indeed, that the word "world" stands for.

> Sieh, die Maschine:
> wie sie sich wälzt und rächt
> und uns enstellt und schwächt.

(I, 18.)

> (See the machines:
> Source of our weakness
> now, and in vengeful rage
> ruining our heritage.)[19]

The machine threatens all we have acquired as long as it dares to be a guiding spirit and not an obedient servant. . . . It is life. It claims to understand this life better than anybody – this mechanism which orders, creates, and destroys with equal resolution. . . .

> *Aber noch ist uns das Dasein verzaubert; an hundert*
> *Stellen ist es noch Ursprung. Ein Spielen von reinen*
> *Kräften, die keiner berührt, der nicht kniet und bewundert.*
> *Worte gehen noch zart am Unsäglichen aus. . . .*
> *Und die Musik, immer neu, aus den bebendsten Steinen,*
> *baut im unbrauchbaren Raum ihr vergottlichtes Haus.*

(II, 10.)

19   Translation as above, p. 106.

Even today, though, existence is magical, pouring
freshly from hundreds of well-springs, – a playing of purest
forces, which none can surprise without humbly adoring.
Words still melt into something beyond their embrace. . . .
Music, too, keeps building anew with the insecurest
stones her celestial house in unusable space.[20]

Nowhere could we find better expressed than in these two verses of the Tenth Sonnet of the Second Part, the reverential love for the
created which men of my generation have seen drying up before
their eyes in so many souls doomed to aridity in the most miserable
desert of self-adulation. The mechanised world thus becomes also
the world of pure consciousness, that which burns without giving
any light and gives light without any warmth. Thus we see a gulf
widening between the masses who are literally *denatured* by a more
and more inhuman way of life, and a very small company of super-
naturalised elect whose life's foundations are more and more fragile and unsteady and who for this reason are in danger of falling a
prey in the end to the most fatal mental disorders, and the worst
inner collapse. I should say that in so far as we can conceive of the
inconceivable, the balsamic influence of Rilke's Orphism upon
those who seek to become penetrated with it, consists in restoring
around and within us (more especially in the interior cosmic space
of the *Weltinnenraum* where this distinction does not exist) an
atmosphere which will develop our faculty for hoping against hope
without which it must be admitted that the Christian message itself,
in the last analysis, would be in danger of losing its meaning and its
quality.

> *Alles will schweben. Da gehn wir umher wie Beschwerer,*
> *legen auf alles uns selbst, vom Gewichte entzückt;*
> *0 was sind wir den Dingen für. zehrende Lehrer,*
> *weil ihnen ewige Kindheit glückt.*
> *Nähme sie einer ins innige Schlafen und schliefe*
> *tief mit den Dingen – : O wie käme er leicht,*
> *anders zum anderen Tag, aus der gemeinsamen Tiefe.*
>
> (*Sonnets,* II, 14.)

20   Translation as above, p. 106

To all that would soar our selves are the grand aggravation,
we lay them on all we encounter, proud of their weight;
what terrifying teachers we are for that part of creation
which loves its eternally childish state.
Could someone but take them right into his slumber and
    sleep
deeply with things, how differently, lightly he'd wander
back to a different day out of that communal sleep.[21]

The Orphism of Rilke gives us one of its most pure secrets here;
the heaviness is not in things but in us. We must get free from it, as
though shaking off a yoke too long endured, so that we can attain
to the reality of things which is candour and participate with our
very being in this imperishable innocence. Elsewhere, in a sonnet
where he recalls the strange fruits of consolation (II, 17), he wonders
whether we have not managed to disturb the peaceful equanimity
of the summer seasons by a false precocity and a premature activity which soon dries up the fruit.

To be sure, a very delicate work of transposition would be necessary to convert all that is here only allusion, remembrance or intuition into the conclusions of discursive thought. I am sure that this
work is not only possible, but should be undertaken by anyone who
wants to get out of the rut in which all Western thought is in danger of sinking at the present time. And I feel I cannot end better than
with this invocation which closes the twenty-sixth Sonnet of the
First Part:

> *O du verlorener Gott! Du unendliche Spur!*
> *Nur well dick reissens zuletzt die Feindschaft verteilte,*
> *Sind wir die Hörenden jetzt und ein Mund der Natur.*

> O you God that has vanished! You infinite track!
> only because dismembering hatred dispersed you
> are we hearers today and a mouth which else nature would
>   lack.[22]

Although the Christian mind might be inclined to see in this

21 J. B. Leishman's translation, p. 115.
22 *Ibid.* p. 85.

only the distorted refraction of a strictly sacred truth in a mythological mirror, it seems to me that this image of a disintegrated God has
the most moving significance for us, Frenchmen and Europeans of
1944; the spectacle of a disjointed world where it does not even
seem to be given to most of us to discern all the scattered currents
of confidence which are ever issuing from the very heart of real
things, this spectacle invites us, indeed, to a reintegration of the
human and of the divine.

I should be sorry, however, to end this second and last lecture
on a note which, after all, was too easy. At the risk of surprising
some of you I feel obliged to close with an invocation which is whis-
pered rather than uttered – an invocation which may find an echo
in the hearts of all of us, Christians and non-Christians alike. Is not
that the very best way of entering into communion with the Angel
of the Elegies or the Orpheus of the Sonnets? In the presence of
enemy forces whose devastating action is more widespread each
day, on the eve of destruction which can reduce to nothing the people and things we live for, let me invoke this spirit of metamorphosis, which can draw forth the unchangeable from our fleeting
world. Let us place ourselves under its guidance for a moment. Let
us allow the hope to penetrate to our hearts that this spirit may
transmute us so intimately ourselves that we shall be able to face
the desolate prospect with a rejuvenated soul, full of acceptance
and in tune with the unfathomable.

Oh, spirit of metamorphosis!

When we try to obliterate the frontier of clouds which separate
us from the other world guide our unpractised movements! And
when the given hour shall strike, arouse us, eager as the traveller
who straps on his rucksack while beyond the misty window-pane
the earliest rays of dawn are faintly visible!

Paris.
January, 1944.

THE REBEL[1]

In certain respects *The Rebel* is the most important work of Albert Camus because it is his most mature work and the one that allows us to understand most clearly the problem on which he has meditated ever since he began to reflect. I speak of a "problem' and not a solution; later we will see why. Moreover it is far from certain that a solution is conceivable – even though the author seeks to persuade himself otherwise.

In general one can say that the development of the thought of *The Rebel* contains three essential phases. The author begins by defining in its purity "the movement of conscience" that is called rebellion or revolt. Then, considering it in history under its metaphysical, literary, and social aspects, he studies, often with great penetration, the conditions in which this movement lost its way in the 19th century and especially in the 20th century. In a final part he attempts to show how revolt can be reestablished in its truth or purity.

It is clear that the pages in which the author attempts to define the essential characteristics of authentic revolt present a special importance. From the phenomenological point of view – which to my mind is the only possible one here – it seems to me that they do not have all the desirable rigor. This is true despite the fact that Camus certainly sees clearly enough to the core of things.

"What is a rebel?" asks Camus. "A man who says 'no.' But he refuses rather than renounces. He is also a man who from the start says 'yes.' A slave who has received orders all his life suddenly judges a command to be unacceptable. What is the content of this

1   A study of Albert Camus's *The Rebel* (1951).

'no'? For example, it can mean that 'things have gone on too long,' up till this point, yes; beyond, no. In short, the 'no' affirms the existence of a border or boundary. One finds the same idea of a limit in the case when one says that the other person transgresses, that he extends his authority beyond its limits; now another authority confronts him and limits him. . . ." But the rebel does not simply oppose another sort of right, the right not to be oppressed, over and above the right he acknowledges. "In every genuine revolt there is a spontaneous and entire adherence of the individual to a certain 'part' of himself. Every act of revolt, at least tacitly, invokes a value."

Without being able to say that they are false, all these formulations seem to me to be vague and inadequate. I would say that the *existential* character of revolt has not yet been adequately brought to light. One loses sight of the essence of revolt when one simply situates it on the plane of judgment or of speech. Revolt is an *act*; it cannot be grasped as such except insofar as it is understood as an act. Judgment or speech should not be considered here, except as they are themselves acts that announce other acts. In a quite general way, one can say that this act always consists in shaking off a yoke, and these words must be taken in their original meaning, I would say, in their "carnal" meaning. I would – somewhat – overstate my point by saying that revolt ought always to be considered in a "muscular" perspective: even when it superficially seems to be only mental, it tends toward a physical culmination. Otherwise it is a mere velleity, a sham, because a merely wished-for revolt is a lie; it is even contradictory to its nature.

On the other hand, Camus is entirely correct to underline the element of value, or more exactly, of justification, that revolt necessarily contains. I cannot revolt without having the absolute assurance that I am right to conduct myself this way and, conversely, that it would be cowardly or ignoble to tolerate any longer what has literally become intolerable, that is, unbearable. It is true to say that there is a point or, if one prefers, a limit, where revolt rises up, which is what the phrase "I am fed up!" means.

But it seems to me that one has to add that revolt presents itself as having a certain unconditional character. It therefore calls into question – entirely and totally into question – the authority of the other who now is treated not as an adversary but as a tyrant, as the very incarnation of abuse. This is extremely important because it allows us to see the existential distinctiveness of revolt. If revolt were only located on an intellectual or rational plane this global rejection could not take place. The rebel would limit himself to saying: "You have exceeded a certain limit. You have transgressed on a domain that doesn't belong to you, I protest against this violation. Go back from this territory in which you illegitimately find yourself, and when you have crossed the border the previous conditions of our relationship will ipso facto be reestablished."

But it is not thus that things ever happen and they cannot happen that way. However, this is not a logical impossibility but an existential one, one that the history of wars and revolutions provides innumerable examples. From the moment when the transgression took place that engendered the revolt, returning to the status quo ante is out of the question. I think we need to go even further. The relationship itself is retrospectively called into question. At bottom it was not really a relationship; it was a de facto, not a de jure, accord. In hindsight the situation now appears as having been infected from the beginning with the possibility of abuse that the recent event only made manifest. To take one example from a thousand, this is why Charles X was overturned in 1830, even though his opponents contented themselves with requiring him to withdraw the ordinances that had started the revolution.

One can therefore say that revolt – because it is an act – is an event that brings in the irreversibility characteristic of history as such.

These observations can help us appreciate how extraordinarily complex each act of revolt as such is. To be sure – I repeat – it is necessary to recall that insofar as it reflects upon itself, it always appeals to an *ideal order* that has been actively misunderstood and denied, to laws that perhaps are unwritten but are nonetheless real and which have been violated, etc. . . . But it is no less necessary to note the properly *existential* character of revolt. This consists in the fact that it is always, that it is fundamentally, the rising-up of an "I" or a "we" ("we" implies the "I," however) who stand up against the one who in every case can be designated "the invader."

In order to justify the use of this latter term, it perhaps is necessary to add the following qualification: one can say that in this case the invader comes not from outside (as in the case of an aggressor) but from within. But how is an invasion that comes from within possible? What is this "within"? Speaking precisely, this requires a situation that has the characteristics of a symbiosis. It is within this symbiosis that transgression – not aggression – occurs. Revolt is the response, not in words or "ideally," but in existence itself to this transgression.

I note in passing that given this perspective I agree without reservation with Camus that it is illegitimate to necessarily equate revolt with resentment. This would be an illegitimate employment of Max Scheler's famous views. But if the preceding analysis is correct it allows us to see how it can happen that revolt in the great majority of cases, and even perhaps always – and even being justified in its intention, in its fundamental *nisus* – has almost no chance of being "pure" in the existential modes in which it is deployed. To explain myself: revolt occurs when a certain situation is judged intolerable; one has to end it at any price. But "at any price" means: by any means. The German term *Rücksichtslosigkeit*, which has no French equivalent, best expresses what I want to say. It literally means that one cannot look back, or have regard for anything. What is essential to revolt is to rush forward, and "to rush" means to do so in a certain way blindly.

If this is true, one ought to take care in speaking about "purity" in connection with revolt. Or more precisely, acknowledge that this word will contain very important equivocations. One can certainly recognize that revolt initially is pure, perhaps always pure at the outset, but one should add that it cannot remain that way. What does one mean by this term "purity" anyway? This word can only be defined negatively, by an absence. The absence of calculation? Or of hatred? Upon reflection these notions grow obscure. On one hand, there cannot be a revolt without hatred of the tyrant qua tyrant. On another hand, isn't it a pure abstraction – at bottom, rather hypocritical – to claim to distinguish between the tyrant as such and the tyrant as a human being? In any event it will be very difficult, perhaps impossible, to find a dividing line between the hatred which is purified by the sentiment of justice and an impure hatred. In the concrete, in each particular case this line will be the subject of infinite debates.

The situation is hardly clearer in what concerns the absence of calculation or self-interest. These words, after all, can be falsely pejorative terms which fail to capture a certain aim or purpose which is quite legitimate.

In any event, it seems to me that in Camus's eyes what internally purifies the act of revolt is the fact that the rebel deliberately risks his life. Now, it seems to me to be fundamentally true to say that this sacrifice in and of itself purifies. What shows this is the inverse situation: the person who remains on the sidelines while exhorting others to perform actions that entail the supreme sacrifice is obviously despicable. (Parenthetically, we should observe yet again the existential character of revolt. I authentically revolt only when I engage myself entirely in it; otherwise it is a sham.) One could also say that it is only by assuming this absolute risk that I can show – not "prove" – my bona fides. Upon reflection, it seems to me that it is in the light of the idea of good faith that the notion of purity is clarified. As is almost always the case, the digression by way of negation is revelatory: bad faith and impurity are, at least in this area, identical.

But someone may be tempted to say that the problem of purity or impurity is only truly posed in connection with the intention or internal disposition. We have already said that revolt cannot be reduced to this intention. On the contrary it is an eruption within existence, and whoever says "eruption" says "violence." In connection with violence, let us leave to the side the more or less sophistical developments of a George Sorel. In general one should look with a maximum of suspicion upon the literature on violence coming from men disposed to exalt it in theory but who remain behind closed doors during the days of tumult. As for myself, I am strongly inclined to think that violence is in every regard a fall, a fall into a world which itself falls short of one in which we can speak of purity or impurity. Must one speak of a fall into an infra-human world? I would hesitate a bit to put it that way. The other side of human privileges, the privilege of being human, we should never forget, is that the man who descends to the level of the animals thereby falls beneath the animals. There is not, and there cannot be, violence without culpability.

It is here that the ethical problem of revolt shows itself to be properly speaking insoluble. I do not believe – in truth, I no longer believe – that it is entirely legitimate to draw arguments from these existentially inevitable violences in order to condemn revolt absolutely. More exactly, I believe that such condemnation cannot be justified except in accordance with certain conditions that have to be further specified. Here the problem opens up a vast philosophical horizon.

On another hand, on the basis of the preceding analyses one has to ask whether the notion of "metaphysical revolt" is to be accepted or not; or more precisely, under what conditions it has meaning. I explain: It is evident that writing allows everything, and we know that certain writers with Promethean ambitions have exercised unlimited powers of spewing bile and invective in this domain. But invective can simply be a rhetorical exercise, and most of the time it is nothing else. If the words "metaphysical revolt" have meaning, they must correspond in some way to the rising-up that we have previously analyzed, the "ordinary" types of revolt. It certainly is not obvious a priori that this sort of rising-up is possible in the metaphysical domain. It may only be a deceptive appearance that dupes someone.

We should observe that this basic question does not seem to have even occurred to Camus. I can acknowledge that at the level of reflection that he operates on, this question cannot occur. However, it is far and away the most important one. It is the one that a philosopher has no right to avoid. I therefore would like to attempt to show how it should be envisaged.

Camus rightly observes elsewhere that revolt against God cannot really occur except to the extent that the notion of "God" has become "personalized." This is only a corollary of what has been said earlier. To revolt is always to revolt against. But that requires revolting against someone, or at least against some distinctive type of reality. I use this deliberately vague expression to assimilate it to the former. How, for example, can one revolt against an anonymous order, against a law that was not enacted by anyone? One can even say that only a person, or personality, offers the necessary "purchase" for revolt. Consider the Promethean myth: for its full meaning, one must take into account that Prometheus rises against Zeus.

At this point one can pose a first question and ask, what *in existence* is capable, even susceptible, of becoming this protest, that is, this accusation? The second term is particularly instructive. To accuse someone is to call him before a tribunal. But what tribunal exactly? Only the tribunal of the conscience (a term I mean in its full amplitude, an amplitude that requires considerable elaboration). On the one hand, we should note that the accuser and the tribunal here appear to fuse or become one. On the other hand, note that the "God" summoned before it by conscience appears to be an idol; one no longer knows it merits being called "God." Further reflection would have no difficulty in showing that in such a situation it is the conscience that has affixed to itself the cachet of the divine.

But let us leave to one side this dialectic. The history of modern thought – (perhaps it would be better to speak of the spiritual attitudes of man before reality or before the universe, as one prefers) – seems to show that as this revolt against God becomes more definite by an inevitable process it tends to transform itself into a denial of God's existence, that is, of the very being one intends to incriminate or accuse. Logically, though, it seems that one has to choose between either believing "enough" in God to be able to revolt against him, or cease to believe in him with the result that rebellion as such ceases to be possible. Rationally speaking, this dilemma seems impossible to escape.

Nonetheless, if we dispassionately analyze the interior life or condition of many unbelievers today, we see that this dilemma fails to capture a fundamental aspect that does not allow itself to be reduced to such an alternative. Again, I explain: What would be logical is that the person who is convinced (whether rightly or wrongly) of the non-existence of God would find in this conviction a consolation or comfort. He would be like someone in political or social life when he saw that the tyrant against whom he rebelled did not exist. We should observe, however, that even on this social-political plane there is something contradictory or incoherent in the position. Revolt expresses the awareness of an abuse. In a general way one can say that the abuse and the awareness of it come together. Supposing that the person who was deemed responsible for the abuse is deemed to be non-existent, would the abuse necessarily disappear? No. One can even ask if the fact of no longer having anyone to accuse would not create in the soul of the rebel not only some sort of disarray, but what I believe we should call an "ulceration." The rebellious conscience becomes the ulcerated conscience.

But if we look closer at the spiritual reality that this phrase indicates, we will see that there cannot be ulceration without resentment. Something, however, is quite singular here. In general, resentment, like revolt, is directed against a sort of aggressive or polemical intentionality. Here, though, it becomes rather diffuse. It seems to be the essence of this sort of resentment that it no longer knows who, or what, it is directed against. Therefore it wanders hither and yon.

In these conditions it is not clear how it is possible to establish anything that would resemble a metaphysics of the ulcerated conscience. Note that in what has preceded we have been led to wander as it were outside the social and political sphere. The resentment that is tied to the fact of not being able to blame anyone for the abuse experienced as such, as abuse, but for which one no longer can find anyone responsible – this resentment, now extended to the cosmic scale, seems to be tied to atheism. We should take care, however, that here too we are firmly in the existential. By that I mean that it is not at all a matter of discerning a notional connection that might exist between the concept of atheism and that of resentment. Rather, it is a connection obtaining between a certain affirmation, or more precisely a negation, and what we can rigorously call an affective attitude. This is found in the beings of flesh and blood that we are. Perhaps the best formulation of this is the following: A sincere atheist is almost inevitably exposed to experiencing a diffuse resentment which according to the individual's particular case will crystallize in a contingent way around this or that aspect of reality.

Perhaps we need to return to the phrase "a sincere atheist" and render its meaning more exact. The sincere atheist, it seems to me, is the man who does not find any traces of a divine presence in the world, such as it reveals itself to him, and who, moreover, believes he detects in the world the existence of phenomena that seem to him incompatible with such a divine presence. This atheism was that of many noble personalities of the 19th century. It excludes the idea that I will not accept the idea that God exists because it would be an intolerable inhibition or encroachment on my own existence. Whatever one might think about this position from a philosophical point of view, the sincere atheist is devoid of that *hubris* which at its extreme tends to merge with a paranoid attitude. None of this stops him from often experiencing deep within himself the diffuse resentment that I talked about. I would be tempted to say that if there are exceptional cases who find themselves wholly exempt from it, these cases are indebted to grace and to it alone. In truth one should see in this diffuse resentment a conscience butting heads with the reality of evil in the world but finding itself at the same time not able to make anyone or anything responsible. This resentment, however, cannot be overcome (this side of true faith) except by means of a generosity whose principle or source cannot be found in the human composite.

Someone may invoke the case of the stoic or of Spinoza who claims that good and evil are subjective qualities and that things are always and only what they have to be, in virtue of a necessity we are unaware of. In the first place, one has to respond that this interior acquiescence (assuming it is truly possible) presupposes the generosity I just spoke of. Moreover, according to contemporary thought such a necessity can only be a myth. I would add that one cannot plausibly find refuge in such a view except on the condition that one has already put to death in himself all the affections that make man truly man and not a sort of thinking mechanism. I am strongly inclined to believe that one cannot eliminate scandal (which unjust suffering, absurd accidents, and the like represent) except by proceeding to a systematic dehumanization which can take different forms, the basest or lowest form being one that is built on thinking that is fascinated, not by science, but by technology and technique in all its forms. This sort of thinking ends in what I would call neo-infantalism, a senile infantilism. Another form, which has nothing in common with the first, in fact is its opposite, is that toward which the contemplative or ascetic tends. Here, though, atheism is surpassed, or at least it is transmuted into something that has nothing in common with what it was at its point of departure. Here, too – here especially – a purification is at work, one whose source cannot reside in nature as such.

If we now concentrate our attention on what I have called the ulcerated conscience, we must recognize that its paradoxical torment consists in the fact that while aspiring to justify itself it must see more or less clearly that it is unjustifiable. One might be tempted to devalue it by maintaining that, after all, it is like, perhaps even the prolongation of, ill humor in daily life. This analogy is illegitimate, however, in the sense that the ulcerated conscience is haunted by anguish, and it is this anguish which gives it its tragic cast. One also has to add that the ulcerated conscience somewhat confusedly tries to transform itself into revolt. It does this, it seems to me, for the profound reason that revolt allows or involves a sort of expansion that by itself it cannot know or achieve. An "expansion," I say, and because of this one can speak of an analogic opposition between revolt and joy. As we said, revolt is not possible except when someone responsible has been discovered or invented. It is here that the transition from atheism to anti-clericalism occurs.

However, it is even more important to seek how in general, or in principle, the transition from atheism to nihilism properly speaking can occur. Nihilism can become, as it were, the "site" of a kind of absolutely generalized revolt. But by this very generalization, by what I would call its septicaemic character, it tends to become unfaithful to what we recognize as its essential motivation: the consciousness of an abuse, of an injustice, that one cannot and must not tolerate.

Here, too, we must repair to the distinction with which we started between the logical point of view and the existential. In theory one can construct a system that excludes any affirmation of a true God, that is, one who is truly transcendent or independent, but which nonetheless avoids nihilism insofar as it recognizes and aims to safeguard values. Before proceeding, we should note that we are in an area where philosophical terminology appears to be a bit shaky. Fichte, for example, indignantly denied being classed among the atheists. He even claimed to be more faithful to the exigence of God than his orthodox adversaries. It was possible to think that way in the deist or theistic climate of the 19th century when the word "atheist" was still felt to be an insult. In our day and age this is not the case, the existential "indexical" has dramatically changed. I make this observation in passing only, though, and only because it shows the misunderstandings to which one is exposed if one limits oneself to using words like "atheism" as verbal tokens, without taking into account the change of existential value to which they are subject.

What controls everything, it seems to me, when one asks about the passage from atheism to nihilism, is the following quite general observation: The sincere atheist finds himself in the presence of an immense void. But here, as always, we must substitute a dynamic view for a static one. This void is a void-in-movement, if I can put it that way, which can englobe or devour the one who observes it. If we go beyond this metaphorical expression, we will see that in reality it is a metaphysical "vertigo" which is capable of taking on two quite different forms. One is suicide, and while this word must first be taken literally, there can also be spiritual suicides that do not necessarily entail physical suicide. There are many ways of destroying oneself. This auto-destruction is nihilism under its most visible aspect. One must also add that, for reasons that are not immediately apparent, it most often is accompanied by the desire to draw others into this self-destruction. The one who has "attained" this sort of despair tends to resent as some sort of outrage the persistence in another of the desire for life.

But the dynamic which is that of the void-in-movement can present itself in a wholly different form as an effort at the divinization of the self. Here the "I" tends to take the place of the God whose non-existence it has proclaimed. But for reasons that reflection has no difficulty in uncovering, I believe, the position of Max Stirner, the purely anarchic position, cannot impose itself upon a world such as ours. It remains at bottom a purely romantic attitude of protest. It is not in this way that one can construct, at least with any chance of success, a defense of violence.

Another nihilism, this one incomparably more dangerous than the former, does not come from the hyperbolic conscience of the individual, but develops itself on the bases of a thoroughly revolutionary consciousness. What is remarkable – and Camus has perfectly shown this in the central part of his book – is that this nihilism is tied to the divinization of history. "Revolt," he says apropos to shigalovism,[2] "cut off from its true roots, unfaithful to man because subject to History, thinks to enslave the entire universe. 'A tenth of humanity,' writes Shigalov, 'will possess the rights of personality,

2   [Publisher's note] Refers to the doctrine proposed by the character Shigalov in Dostoevsky's *The Possessed*.

and will exercise an unlimited authority over the other 9/10s. The latter will lose their personality and become a herd; trained in easy obedience, they will be restored to original innocence and, as it were, to the primitive paradise where they will work eternally.'" As Camus says, the "theocratic" totalitarians of the 20th century are clearly announced.

But the proper task of philosophical reflection consists in asking about the meaning or the properly metaphysical foundation of this opposition between man and history. It is at the heart of Camus's book, but philosophically speaking it is not adequately elucidated. The question he does not ask (or perhaps which he privately answers in the negative) seems to me to be the following: In order for this opposition truly to have a meaning, does one have to reestablish history's vertical dimension, the relation of man to God, in addition to the horizontality of history? Now, to be candid, it certainly could be the case that in order to effect this reestablishment one would have to liberate oneself from traditional categories, in particular those pertaining to causality, which for so long have burdened theology. In any event, for what I just said to have some meaning it is necessary, I believe, to place oneself directly, I would even say *dramatically*, before the situation of the rebel. What complicates everything – including my exposition and analysis – is the sort of inextricable imbroglio that tends to occur today between social revolt and metaphysical revolt.

The views of Christians on the extreme left today are very revealing in this connection. In their ardor to denounce the implicit pact between the defenders of the existing social order and the official representatives of religion during the greater part of the 19th century, they adopt a symmetrically opposite position and try to show that true religion is on the side of revolt or revolution. To be sure, no one today would attempt to rehabilitate the social and religious conservatism of yesterday. Still, one should restrain oneself from the too-categorical approvals, and the wholly pitiless condemnations, to which Camus delivers himself. Such is the case when he says apropos to the 19th century bourgeoisie that by its *essential* corruption and its dismaying hypocrisy it aided the *definitive* discrediting of the principles it proclaimed. The truth, no doubt, is infinitely more complex and needs to be appropriately nuanced. In truth, the bourgeoisie that Albert Camus talks about is a myth. Among many of those whom he categorizes absolutely there were admirable virtues, even despite a widespread blindness to the humanly atrocious conditions engendered by the dawning industrial civilization. Above all, though, one has to resist the temptation to ascribe to one camp or party all the virtues that one refuses to the other.

It is of course right that the Christian commits himself to denouncing abuses and to the extent possible attempts to correct them. Mere words, as we said, are tantamount to hypocrisy or a lie; they literally "ring false." Acting to correct abuse is certainly better than merely deploring the abuses or presenting them as God's mysterious will to test people. And all this is particularly true for the priest or cleric. Not only is this right, it is "just" in the biblical sense. But none of this means that Christianity can transform itself into a philosophy of revolution without suffering a frightful alteration. This point is so important (and so difficult) that we must stop here for a moment and recall once again the fundamental principles in question. In particular we must return to what was said at the beginning concerning the inevitable *impurity* of revolt or rebellion or revolution.

Here one can encounter a hypocrisy no more justifiable than that denounced by far-left Christians when they unmask the powers-that-be. The hypocrisy consists in theoretically regretting – regretting with one's lips and utterances – the "excesses" to which revolt always leads, but nonetheless – and with glad heart – taking part in them and even, sometimes, merely approving of them. I recall with sadness a thoughtless religious who laughingly recounted to me during the German occupation that one night some fellow "patriots" had bayoneted a German soldier and threw him into the Seine. One has to say unequivocally that such a gleeful attitude is incompatible with Christianity. In the same way one has to denounce the sort of "fraternization," I would even say *complicity*, that often occurs between "progressive" Christians and dictators and their regimes – as long as the latter are of the "good sort," that is, on the Left. (A side note: we really need to get rid of this distinction of "the Right and the Left," because of the grave confusions to which it gives rise.)

The more I consider the phenomenon of revolt, the more it seems clear to me that from a Christian point of view it presents a properly "crucifying" character. That is, for the Christian it presents in a more intense, more acute manner, the very characteristics found otherwise in life. Thus it is extremely important to determine the conditions for legitimately posing, and pursuing, the question. Here is what I would say: In this domain we are never allowed to forget, to make abstraction from, our concrete conditions of insertion in the world. There are things that relate to us, that regard us, and those that do not. If they do not regard us, it is because they imply (an) experience we have not shared. They cannot become matter for a decision by us.

To take an example that is both temporally removed from us and yet still retains contemporary relevance: I would say that the French did not have to take up a position in the Spanish Civil War, and the position they did adopt had the character of being a shocking intrusion. The only justifiable action, I believe, would have been one that tended toward reconciliation and pacification. But for a Spanish Christian on the other hand, the question was posed and, to use the term I employed earlier, was "crucifying." It is no less certain that a similar problem *could* arise here in the future.

The term "problem" is unfortunate, even inappropriate in this context. As I said in another place, there is no problem where there is no solution, i.e., a possible satisfactory result. But in the order of "crucifixion," "satisfactory" is strictly speaking inconceivable. This being unthinkable is itself constitutive of the tragic condition of man. It further follows from this, that in the extreme situations when this condition shows itself, it is impossible to speak strictly of "obligation." About them, no one has the right to say categorically: if you find yourself in such a situation you are obliged to act in this way and not that way. . . . The "crucifixion" here is precisely this absence, which seems to be a dereliction.

On the other hand, there is every reason to think that a judgment can and ought to be made on the *means* one employs, regardless of the option one chose. And perhaps even more importantly, on the *spirit* in which one will use these means. One must firmly resist the widespread view today that the ends justify the means. On the contrary, the value of the end is deeply uncertain, but in the vast majority of cases the means can themselves be judged, and most often judged as being evil or bad, absolutely speaking.

One therefore should not hide from himself the fact that in the domain of practice such considerations almost always lead to conundrums, to excruciating impasses, impossibilities, or contradictions. At this juncture, therefore, we should examine non-resistance as a kind of sublimation of rebellion. Without question there is something seductive in such a view. But here, too, one must ask, in what conditions, in what context – social and religious – can non-resistance be not merely ratified but simply entertained? Because of various constraints, all that I can say here is that in the perspective of western moral consciousness and in a world more and more subject to the omnipotence of technique, it tends to present itself, if not as a lie, at least as a delusion. One very much has to fear the emergence of a type of hypocrisy that is not any better than those that have been critiqued above. This is the case, to give an example in passing, of the self-proclaimed "neutralists" who, in truth, are pure defeatists.

The next point is not merely parenthetical, but rather touches upon the core of Camus's book. It is impossible not to recognize the total lack of proportion between, on the one hand, the admirably vigorous and pertinent critique he delivers against the contemporary deviations and perversions of the authentic attitude of revolt and, on the other, the positive conclusions he wants to arrive at. He does not succeed in connecting them, it seems to me. Here are some revealing passages. On the one hand, one cannot but subscribe – I would say without reservation – to the thought or intention they reveal. On the other, if one thinks concretely about their chances of being adopted, one has to say that they are practically nil. For example, one reads in a chapter entitled "Revolt and Murder": "Absolute non-violence negatively grounds or enables servitude and its violences. On the other hand, systematic violence positively destroys the living community and what we receive from it. In order to be fecund, these two notions must have limits. In History conceived as absolute, violence is legitimated. As a relative risk, it is a rupture of communication. For revolt, therefore, violence must preserve its provisional character, it must always be connected – if it cannot be avoided – to a personal responsibility, to an immediate risk." In other words, in no case is someone permitted as it were *to install* himself in violence. Moreover, as we saw earlier, we cannot employ it while exempting ourselves from the risk of death.

It is in the same spirit that the author observes a bit later that "measure" is not the contrary of revolt. He even adds that it is revolt which is the measure, that it raises, defends, and recreates measure throughout History and its disorders. The very origin of this value (measure) guarantees that it must be imperfect. Measure born in violence can live only by the latter. It is in constant conflict, perpetually raised and mastered by intelligence. "We all carry in ourselves our penal colonies, our crimes, our ravages. But our task is not to unleash them on the world, but to combat them in ourselves and in others. Revolt, the age-old will not to submit of which Barrès spoke, is still today the principle of this struggle. Mother of forms, source of true life, it holds us upright in the amorphous and wild movement of history."

It is most inadequate to say that these words and lines are beautiful, one has to salute the great soul that expresses itself here so directly and nobly. It seems to me, however, that despite all that, on the metaphysical plane – which, after all, remains primary – they conceal a subtle and dangerous error. I do not think that one can affirm that revolt is "the very movement of life," or that it is "the mother of forms." The truth is much more complex, and Camus here seems to me to commit an illegitimate extrapolation. To be sure, it can be true, at least in general, to say that in the world in which we live life is everywhere trampled on, and that therefore every sincere and genuine taking-up of a position in favor of life necessarily presents itself as a revolt or rebellion.

This, however, in no way entails that life itself is essentially revolt. In the last few pages of his book Camus says that revolt cannot do without a "strange love." But one must go infinitely beyond that. One must say that in all respects, and speaking absolutely, love is primary; this is true in a fundamental sense, one that exceeds even that painful human "fraternity" of which our author has such a keen sense. This love is the love of being and, as much as we can grow closer to it, is inseparable from it.

This means that revolt is not and cannot be the final word. It seems to me that it can only present itself as a tragic *recuperation*, somewhat sinful itself because of what has been lost already by sin. We might even say that this recuperation in its *essential* modalities is appropriate to the status of man insofar as he is a sinner. This to my mind has a precise meaning. It means that the man who is not a saint does not have to pretend to sanctity the way that pacifists and non-resistants do. If he does, he necessarily (perhaps involuntarily) becomes the accomplice of the violent. Short of sanctity, therefore, the non-resistant risks placing himself below the rebel.

Nor does it follow that we can therefore proceed to a canonization of the rebel. As we saw at the beginning of this study, revolt or rebellion presents a radically contradictory character. It is a disorder at the service of order (but a disorder nonetheless). To be sure, it is a disorder that, all things considered, is preferable to the one that consists in maintaining an *appearance of order* which is but injustice and lies.

But one must add – and on this point I necessarily find myself in disagreement with Albert Camus – that only authentic *transcendence*, that is, vertical transcendence, can constitute the sort of permanent invisible counterweight without which revolt, even when it is conceived with the profound honesty we admire in Camus, cannot fail to fall into despair. Of this transcendence, holiness or sanctity, that of Christ himself and the martyrs is the permanent witness offered to our consideration. For humanly speaking, revolt's chances are nil. Revolt is destined to be crushed between, and by, the equally blind powers it attempts either simultaneously or successively to rise against. To be sure, it is not an obvious contradiction that despair should have the last word. It certainly is a possibility that thought does not have the right not to consider. The truth is perhaps sad, said Renan (if I remember correctly). But Albert Camus is not Ernst Renan. In Camus's soul has never burned the vengeful fire that consumed the author of *The History of the Origins of Christianity*.

Everything, including his style, shows that for him, despite everything, despair does not have and cannot be the last word. I am not going to say, because it would be too facile, and because such characterizations are suspect, that Albert Camus is a Christian who does not know it. What *is* true, I believe, is that what stops him from adhering to what I would call the true religion – in contrast to all the idolatries of whatever sort – are the "materializations," whether theological or institutional, which *for him and for a multitude of others* "intercept" the true light, the unique Light, which enlightens everyone coming into this world.

Translated by Paul Seaton

PASCALIAN PHILOSOPHY[1]

Among the swirling, confused thoughts stirred in me by the eyewitness accounts of those who, often miraculously, have returned from the extermination camps, there is one that dominates the reflections I want to propose today. It seems to me that the dogma of the resurrection of the body can find, as it were, its "pledge" in the nameless horrors that took place day after day, year after year, in these laboratories of the devil. This is the same dogma that is often hidden away, even by real believers, or reduced to a formula designed not to attract attention. This dogma, though, is both paradoxical and salvific. I mean to say that by the mediation of the survivors, but also by paths both more direct and more mysterious, all "flesh," not only that which was tortured but that which was systematically denigrated, reclaims its rights. In the face of such horrors, we cannot content ourselves with speaking in the abstract, putting forth the pale "demand" that certain moralists deliver at the end of their ethics. With respect to these victims and those who devoted an unfailing love to them, we cannot content ourselves with a bloodless (and, truth be told, unthinkable) "happiness" that a disembodied spirituality promises souls delivered from the shackles of the sensible. It is not the soul, but the body itself which, albeit mutely, calls for – which demands – the transfigured state which the resurrection alone will reestablish in its "profane" dignity.

To be sure, I am well aware that many qualifications are needed here. One cannot even for one instant – unless one wants to go beyond the Christian worldview – speak of "a right." "Right" perhaps is only conceivable, strictly speaking, for subjects taken

1   Réforme, April 20, 1946.

as abstract entities. How can the body have a right? More essentially, how can a creature claim a destiny that so exceeds the strict limits of the world in which it is called to exercise its poor faculties?

In truth, the sole justice of which I will speak here is based upon the Promise, that is, in the final analysis upon the Incarnation and consequently, upon grace. And if we can legitimately affirm such grace in its transcendence with respect to any humanistic reduction, vis-à-vis any possible psychologizing, this is because of the Resurrection of Our Lord. St. Paul's formula is the key: If Christ has not risen, our faith is in vain. It is only from this privileged fact (privileged because alone among all historical facts it is truly *enlightening*), from this "pivot" of all faith and all hope, that in the face of so many atrocities we can affirm the restoration of tortured flesh in its fullness as a glorious body.

All this runs the risk of seeming, at first glance, rather foreign to philosophical thought as such, taken strictly. But is not this merely an appearance that an even deeper reflection needs to dispel? In another study that I devoted to hope, which in principle was purely phenomenological, I attempted to show that hope is entirely structured around the claim "As before, but otherwise, and better, than before." It is based upon a supra-logical connection of a "return" and a "pure novelty." As I tried to show, it has to be so, if hope is always called for by a situation that can be likened to an exile or a captivity. All those who have experienced captivity at some deeper level have had the sentiment that it was preparing them to lead a renewed life, in which they would somehow reap the spiritual fruits of the ordeal experienced and borne. But if this is so, must we not recognize that all authentic hope is constituted on the model of the absolute hope, which is the hope of resurrection? It is not so much a question of my personal resurrection, since I have too much reason to doubt my own titles to a substantial "perenniality." It rather is hope of *our* resurrection, that of all the beings who form with me a community to which I really cannot assign limits because beyond my personal horizon it joins, if not the entire human race (a positivistic abstraction), at least with the Mystical Body.

But [. . .] the most decisive lesson that can be derived from the terrible experiences to which I referred in the beginning (and from which no one will ever have the right to completely withdraw his thought), is that outside of a positive or real religion announcing the resurrection of the body, there is only room for absolute pessimism. Schopenhauer only provided a pale version of this. For him there still existed some possibility of escape. I will not talk about the contemporary thinkers like Sartre who ensconce themselves most gladly in a despair more verbal than truly felt and to which they claim to find a counterweight in a "liberty" that is nothing more than our nothingness, "our lack of being" as they put it. There certainly is nothing there to found values and nourish human elevation. At this point, I believe, one has to recognize that between absolute pessimism and absolute hope all else has collapsed, carried away by an irresistible avalanche.

I agree, however, that it can be dangerous to pose such a dilemma, that one runs the risk of plunging into deep discouragement souls which try with all their might to resist despair, without having anything – at least visibly – that resembles absolute hope. What do I know? If we are candid, do we not recognize that there is no one among us who at least at certain times does not find himself deserted by that Confidence which alone makes this world habitable? It belongs only to prayer – I here am addressing those who find prayer difficult, those I know well – to obtain [the grace] that this Hope might daily rekindle in us and that it might illumine those who travel in the dark.

Translated by Paul Seaton

DEATH AND IMMORTALITY[1]

It is not as a theologian that I propose to speak here of death and
immortality. It is not even certain that the notion of immortality
derives from theology, as is unquestionably the case with resurrection. I will speak as a philosopher and, I add, as a philosopher of
reflection. People too often misunderstand the relations obtaining
between my thought and French philosophy of the 19th century (I
have in mind Maine de Biran and those who continued his work).
To my knowledge only the philosopher Ian Alexander has brought
these connections to light.

If I insist on this "reflective" aspect of my thought, it is in order
to make clear from the beginning that I am not going to launch
myself into any fantastic speculations about "the Beyond," about
"the mystery of the Beyond." To be sure, to my mind it is most
important that this mystery be *recognized*, and recognized in its
enlightening and liberating value. I believe that many of the most terrible ills from which humanity suffers, many of the errors and even
most noxious perversions we observe around us, are intimately tied
to the widespread obscuring of the meaning of this enveloping mystery: without it human life loses more than one of its dimensions,
including its density and its fullness. But this is not a reason for me
to subscribe to this or that spiritualist or theosophic view (some,
however, have made me a champion of such views!). My position, if
I dare say, is extremely nuanced in this area, and I hope to show in
the last part of this analysis how far one can go in this direction, but
also what are the limits within which I intend to keep myself.

1   Unpublished, 1959

The first question upon which I wish to reflect can be initially formulated as follows: How am I situated vis-à-vis death and more precisely my own death?

But immediately this question reveals itself to be extremely ambiguous. Is it a matter of knowing how *I*, i.e., this person who is inscribed in the registers of the civil State, with the empirical individuality proper to him, who lives now, with the paths that lead him from birth to the grave, how *I* situate myself vis-à-vis my death? The words "situate myself" upon reflection also show themselves to be equivocal: Do they refer to the entirely subjective way I react to the idea of my own death, the fact, for example, that I fear it, or that I await it with confidence (even if I do not see it as a liberation), or that I am indifferent to it? All this only presents a psychological interest and really is foreign to my aim, which my first formulation rather poorly expressed.

I therefore need to "departicularize" (at least provisionally) the subject – the "I" – who poses the question. Immediately, however, another difficulty arises. This departicularization can be pushed so far that it would be something like a Kantian or Fichtian transcendental ego who asks about death *in persona mea*. It is clear that this limit-possibility of thought should not enter into the investigation. The "I" who considers his own death is not and cannot be a purely abstract being like the transcendental ego. From the outset one must reject the idealist attempt to defend immortality by alleging that the thinking subject considered in its essence cannot die. The truth, I would answer, is that such a subject cannot even live. It is a fiction that should be left to an outdated philosophy. If it does have some value, it is only in the domain of epistemology, of a theory of knowledge, while maintaining that it can be rigorously separated from a philosophy of the concrete – something that seems to me to be far from certain.

This leads us therefore to an important observation: the departicularization I am talking about can only be partial. The one who asks himself about death is a man among other men; he refers therefore to a certain situation common to us all, all us human beings. (The question remains open whether there are other beings who might not be subject to mortality, to *having-to-die*.)

This *having-to-die* which is mine, which is *ours*, is known by induction, but it also can be derived deductively from the nature of the organic body which is mine. All this belongs to the order of *knowledge*: I know, I've learned, that I will die. It also can be the case (but this is more doubtful) that I carry within myself, beneath or beyond all knowledge, something like prescience of this death which will be mine. But one has to agree that if this prescience manifests itself, it is only at certain times or perhaps at a certain period of life, while at other times I have the contrary awareness (whether this is or is not an illusion doesn't matter) of not having, not being able, to die. Taken in themselves, these are contingent experiences – *Erlebnisse* in German – the value of which I am not in a position to judge.

I have spoken of the organized body. When I say that I *know* I have to die, I am thinking about the destiny of this body. But this certitude, which bears upon an object and hence is "objective," is it equivalent to, does it join with, an existential certainty about the "I" that is presently asking about death? Posed this way the question becomes quite obscure. When I say that I know that I am destined to die, it does not seem that I simply want to say, my *body* will cease functioning and will decompose. This reductive interpretation radically alters the meaning of my certainty about having to die. But it would not be exact either to say that I *know* that I cannot or will not survive this destruction of my body. To claim this, to grant it the status of *knowledge*, would be to introduce a kind of dogmatic assurance that is not and cannot be given to reflection as such. (On this point, one must abstract from what I individually, as this or that person, as a believer, for example, might think.) Nor would it be legitimate to introduce a contrary certainty, that of a dualism between my body and me. Perhaps one should say that this *having-to-die* implies a confrontation with something unknown, but that this "something" presents itself as a end-term or an absolute limit – if, that is, this "something" is considered in a purely worldly perspective, in terms of what the world contains of obligations and of possibilities.

The reader may be surprised to hear me talking so vaguely about "something." This is because every further specification seems to be arbitrary. This would be the case for the words "event" or "happening," for example, which Heidegger uses. My death seems to be much less something that will happen to me than what will end the possibility of any further happening. The word "confrontation" is also extremely important because it indicates at least the possibility for me to take up a position vis-à-vis my death-to-come, and to conduct myself before it in a determinate manner. In the foregoing I use the term "possibility" only in a negative sense. It does not exclude that I might remain somehow "inert" before my death-to-come, without this inertia being deliberate or even conscious, and without it being able to be qualified even as an "attitude." But what is true is that if I have attained to a certain stage of reflection I recognize that *I must take up a position*. This is a use of my liberty, but of a liberty that includes the power of denying itself. I said as much in a communication I made to the International Congress of Philosophy in 1937. Here is a passage from it.

> In the midst of the clouds that envelop the future, *my* future, one certainty remains invariable: I will die. My death alone, in what awaits me, is not problematic, not a "problem." What is it? My death is not yet a fact; is it an idea? If it were, I should be able to conceive it, but that is impossible. I cannot comprehend it in thought and imagine it as having occurred except by placing myself in the place of *someone else* who survives me and for whom what I call *my* death is *his* death. . . . Thus, this certain death hangs "over" me. My situation differs in nothing from the condemned prisoner enclosed in a cell whose walls gradually close in. There is nothing in my actual existence which cannot as it were be reduced to nothing – Sartre would say, "shrunk" to nothing – by this supervening "presence," death looming "over" me. In this situation, overcome by vertigo, how could I not succumb to the temptation to put an end to this "looming," this frightful and yet indeterminate presence, and deliver myself from this always imminent torment?
>
> In this way, I continued, there is constituted for me a "metaproblematic" of *no-longer-being*, which at the same time is a structural condition for despair, which can only be eliminated by suicide.
>
> Now, it was quite illuminating when I attempted without success to make the members of the Society of Philosophy of Oxford understand this a few years ago. They declared that

such an attitude was blameworthy, even shameful, without understanding that it was not a question of making a value judgment but only of recognizing that this *possibility* of radical despair was implicit in my condition of being mortal. And that this seemed to me to be of the greatest importance for the study of certain psychoses.

What should be the role of reflection here, if not to recognize that this abyss which seems to draw me to itself, in a certain sense *is my own liberty which created it*? In truth my death is nothing in itself or by itself. The power of annihilation with which death seems to be invested, it doesn't possess except with the collusion of a liberty which betrays itself in order to bestow it. It is this liberty and it alone – which can exercise itself like a power of obfuscation capable of hiding from my sight the inexhaustible wealth of the universe. It therefore is my liberty which becomes a power of occultation. At the same time, if we can speak of an "ontological counterpoint" to death, it cannot be either life itself – which is so inclined "to cut a deal" with that which destroys it – nor any sort of objective truth. This ontological counterweight can only reside in the positive use of a liberty that refuses that ruinous deceit by which it confers on death a power it alone can possess. In that case liberty changes meaning and becomes adhesion and love – and thus death is transcended.

I remain fundamentally in agreement with this text written more than twenty years ago. However, in the light of the terrible experiences which have occurred since then, I feel the need to add today the following: it has been given to us – alas! – to see techniques of killing developed and perfected that reduce the "space" where this liberty can exercise itself, reducing it to the point of practically annulling it. "Each one of us," I wrote in *Men against the Mass Society*, "if he does not want to lie to himself, or sin by an unjustifiable presumption, must admit that there exist concrete instruments and techniques that can be brought against him and strip him of his sovereignty, or even of control over himself, that at other epochs – let us recall the stoics – we would be justified in regarding as inviolable."

One has to add, nonetheless, that a meditation like the one I am engaged in here implies a "space," perhaps better put: a "margin" of security, without which liberty would be extinguished.

The preceding reflections lead us to recognize that it is impossible to agree with Heidegger's thought in *Being and Time* according to which *being-for* or *toward-death* is a structural given of the being that I am. One needs to take stock of the very words Heidegger employs: *Sein zu Tode*. I have often remarked that the relation – if there is one – translated by the preposition *zu* is far from univocal. If it is, it is uniquely "for" my body – and on the condition that it be looked at in a purely biological perspective. But as soon as I reintroduce myself as an incarnate being, the ambiguity of the relationship evoked by the word *zu* appears in plain sight. In passing, let us observe that one cannot translate it into French without having the ambiguity appear. If one speaks of being "for" death, the word "for" seems to correspond to a finality or end that certainly is not implied in the words *Sein zu Tode*; and if one translates *zu* by "toward," one leaves the French language because "toward" presupposes a movement, a direction, that the word "being" does not.

In my eyes this is only an external sign of something more profound, that is, of a basic indetermination. One can understand as inherent – but not necessarily – in the word *zu* the idea of "condemnation" – such as is so powerfully expressed in Brahms's *Requiem*. But even this idea of condemnation can be emptied of ethical-religious meaning, and one therefore finds oneself in the order of law, of *Gesetz*. But when it does, the term leaves the existential order to take its place in a natural order – one of which man can only be a part. Only, as soon as I say "I" don't I thereby place myself somehow outside of nature?

The conclusion to draw from all this can only be expressed negatively. If I consider myself as a subject instead of naively identifying myself with my body conceived as an object, I cannot determine in a univocal manner my relationship to my death. This has to be chosen, it is to be determined, even in a certain way invented.

But we should not fail to observe that if this is so, it is because the relationship between the "I" and what I call "my body" is itself not determinable in any univocal fashion. It belongs to me to determine this relationship. For example, I can conduct myself vis-à-vis my body in such a way that materialism is verified in my life (and even in my being). On the other hand, by the way in which he triumphed over his physical trials, Bergson in a certain way provided the proof of his own invincible spiritualism.

We now must show that what has just been said about my relationship to my own death is even more evident when it is a question of my relationship to the death of others. We shall try to be as concrete as possible.

It manifestly belongs to what I am *being among others*. (We do not have to determine whether it belongs to my essence or my existence, or even if this distinction is applicable here.) Only, if I try to concretely examine what this means I see that this apparently simple affirmation expresses a very complex reality, one that does not allow itself to be assimilated to the condition of being one "unity" among other "unities." We must note that in this domain we have a wide-ranging register that bears upon both the nature of the "among" as upon what I call *grosso modo*, "the other." Certain beings constitute for me a milieu (e.g., familial, professional) which constantly nourishes and supports me and outside of which I would find myself literally lost. Others have with me relations I could call "everyday" (a contractor, a bus driver). Finally, the great number are only passers-by whom I encounter but who are for me as if they didn't exist. In this last case, the word "among" loses all existential meaning. On the other hand, I note that the word "other" (or "others") is not affected with the same mark.

These preliminary observations are most important if I want to understand what it is to survive. The word "survive" does not have a real sense except when it is a question of those near and dear to me, or of those who have a relationship with me, such as teacher or student, or those who share with me a creative effort in this or that domain. To the beings related to me in these ways there can be meaning in saying, eventually, that I survive or live on. But it is certain that the fundamental problem arises for those to whom I am united by friendship, affection, or love, when their disappearance consists, as it were, in a personal injury or harm. This is one of the "givens" of life that I have reflected upon for almost fifty years. This is what I was led to recognize publicly in 1937 in the communication I already referred to, that before the abyss created by the disappearance of a beloved one, I experience a different sort of disturbance than what I feel before my own "having-to-die." One that is more profound. In the case of my own death, I can exercise a sort of narcosis, especially if I detach myself from the world, or if I see the world detach itself from me. But grief, if it is genuine, excludes such a possibility. It would experience it as a betrayal.

The objection that will be made to these reflections is easy to foresee. Here, it will be said, you are only talking about simple subjective dispositions, merely psychological experiences, that change nothing in the reality of the thing. But, I answer, what is really envisaged by the word "reality"? Is it the verifiable process by which the body – that of a living being like any other – becomes a cadaver and decomposes? However, to reduce what one calls "reality" – even the reality of death – to this process is, whether one is aware of it or not, to become a prisoner of the crudest materialism. This is so obvious that I am almost embarrassed to have to say it. When we today speak of those deceased called Molière, Mozart, or Rembrandt, it is obvious that it is not their long-since-destroyed bodies that we have in mind. It is true that my opponent will shrug his shoulders and inform us that what presently remains, what one can talk about at present, is the *works* of Molière, Mozart, or Rembrandt. And these subsist thanks to material elements, up until our own day.

This response is both correct and superficial. What perdures through these material elements is a spirit, is thought. And this spirit or thought must be sufficiently "in accord" with ours for it to be able to speak to us. History shows us ruptures in which a language no longer speaks to other human beings. Even if we leave to one side the possibility of rupture, the word "survive" itself contains ambiguity. If it is true that chronologically we live after Molière and Mozart, it is also true in an infinitely more profound sense that it is they who survive us, with the prefix "sur-" having pretty much the same meaning as "super" or "supra," that is, "above." It is from "above" that they enlighten us.

Everyone, or almost everyone, will be obliged to recognize the foregoing, but some will refuse to grant it a metaphysical importance. They will want to leave things at their most vague, when it is important to specify what this "spirit," this "thought," is that they admit continues to exist. They probably will say that it is not the spirit or thought of the individual Mozart or the individual Molière, whatever their destiny was after they died.

Returning to an earlier example, what must be acknowledged, and in a most explicit manner, is that grief does not allow itself such indetermination. When it is internally animated by love it seems to be accompanied by this 2nd-person affirmation: "You cannot have disappeared like a vapor disappears; to admit this is to betray you."

To be sure, there is a type of philosophy that disdains this sort of affirmation and likens it to what the British call *wishful thinking*, a mode of thought that is at the service of a desire. This is particularly true of the Spinozistic mode of philosophy which sees in it an illusion pure and simple, born of falsehood about the nature of things. He or she whose disappearance, whose annihilation even, seems to me to be unthinkable or impossible to admit, in this view is only an ephemeral assemblage that has dissipated.

But it is here that the distinction between the objective and the existential assumes all its value. There is no meaning in saying that the being whom I loved was an "assemblage," that is a characterization applicable only to things. But love can address itself only to a subject, that is, to a being capable of loving in its own turn. There is no love worthy of the name without, or outside of, a certain dimension to which I have given the name of "intersubjectivity." It is in function of this dimension, and only in this way, that the question we are circling around can be approached.

Therefore to speak of being "for" or "toward" death as Heidegger does is, in reality, whether he knows it or not, to hold to an existential solipsism; the death of the other is treated only as an event at which I assist, perhaps only attend, and which even if it concerns me does not affect me in the vital meaning of the term. As Valentine, one of the characters of my play *Horizon*, says about a man she loves and who just died in an accident: his death is mine. This cry is the spark that shoots from absolute grief. The tragedy of the survivor is here: the one struck by death seems to continue to live in him, the survivor carries within himself this contradiction, he is this contradiction. But the one who lives this condition attests existentially to the falsity of the Spinozistic view; he shows that this view comes from a "place" outside of the intersubjective dimension, one that Spinoza never glimpsed.

A long time ago I believed that it was my duty to note that Spinoza, in a famous proposition of the *Ethics*, has confused desire and hope, thus obscuring what the latter has that is specific, that by which it can be considered a theological virtue. How can desire be so treated? But there is another confusion, one that is equally injurious: Kant's concerning immortality as a postulate of practical reason. In his extreme anxiousness to exorcise everything that is rooted in the sensible and in sensibility, Kant seems to me to have radically misunderstood the fact already brought to light, perhaps by Plato, certainly by Saint Augustine and all those who followed him: that love as such presents an incomparable dignity, by which it places itself well beyond the givens of the mere sensibility. Before I continue, though, I need to indicate an equivocation in the word "sensibility." It has caused a great deal of confusion in psychology.

What the mystics have recognized long before the philosophers is that love and hope are inseparable. No hope is possible for a being without love, only lusts and ambitions (every ambition aiming to procure satisfactions of a certain order). But what place can there be for such satisfactions after death? Isn't it obvious that death puts things back in their place, that it "smooths the wrinkles"? Isn't it precisely these "wrinkles" that we have in mind when we point to the merely ephemeral advantages of the person who has achieved fortune, power, or celebrity? But hope – and this is its mystery, the very mark of its transcendence – hope aims beyond this "wrinkled world" to which we belong. And the very fact that it finds *in us* its root is, as it were, the gauge of what it announces. It is from heaven, while desire is of earth, and it is only in heaven that it can find its fulfillment.

But what does that mean? Some will say that the word "heaven" has no meaning. Do we imagine, he will ask sarcastically, that in and through death we embark upon some sort of migration toward another planet or galaxy? And if we do not mean this sort of mythical mumbo-jumbo, what does the word signify?

We should not be daunted by this sort of aggressive questioning. But let us gather ourselves before responding.

One way of responding, it seems to me, is the following: Whatever the speculative errors idealism might be guilty of, it at least has the immense merit of having rendered a fundamental truth accessible to human intelligence that Christianity for its part revealed from the beginning. There is a sense in which the soul surpasses the visible world and in which it becomes "interior" to it: the visible world, including the astronomer's heaven with its thousands of constellations, *can become a symbol*. The greatest act of transcendence of which the human spirit is capable perhaps consists in the reversal by which the visible becomes the symbol of a spiritual reality, upon which it appears to be dependent. Here I limit myself to reiterating a claim that is at the heart of every mysticism and perhaps of every theology worthy of the name. What is important to note, though, is that even the person who has never had any mystical experience can, on the basis of his own experience, go in the same direction, if his is sufficiently profound.

Perhaps it is worthwhile recapitulating our steps to this point.

In the first place it is not true, it is not true in any way, that I have to see myself as *destined to death*. Here there is no univocal relationship able to be recognized by everyone. If this type of relation exists, it is vis-à-vis my body understood as an object, that is, insofar as I detach it from the mysterious connections with the subject who I am. Moreover, between this I-subject and my body there are no univocal and universal relationships of the sort that is true, for example, in the area of causality. My relationship to my body is one that I have to establish, to invent; in this area physical sickness presents a special importance. We all know that someone subject to a sickness can transmute it from a simple suffering to something sublime.

In this perspective, death – my death, that is, the death of a human being – already appears to be something mysterious. In other words, we would be wrong to confuse it with the implacable process of degeneration whose "site" is the body. "Implacable," I said: the appearances tend to make us judge thus. But certain indications that each of us can recognize by exercising reverent attention can lead us to conjecture that the Mercy that infinitely surpasses the limits of our understanding can, as it were, "infiltrate" through the chains of determinism. I do not insist, though, upon this point and only point to the "overtures" that such experiences can bring to our thinking.

A bit brusquely, I admit, I then moved to the problem (if one can put it that way) that the death of a beloved poses to me. Contrary to what the vast majority of philosophers seem to have thought, I claimed that this problem is more essential and more tragic than my own death. The latter can be, if not resolved, at least transmuted by a certain "moral anesthetic." I can bring myself to consider my own death as the rest or repose to which I aspire after the exhausting labor of life. But this anesthesia loses all its power as soon as I am in the presence of another's death, if, that is, the other was truly for me a "you." A bond is insufferably broken, but without totally being broken, because even with the sundering, and perhaps even more so than when the other was alive, I remain indissolubly tied to the one who now no longer lives. What is insufferable or intolerable is precisely this contradiction. This is a scandal which can cast over all of reality the infamous shadow of absurdity. But here, too, and even more so than in the previous case, liberty can intervene, the only true liberty – truly positive liberty – which is connected with love. To be sure, "love" possesses a wide register that goes from possession to sacrifice. In making this distinction between possession and sacrifice, I echo what Doctor Stocker said from a neo-Augustinian perspective. Now I need to specify the profound meaning of sacrifice. To do so, I will present examples drawn from my own dramatic works, which revolve almost entirely around the themes I bring to your attention.

Take Aline Fortier, a character is *La Chapelle ardent*. She is a woman who remains, as it were, "riveted" to her dead son. Identifying herself with him in her imagination (and falsifying him along the way), she tries to turn his fiancée from the man she is about to marry and to marry a sick man, whose death cannot cause jealousy. She is a limit-case example of what possessive love can do when it attempts to tighten its hold on its object, even after death. Werner Schnee in *Le Dard*, who is faithful to the end to his friend, a Jewish pianist who is killed by the Nazis, is at the opposite pole: an example of pure devotion and sacrifice, as is Simon Bernauer in *Le Signe de la croix*.

Here too, however, I need to anticipate an objection. What prevents, someone will ask, all of this from occurring exclusively in the consciousness of the survivors, that Aline's son, Werner's friend, finally aren't simply the idea the survivors have, or make, of them? This leads us to question a distinction that we have so far taken for granted, but to which we have given somewhat imprudently an absolute value. The distinction is between what is "in us" and what is "outside" us.

It goes without saying that at the level of ordinary experience, the experience which guides, even commands, our actions, this distinction is indispensable. It also is indispensable at the level of persons; this is one of the contributions of the Incarnation. I've been driven to the station by a dear friend; I've said good-bye to him. Now that he is gone I ask myself where he is and what he is doing? I possess certain empirical means of contacting him, of getting news from him, and for giving him news of me. It is normally not said (except if certain exceptional conditions are realized, of which I am not the master) that it is possible for us to come together (when we are apart) outside of these well-traced paths. This however is not the whole story. For example, today the reality of telepathy does not seem able to be denied, at least in good faith. But one also has to recognize that in our world everything for the most part occurs as if telepathy does not exist, as if we depend on these imperfect means – letters, telegrams, the telephone – in order to communicate. But one does not have to push reflection very far to see that this neatly surveyed world, where synchronizations are possible, is not the totality of the world, that it perhaps is only the most superficial sector. I only need to concentrate my attention on what is rather artlessly called "the unconscious" and "the subconscious" to see that in the regions to which these words refer it is not possible to draw boundaries between mine and thine. "You, yours? I, mine?" asks Claire at the end of *Quatuor en fa dièse*. "Where does the personality begin?" How could this question not occur when we enter the country about which we know almost nothing, but where the encounter between the living and those we call – with a murderous and desecrating sort of language – "the dead"?

This shallow, disparaged, brook, death, wrote Mallarmé. We again find, but at an infinitely more intimate level, what I said earlier about Molière and Mozart: We are "survived" by those we believe we outlive.

An unverifiable assertion! is what my opponent will say. But we need to take care: In what conditions is controllable verification possible? I believe that I showed many years ago in my first *Metaphysical Journal* that all control implies a triadic relationship, or the possibility for a "you" to become a "he" over whom one exercises influence. But love, insofar as it liberates itself from all possessiveness, can only manifest itself on the plane of the Dyad; hence the conversion from "you" to "him" becomes impossible. It is on this plane that the inhabitation of a living being by the "departed" occurs. As a sort of counterproof, one could bring in the role of suspicion, distrust, and the need for control found in Proust's writings, especially in *Albertine disparue*. With these we are on the plane of fanatically desired possession, one that is never consummated. In contrast, the more that we elevate ourselves to sacrificial love, the more we tend toward that dyadic relation where all control is overcome and even rendered meaningless.

We should make sure that we do not excessively simplify, though. If a "departed" purportedly manifests himself to me by some external means and pleads his genuineness, it is inevitable that I feel the need to verify and hence in some sense control. But where communion is realized, where the presence of the deceased continually "irrigates" the survivor to the point where it no longer matters whether it is "you" or "me" who speaks because we have become "one," in that state the very idea of control becomes moot.

Now the reader can understand why at the beginning I made clear that I would not attempt in any way to imagine, much less to describe, the "Beyond" and what might occur there. I do not deny that from another point of view different from my own this might be possible. However, it does seem to me that in the midst of this strange life that belongs to us, we are constituted and "placed" in such a way that the Beyond must remain the Beyond. It is, paradoxically, only on this condition that the Beyond can become present to us, that is, as a mystery of which (short of theology) we can only have intimations. Even in this almost total night that surrounds us, whose darkness at times risks overwhelming us, nonetheless there are intimations – signs – that come to meet the expectations and demands which we have and which we are.

But experiences of this sort, other depressing experiences teach us that they can be not only frustrated but even become undetectable to those who have them. The curse characteristic of the world that tends to take shape around us is that with all of its density and authority it tries to make this demand seem absurd, seem superstitious, if not infantile. And this world, alas, finds an accomplice in whatever in us tends toward despair.

If my work taken in its entirety has a meaning, it is to show that a philosophy is possible that can lend comfort and support, even stimulate, such experiences, one that can teach men how to breathe, or can awaken them, like a mother awakens her little child when the time has come to feed him. To awaken, to feed, to teach how to breathe: these essential life-functions have their exact correspondences at the level of philosophy, of the only worthwhile philosophy in my view, which aids us in living and which perhaps prepares us – who knows? – by the paths of "learned ignorance" for the ineffable surprise of the eternal tomorrow.

I know that nothing resembles less an exposition of the classical sort than my reflections here. So perhaps a few more words are necessary to clarify the nature of this investigation. I have said this many times since my conversion to Catholicism. I have been led to regard myself and conduct myself as a philosopher of the threshold, addressing much more those who seek in the darkness, often in anguish, than those who have attained an unshakeable faith and therefore have no need of me. But even with the latter we could point out the "not-yet-evangelized parts" of ourselves that Paul Claudel spoke so well about. It is as a philosopher of the threshold that I wanted to speak today. The openings that I have tried to discern in the prison in which we find ourselves – it is from the point of view of the prisoner that I have tried to look. Viewed from the other side, the light of Revelation, these openings grow even larger.

It belongs – and this I say as a Catholic and not as a philosopher – to theological reflection to concentrate on the central questions I have only touched upon today. It needs to do this not only for speculative reasons, but also for a motive that seems to me to be infinitely more pressing: in order to address the unspoken distress of countless souls today who risk seeing themselves caught without hope in the vise of a pitiless world, one which even the promise of interplanetary travel cannot make more habitable.

Translated by Paul Seaton

RELIGIOUS EXPERIENCE AND INTELLIGIBILITY IN THE WORK OF GABRIEL MARCEL

Pierre Colin

Gabriel Marcel, philosopher of religious experience? Nothing guarantees that by presenting him in this way one will not impose on his thought the limitations of an external characterization, one that in the final analysis is inadequate.

Nonetheless, the two elements of a philosophy of religious experience seem to be brought together in his work. First of all, Gabriel Marcel reflects upon lived experience. He did so at least from the moment he first had the idea, and then the practice, of a "concrete philosophy," "a philosophy of the concrete." Next, even when biographical circumstances (the absence of religious faith) did not incline him in this direction, from the start Marcel's reflection was oriented toward the religious problem, which remained the center of his preoccupations.

The difficulty first of all is semantic. Marcel did not use the expression "religious experience." And if the word "religion" is found in the index of his *Metaphysical Journal*, it is displaced by the word "faith," which invokes more clearly the free act of the believer. Later this word will be inscribed in two registers, the philosophical register of "creative fidelity," and the Christian register of the three theological virtues: faith, hope, and charity.

The difficulty however is not merely semantic. We do not find in Gabriel Marcel a phenomenology of religion, with religion taken

in the ensemble of its historical manifestations. Nor do we find anything comparable to William James's interest in the psychological
diversity of religious experience. Gabriel Marcel's phenomenology,
moreover, is not descriptive but reflexive.

Texts concerning mystical experience are few. But when we read
them we immediately grasp the central point of Marcel's thought:
the project of a philosophy of experience that yields nothing to
empiricism.

For Marcel, as for Bergson, mysticism represents an experiential
grasp of God, or faith lived in the mode of direct experience. In an
article published on the 80th anniversary of Bergson, Marcel
praised the author of the *Two Sources of Morality and of Religion*.[1] But
he refused to seek in mysticism "the means of approaching, as it
were experientially, the problem of the existence and nature of
God":

> I will not insist on the serious reservations an empiricism of
> this sort raises; there is every reason to think – to speak in
> passing – that if there is a mystical experience, this experi-
> ence cannot bear upon a determinate object, one capable of
> being described. The categories here are entirely different.

This parenthetical remark sends us to a text of the much earlier
Metaphysical Journal. In it Marcel asks if it is legitimate to translate
faith by an existential judgment, to move from it to a judgment of
real existence. Long before Bergson he envisages the possibility of
finding in mysticism an experiential foundation for the affirmation
of God. But he rejects this hypothesis.

> While believing that one affirms (in existence or objectively)
> the absolute independence of God, we, on the contrary, bind
> him to immediate consciousness. I had never seen so clear-
> ly the antinomy. All this means that the problem of God can
> only be posed in terms of experience, in mystical terms; but
> at the same time, posed on this plane it is destined to receive
> a negative answer.

To be sure, the impasse is provisional. Marcel has not yet elaborated his distinction between existence and objectivity, which will

1   Qu'est-ce que le bergsonisme? *Temps present*, June 30, 1939.

introduce other problematics. But the text does mark a point of no return. Marcel henceforth will always reject, not mystical experience, but the empiricist – hence, objectifying – interpretation that philosophy is tempted to give it.

For the philosopher of existence reflecting on religion, the central and undeniable "datum" is and remains the witness and testimony of "the person who experiences the presence of God."[2] But by specifying that this presence is less felt than recognized, Marcel indicates the problem posed to the philosopher: How to speak of this experience without reducing to an empirical "datum" what the believer receives as a "gift"?

What is at stake is the very idea of a "concrete philosophy." Marcel declares that such a philosophy is inconceivable "without a reflection as strict, as rigorous as possible, exercising itself upon the most intensely lived experience."[3]

The same movement causes the two poles – the pole of experience and the reflexive pole – of his philosophy to emerge. The intensity of life and living is required: it is what sets thinking in motion. But concrete philosophy cannot be an *immediate* description of "the lived." Experience does not find from the outset its adequate language. As Paul Ricoeur said so well:

> There is not a theme in Marcel's thought that isn't "won" by
> an initial movement of reflection, where he discerns an
> obstacle, a principle of hiddenness, both opposed to the dis-
> covery of the fundamental experiences which in their turn
> oppose resistance to resistance.[4]

Marcel's philosophy develops via the conjunction of two types of experience. To be sure, the experience of life, of the difficulty of living, since this is what provokes questioning. But no less important is the experience of thought. In a first statement, let us call this the experience that thought has of itself. Later we will have to subject the formula to criticism.

Returning, or turning, upon itself, thought attains to the "sec-

2   *Le Mystère de l' tre*, Aubier, 1951; t. II, p. 177.
3   *Du Refus à l'Invocation*, p. 89.
4   "Réflexion primaire et réflexion seconde chez Gabriel Marcel," *Bulletin de la Société française de philosophie*, April-June 1984.

ond reflection" which frees experiences from the systems of interpretation of "first reflection." It is in this way, and only this way,
that philosophy becomes capable of apprehending the existential
core of faith without altering it by objectification.

A double itinerary, philosophic and religious

In his Gifford Lectures of 1949–50, Marcel sought to bring his
thoughts together into a quasi-system. The result was *The Mystery
of Being*. Now, this effort at synthesis does not dispense one from
reading the *Metaphysical Journal*, where one sees how Marcel's
thinking arose and developed by always posing new problems to
itself.

To be sure, in 1914 when the young agrégé took notes in view of
a thesis on religious intelligibility, he was not thinking that the day
would come when he would publish them in their original form.
He resolved to do so in 1927, having noticed a certain inability to
systematize. Doubtlessly he also did so because he recognized in
the literary form of a journal the mode of philosophical writing
appropriate to the rhythm of a thought always in search of itself,
never stabilized in a result.

The resistance of Gabriel Marcel to systems is well known. So,
too, is the essentially "itinerant" character of his thought. But rather
complex problems arise when one notices that the itinerary was in
fact double, and that their respective periodicizations do not coincide. The important moments of the intellectual itinerary exist in
disjunction from those of the religious itinerary.

In one sense, the latter began very soon, from Marcel's infancy,
which was marked by the death of his mother when he was four,
although it took a long time to develop. It was in 1929, when he was
fourteen years old, that Marcel converted to Catholicism and
received baptism. This was the decisive stage, or step, of the religious itinerary. But the recent publication of his correspondence
with Father Fessard, s.j., shows that long after his conversion
Marcel had to overcome periods of personal and religious disarray.[5]

The first philosophical essays manifest a clear advance of the

5   Gabriel Marcel, Gaston Fessard. *Correspondance* (1934–1971), Beauchesne,
     1985.

intellectual itinerary over the religious. Even though Marcel did not yet identify himself as a believer, he had enough interest in faith and in the intelligibility of which it is the source to conceive the project of a thesis on the subject. However, the experience of belief was only accessible to him indirectly, through the witness and testimony of others.

In the later years of his life Marcel often returned to this past, as if it contained an enigma that had never been entirely deciphered. We possess several retrospective texts in which he tried to understand the awakening of this philosophical interest, but also personal or existential, in Christianity.[6] We will return to this problem – and the answers Marcel gave to it – in the second part of this exposition.

But we need to indicate right away a striking contrast. As much as Marcel continued to value the encounters and experiences that wakened his interest in religion, just as much he found his first philosophical writings – which witnessed to this interest – to be inadequate. The *Metaphysical Journal*, published in 1927, contains two very distinct parts. The dialectical austerity of the first part eventually disconcerted Marcel and it seemed to him that the notes taken in 1914 were written by another. The interpreter thus has a delicate problem. Should he follow the author's retrospective quasi-disavowal? Should these early pages be left to a buried past, without any interest or assistance in understanding the subsequent thought and work? Marcel himself provides the answer I adopt. In the preface of the work, Marcel refused to separate the two parts of his journal because, he said, the first contains "the logical infrastructure" of the second part.

In any event we will operate on the assumption of a structural homology between the teaching about "the unverifiable absolute" in the first part and the theme of the 1937 communication delivered to the Descartes Congress: "The transcendent as metaproblematic." In both cases, reflective mediation asserts the transcendence of faith, or of "mystery," vis-à-vis the order of knowledge, of "problems."

6   "Regard en arrière," *Existentialisme chrétien, Gabriel Marcel*, Plon, coll. "Présences," 1947.

To be sure, I have no wish to deny an important fact. The first part of the *Metaphysical Journal* remains immured in the context of an idealism it nonetheless attempts to overcome. In notes made between 1919 and 1923, which constitute the second part of the journal, and with the article "Existence and Objectivity" which was added to the journal when it was published, Marcel elaborates a new philosophy, one animated by the two poles of existence and being.

This marked caesura in Marcel's intellectual development poses a new problem. It was more than ten years before his conversion that Marcel laid the foundations for the subsequent development of his thought. Here, too, the intellectual preceded the religious.

Perhaps one should take cognizance of these facts and draw a general conclusion. Unlike what happened with, say, Maurice Blondel, one cannot say that for Marcel Christian practice preceded and engendered the reflective regrasping of lived experience. But must one say the converse, that philosophical activity prepared the religious discovery? We will see that this isn't entirely correct. But it has its value nonetheless.

Without any doubt it was the experience of life, the difficulty of finding within it a stable position, that provoked Marcel to think, and to think about religion. This did not stop him from initially moving in a purely intellectual "space," that of idealism, within which he searched a way out, a way forward. But also the "space" constituted by his own thought, by exposing it to questions that tested its possibilities, and which caused him to discover its limits, at least provisional ones.

The general contours of his procedure were therefore the following: Marcel posed the hypothesis of a properly religious intelligibility and he then sought to lay bare the conditions that would allow him to define and to justify it. This meant that one had to radically distinguish knowledge from faith. But either faith thereby remained entirely foreign to the life of thought or one must also understand the passage from *I think* to *I believe*. This required articulating the human act of liberty and grace, understood as a "radically independent power."

The philosopher speaks in this way of lived experience. But religious experience is not yet his. Or better: he does not yet see what in his own experience causes him to participate already, if indirectly, in the faith about which he speaks. But by constructing this system of hypotheses he prepares, without knowing it, the philosophical expression of what the development of his religious life will allow him to discover.

And one day the language of "grace" will find its concrete fulfillment in lived experience. Thus we find the point of encounter of the two itineraries. This is found in the part of the *Metaphysical Journal* published in *Being and Having*, in particular in a text dated March 5, 1929, which is a few days before his baptism.

> I no longer doubt. Miraculous happiness! This morning for the first time
> I had the clear experience of grace. These words are frightening but true.

From this date new possibilities offered themselves to the philosopher. Henceforth he could directly consider a well-identified religious experience. But the distance between the philosopher and the "lived" was not thereby suppressed. On the contrary, it was from his conversion that Marcel elaborated his ontological problematic, which was only sketched in the second part of the *Metaphysical Journal*.

We will see a bit later how this ontological problematic allowed him to establish a new relationship between metaphysics and sanctity. First, though, we will return to the question we raised earlier, the origin of the religious interest in the young philosopher. The study of this question will allow us to grasp the "fundamental assurance" which underlays the double itinerary, philosophic and religious.

The fundamental assurance

In his first philosophical essays Marcel undertook the work of turning thinking upon itself, which would enable it to understand the transcendence of the act of faith. But where did the initial attraction come from which moved and guided the investigation? Put another way: how did religious reality "impose" itself upon the young man who had received an agnostic education?

As we said, Marcel himself posed the question in several

retrospective texts. He invoked the witness of certain believers whose faith seemed undeniable to him and raised a problem for him. But he also underlined the role of two personal experiences, intensely experienced. On the one hand, his reaction to the death of loved ones; on another, musical experience, considered as a religious experience (in a sense to be determined).

Marcel's mother died when he was four years old. He thus experienced very early on the existential "fracture" wrought by the disappearance of a loved one. All his life and all his thinking were marked by it. The question of death will appear in all his philosophical work, but also in his dramas. What needs to be underscored is his reaction to the trying experience. To the brutal fact of death and the separation that appeared to be definitive he opposed the interior power of a conviction, one that was independent of both rational justification and religious belief.

This conviction was that the dead remain "present" to us and in a way that goes beyond the simple "maintenance" of "being remembered." The dead live always, they wait for us, we can hope to rejoin them after our own death. Here we come to a deeply felt experience. It did not however inscribe itself in a preestablished framework of a regular belief system, such as the Christian faith in the resurrection. One has to comprehend it in order to understand the meaning of the term "religion" for Marcel.

The affirmation of the presence of beloved dead was intensely felt and lived but in the mode of an experience that transcends all empirical critique. When reflection tries to approach this existential core, it has to refer to the order of "the unconditional" which characterizes what Marcel later will call "creative fidelity."

In addition, the philosopher experienced the "pull" of "metapsychic" experiences which he engaged in during the first world war. This fact poses a complex problem. We will have to limit ourselves to a few schematic indications.

Marcel thoroughly excluded the type of rationalism that denies in principle the possibility of such experiences, or which deprives them *a priori* of any value. In contrast, the reflection on these experiences nourished his philosophical conceptualization, especially in the second part of the *Metaphysical Journal*.

In order, for example, to take into account telepathy, but also in order to characterize the mode according to which a medium offers the mediation of his own body to the deceased trying to express himself in this life, Marcel formed the concept of "sympathetic mediation." This concept was opposed to "instrumental mediation" and allowed him to conceptualize the experience of "feeling." In other words, the reflection upon metapsychic experience played a secondary, but decisive, role in the constitution of his existential philosophy.

This role does not by itself imply that Marcel recognized the reality of the interventions of the dead. The phenomenon of the evocation of the deceased remained for him essentially ambiguous. He could neither simply deny them nor find in them a proof of immortality.

The phenomenon of the evocation of the dead is above all ambiguous at the level of the intentions of those who give them-selves over to these experiences. Are they disposing themselves to receive an eventual gift or are they attempting to capture, to master, the unknown? In the second case the desire to know can only degrade the "presence." This is what characters in *L'Iconoclaste* become aware of. To be sure, they passionately desire "to see, to hear, to touch," but at the end of the play the light that shines upon them is that of "mystery" incompatible with the search for a knowl-edge that, in truth, "exiles far away everything that it believes it captures."

The advantage of the dramatic presentation over philosophical reflection here is obvious. It merits being underscored, even if it is already well known. By putting human conflicts on the stage Marcel subjected lived experience to a first elaboration in thought. Then came the conceptual "reprise."

Later, according to the formulation of *Homo Viator*, "I hope in You for our sake," Marcel established a definitive link between faith in God and the religious conviction that had always underlay his philosophical reflection. The passage from which this line is taken summarized Marcel's reflection on religious experience by uniting hope and charity.

> Hope is essentially, one can say, the disposition and avail-ability of a soul engaged deeply enough in an experience of communion to be able to accomplish the transcendent act by

which it affirms living permanence. This very experience of communion is itself the gauge and first fruits thereof.

The assurance which grounds the affirmation is first on the existential plane. And it was so for Marcel. But the entire development of "second reflection" was necessary for philosophy to establish the status of an act of hope that transcends both the certitudes (or uncertainties) of speculative reason and the postulates of practical reason.

Hope for salvation, belief in a Beyond, will only gradually inscribe themselves in the context of the Christian faith. But from the beginning they are "religious." This, however, was not the case for musical experience, which Marcel nonetheless thought had played an essential role in his initial relationship with religion:

> Perhaps my entire philosophical inquiry was but a huge
> detour by which I rejoined something that had been given
> to me immediately in the mode of musical experience.[7]

In other circumstances Marcel went so far as to say that in his youth music put him in the presence of religious witness. The reference to the two *Passions* and the *Cantatas* of Bach might suggest that he has in mind the properly religious content of these works. But in other texts invoking Mozart, he specifies that he does not primarily have in mind the author of the *Requiem*. The first interpretation therefore would be too narrow. We therefore have to seek for a less direct, less simple, relationship between religion and music, one present in some particularly revealing works.

A text of 1959, "Music in my life and in my work." More than any other art, music combines the sensible and the intelligible, without the aid of the conceptual. It is the "bearer of truth," even though it doesn't reveal any particular truth, i.e., reducible to an objective content. It therefore is the very type – the privileged species – of experience that obliges us to think the transcendence of Truth – or of the Spirit of Truth – vis-à-vis the order of truths that are the object of knowledge.

Of music, Marcel says that it gives to the person who allows

7   *Kierkegaard en ma pensée*, in *Kierkegaard vivant*, NRF, coll. "Idées", 1966, p. 71.

himself to be "grasped" by it a "mysterious assurance." The word "assurance" is important, but what does it mean? Once again, one must exclude the possession of some content and the type of certainty inherent in such a possession. But because this assurance "carried" Marcel's philosophy, we need to seek to understand it.

I propose the following hypothesis. I base myself on a text of his youth that seems to me to have the value of a "matrix" for the entirety of Marcel's thought. It is found at the end of his thesis for advanced studies, later published as *Coleridge et Schelling*.

In it Marcel invokes the possibility of "a philosophy that simultaneously refuses to see in the world merely an ensemble of abstract relationships and to consider it as subject to a blind 'becoming.' Moreover, it maintains that what there is in us of 'better' and of 'superior' cannot be without absolutely any relationship with the core of things; there must be some deep analogy between the internal principle that animates them and the wellspring of our own activity."

Marcel's philosophical project therefore aims to overcome the opposition between a rationalism concerned with abstract intelligibility and a philosophy of the absurd. The overcoming effects itself by combining two distinct but complementary moments.

The first moment: the affirmation of a human order with meaning and value. We "hierarchalize" our activities, discerning what makes us attain to the "better" and to the "superior." This important humanistic affirmation is at once necessary and insufficient. How can we go beyond it? Not by posing the exigency of something "more" but by returning to the principle of our own spiritual dynamism.

Hence, the second moment: under the modest form of a double negation, which shows that we are not in the order of knowledge, philosophy affirms that our values cannot be without some relationship "with the core of things." In the same movement one poses the Principle and affirms that it cannot be alien, indifferent, to that by which our life acquires meaning. Between the Principle of being and ourselves there must be a "connivance" such that we can relate the spiritual dynamism which makes us tend toward better and superior to this Principle.

Our hypothesis is that the "mysterious assurance" dispensed

by music can be understood in function of the text we just read. Music makes us communicate with the highest forms of human spirituality. But even more so, and above all, it is in musical communication that the "connivance" between human creation and the very Principle of being is attested to.

The last phrase, Principle of being, sends us forward to the later position concerning "ontological mystery." In texts in which this view is present one finds a conjunction – rather problematical for Marcel – between *assurance*, which is always maintained, and *intuition*, which is put forward but not without reservations.

As a matter of fact, the text of 1959 on musical experience employed the word "intuition." To understand it, however, one should follow the history of the word in Marcel's work. This begins with its privileged use in a youthful text, one before the *Metaphysical Journal*, a 1912 article on "The dialectical conditions of a philosophy of intuition."[8]

Even then, Marcel finds himself confronted with the problem of the articulation between dialectics and intuition (between knowledge and faith). We should note that he seeks the dialectical conditions, not of intuition *tout court*, but of a *philosophy of intuition*. What he means by the latter: "every doctrine that affirms that being can be attained by intuition and only by intuition."

Conformable to his method, Marcel does not establish the reality of this intuition, but he seeks the conditions that would allow one to think it and to determine its value. Without going into the details of the argument, we will report the conclusion. On one hand, it marks the highest point that Marcel then attained: the transcendence of thought as such, vis-à-vis "discursivity." Thought, insofar as it is an act, it is irreducible to "absolute knowledge." On the other hand, this same conclusion opens the inquiry which the *Metaphysical Journal* will pursue:

> Intuition itself at bottom reduces itself to the act by which thought affirms that in itself it is transcendent of what in it is only pure objectivity. In short, it is an act of faith, and its content cannot be explained except by a practical dialectic of participation, by which thought, via successive creative

8   Revue de métaphysique et de morale, 1912.

steps, surpasses the world of knowledge and approaches the center where it must freely renounce itself in order to yield to "Him who is."

In the commentary he gave to this article, Fr. Dubarle showed very well how for Marcel at that point it was a question of breaking out of the enclosure of idealism, above all, the neo-Hegelianism of Bradley, who sought the reconciliation of appearances in "absolute knowledge."[9] This context, though, is still that of the first part of *Metaphysical Journal*, but this one directly treats faith and its transcendence vis-à-vis knowledge. Except for rare passages, it is not the word "intuition" that guides Marcel.

It returns much later in *Being and Having*. It does so in a paradoxical phrase, since Marcel ventures the theme of a "blind intuition," one that isn't in control of itself, such that reflection cannot grasp it except via thoughts that benefit from its light.

> I have to admit that – let's say, at a certain level of myself – I confront Being. In this sense, I see it, in another, I cannot say that I see it because I do not grasp myself as the seer. This intuition does not reflect itself nor can it be directly reflected. But by returning toward itself it illumines an entire world of thoughts that it transcends. Metaphysically speaking, I do not see how one can account for faith any other way.

In *Concrete Approaches to the Ontological Mystery*, Marcel once again hesitates before the word "intuition," but finds the word "assurance" especially important.

> It would be better to say that we have here an assurance that underlies the development of thought, even discursive thought; we therefore cannot approach it except by a movement of conversion, that is, by a second reflection.

All the conceptual apparatus is thus in place. It now becomes possible to understand retrospectively the role musical experience played in the life and thought of Marcel. In the 1959 text he invoked

9   "Le franchissement des clôtures de la philosophie idéaliste classique. La première philosophie de Gabriel Marcel, 1912–1914," *Revue des sciences philosophiques et théologiques*, April 1974.

"the exhausting inquiry" conducted in his first philosophical writings. At that time, though, he would not have been able to say what sustained or oriented this inquiry. After the fact, he understood that music then constituted "as it were a permanent guarantee of that reality that I attempted to attain by the dry paths of pure reflection."

The ontological problematic is given all its import in that declaration. In and by music, Marcel already experienced – without being able to reflect upon it – the original affirmation, which he later will say affirms itself in us more than we affirm it. The "mysterious affirmation" dispensed by music engenders the reflection – moving from first reflection to second – that finally will enable him to articulate the meaning of this fundamental and foundational experience.

The saint as metaphysical marker

Until now we have not considered the religious context of Marcel's first writings. His agnostic education kept him from any personal investment in the theological controversies of the period. It remains true, however, that his initial posing of the religious problem was relative to this context.

In 1914, under the title *The Invisible Threshold*, Marcel published his first two dramas: *La Grâce* and *Le Palais de sable*.[10] In the preface to them, he did not hesitate to define religion:

> Considered in its essence religion is not an objective credo bearing upon transcendent realities, no more than it is a code of moral precepts. It is faith in the absolute value of life, not the divinization of a natural phenomenon but the affirmation that there is no true reality except what belongs to the spirit, and that the rest is not.

Progress in reflection led Marcel to go beyond this definition of religion which was still too bound up with a certain idealism. That he gave one, though, is significant. It is also clear that the two exclusions at the outset are as well. The first aims at Catholic dogmatism, the other at liberal Protestantism which reduces religion to morality.

In this regard it is interesting to contrast this first philosophical

10   Grasset, 1914.

effort of Marcel with a form of liberal Protestantism which itself defends the specificity of religious experience. I do not know if Marcel read Auguste Sabatier's *Esquisse d'une philosophie de la religion d'après la psychologie et l'histoire* (1897). Be that as it may, the similarity of certain formulations is rather striking.

After having "concentrated" religion in the act of prayer, Sabatier writes: "Religion is nothing if it is not the vital act by which the entire human spirit tries to save itself by attaching itself to its principle." Such a sentence would not be out of place in the first part of *Metaphysical Journal*.

Marcel in fact tries to extract the anthropological meaning of faith in divine Paternity. Sabatier attempts a transcendental genesis of religion, one that follows in Kant's wake by addressing the need to overcome the dualism between the natural world and the moral world. Similarly, Marcel understands faith as the act which poses beyond knowledge the unity of what I am as a thinker and of what I am as a body inserted in the world.

> The act of faith is that by which the cogito transcends itself, that is, the act by which the spirit constitutes itself by posing in God the unity of the *I think* and the empirical content to which it is tied (i.e., the world).

These textual similarities do not deny the methodological differences of the two works. Their real interest and importance is connected with the position that Sabatier then occupied in France at the time, which was at the center of theological controversies. His description and valorization of religious experience constituted a capital point of disagreement between Catholicism and Protestantism, but also within both Christian confessions.

On the Catholic side, the "modernist crisis" was provoked by the exegetical and historical positions of Alfred Loisy in his *The Gospel and the Church* (1902). But when the encyclical *Pascendi* (issued by Pius X in 1907) reconstructed the modernist system in order to condemn it, it devoted itself entirely to certain philosophical underpinnings. Starting from a global concession to a "phenomenalist" agnosticism, the modernist as a believer had no choice but to refer faith to a vital religious immanence. This entails a double relativizing, at once metaphysical and historical, of dogma.

Seen this way modernism appeared to be the infiltration into Catholicism of the same type of philosophy of religion developed by Sabatier. This proximity caused the longtime exclusion of the phrase "religious experience" from the Catholic lexicon. If one refers to the courageous book of Fr. Gardeil, *The Structure of the Soul and Mystical Experience* (1927), he shows the difficulty in articulating mystical experience in the framework of Thomas's epistemology.

Discovering philosophy in 1905–1906, received into the course of aggregation in 1910, if Marcel had been raised as a Catholic he would have personally experienced the modernist crisis. On the other hand, if he had been raised a Protestant he would have participated in the conflict between liberalism and orthodoxy. His agnostic education dispensed him from a direct engagement in these theological controversies.

But it would be false to conclude that they did not affect him. In truth, these controversies are present as the background of his first dramatic works and his first philosophical essays. This is true at least in the rarefied form of the conflict between religious objectivism and subjectivism.

His familial milieu and his personal preferences initially inclined Marcel to Protestantism. However, it was to Catholicism that he converted in 1929. The notes for *Being and Having* witness to his efforts to come to terms with neo-Thomism, especially through the reading of Fr. Garrigou-Lagrange. But the failure of these initiatives show that he remained, and always remained, a stranger to a certain philosophical-theological objectivism.

On the other hand, his attraction to Protestantism did not stop him from fearing, and from rejecting, the subjectivistic tendencies developed in liberal Protestantism. The problem was even more acute for him as religious subjectivism overlapped with the idealism he initially embraced, then sought to escape.

This is the context of his notes of 1914. At the level of his intention, things are clear: Marcel wanted to overcome the opposition between objectivism and subjectivism, which would only occur, he maintained, if faith was erroneously situated on the plane of knowledge. Thus one can understand his views concerning "the unverifiable absolute," which elevates faith above both objective knowledge and subjective opinion.

However, if Marcel established in that way "the logical infra-structure" of his further reflection, it is permitted to ask if what he actually achieved in the first part of *Metaphysical Journal* fulfilled his intention. There are two objections, ones, moreover, that Marcel himself has raised.

The first consists in wondering whether one can actually conceive faith when one raises it in this way above knowledge. The most important notes in this regard are those of the 10th and 11th of February, 1914. What is faith insofar as it transcends reflection? Marcel presents it as an act that "illumines with a sudden ray the 'nothing' of its genesis and of its posterity." Not without hesitation, he speaks of a moment of intuition: "I agree to speak here of 'intuition' if one insists." But the illuminating ray of an intuition implies a double negation, bearing upon an antecedent reflection (which prepares the act of faith that transcends it) and on a subsequent reflection (which attempts to conceive the act of faith supposed complete).

Marcel was very well aware of this difficulty. "If reflection on faith destroys itself, how can faith remain a thought?" Put another way, can faith conceive itself without becoming what it denies insofar as it is faith? What then becomes of the "religious intelligibility" upon which Marcel wants to address his philosophical reflection?

The note ends with a voluntaristic appeal that Marcel himself was not satisfied with: "To the dualism of faith and the thought of faith is substituted the idea of a will to believe, this will conceiving itself as bound to an obligation." Instead of overcoming the opposition of objectivism and subjectivism, this text commits us to an unstable position, one with two possibilities. We can return to subjectivism, if the will to believe is purely individual, or we can return to objectivism, if this will to believe inscribes itself in a dogmatic framework. To be sure, Marcel will always maintain that faith is an act of human liberty corresponding to the call of divine Liberty. But the notes of this period find a stumbling block in the problem of grace. Marcel will not find a way out except much later, in his ontological problematic.

The other difficulty concerns religious history or the role of the historical in faith. The seriousness with which Marcel takes this question shows that his reflection focuses especially on the

Christian faith, with its founding reference to Jesus Christ. But with "the historical" comes the need for verification. Or rather: the legitimacy of this need. How can one maintain at the level of the "unverifiable absolute" the historical content of Christian faith?

> It seems that religion cannot actualize itself except by affirmations that contain a relationship with history and thus contain the seeds of death. The solution I see is the following: with a saint, for whom everything is contemporary, vis-à-vis for whom everything is ordered (Christ taken as the Idea), this historical basis is not necessary, eternity is one with the present, it is present.

Is this solution satisfactory? Or does the idealistic projection into the absolute of sanctity, does it betray an intellectual difficulty going back to the first *Metaphysical Journal*? Perhaps one can admit that the dualism of appearance and reality is entirely overcome in the saint for whom "subjectivism no longer wants to speak and which becomes identical with the most naïve objectivism." But is this really "in the saint" or in the ideal image that we form of him? In any case, the solution does not work for the rest of us who are not saints, who at most are trying to attain sanctity. No one, least of all Gabriel Marcel, can be satisfied with a solution that would be viable only if we overcame – totally surpassed — our condition as "itinerants" (*iter* being the Latin word for path or journey)! In short, it remained to think the meaning of faith for the *homo viator*, man the wayfarer, we all are.

Much later Marcel will reprise the reference to sanctity. But between times, he will have elaborated the ontological problematic which allows him to inscribe this reference in(to) our questioning and our itinerary as concrete human beings. We will refer to two texts.

The first comes from *Concrete Approaches to the Ontological Mystery*. It occurs at the end of a long meditation on unreceptivity. In the world we ordinarily consider the "normal" world, each one of us concentrates upon himself, in such a way that if he does open himself to the outside he does so in a utilitarian manner, in function of various interests. But encountering someone who is truly open and receptive – a saint – opens a breech in this egocentric topology. He causes us to discover, in what we call "the normal order," the subversion of a superior order; this encounter may call us to what we call "conversion." It belongs to the philosopher to think about such an experience.

> Reflection upon sanctity with all its concrete attributes seems to me to possess an immense speculative value. One would not need to push me too hard for me to say that it is the true introduction to ontology.

Without the holiness present in certain beings, whose value as "witnesses" is decisive (witnesses to faith, witnesses to hope, witnesses to charity), would philosophy be called – "provoked" – to pose the ontological problem? Or at least the type of ontological problematic that Marcel will develop in the 1930s, after having sketched it in the second part of *Metaphysical Journal*.

On the occasion of a conference devoted to the thought of Fr. Lucien Laberthonnière, I retraced the texts which showed that Marcel had begun to elaborate his ontological problematic at the time he was reading Laberthonnière's *Essays on religious philosophy*. In them the problem of being and the problem of salvation, taken in the general perspective of a "metaphysics of charity," were already joined.

For Marcel as for Laberthonnière, "it is a question 'of being' and not of 'being'." Already the major theme of "ontological exigence" is sketched.

> Being is what does not deceive, there is 'of being' from the moment our expectation is fulfilled; I am speaking of that expectation to which we give ourselves entirely.

Must one say that in raising the question of being, the philosopher turns his back on the "fundamental assurance" we talked about earlier? Not exactly. This is because the way in which Marcel poses the problem of being is closely related to the experiences of plenitude that ground this assurance.

But to note this is not to minimize the interrogative *force* of the question of being. The question's stakes are too important for the philosopher to consider it as resolved in advance. The world in which we live, moreover, offers too many motives for a despair that is always possible. Everything *could* only be a play of appearances, without any ultimate significance.

In order to exorcise this despair, there is no other means than to seriously put to the test – in order to verify its value – everything that seems to us to be solid, coherent, likely to assure us being. In this way we rejoin the "definition" proposed in *Concrete Approaches to the Ontological Mystery*:

> Being is what resists – or what would resist – an exhaustive analysis brought to bear on the givens of experiences and which would try to eventually reduce them to bare elements deprived of intrinsic value or meaning.

It is not surprising that the rest of the text contains an allusion to Freud. Conducted rigorously, the "debunking" analysis whose principle Marcel states cannot fail to encounter the "masters of suspicion." But their perspectives are obviously quite different. With Marcel, the "critique" of life and its illusions remains motivated and supported by the exigence of discovering what is *really* capable of causing us "to be," and by the "fundamental assurance" that such a discovery is possible.

This is what the experience of the saint attests, an experience we find discussed in a final text taken from *Being and Having*:

> In any case, what I perceive is the hidden identity of the way that leads to holiness and the path that leads the metaphysician to the affirmation of being: and above all, the necessity for a concrete philosophy to recognize that there is only one and the same path.

By speaking of a "hidden identity" which one discovers en route, this text contains both a difference and a proximity to what we have seen earlier. Marcel has progressed since the first pages of the *Metaphysical Journal*. We no longer have direct reflection on faith. The philosopher has taken up the "distance" vis-à-vis religious experience that permits him to elaborate an ontological problematic with its own consistence. And this distance is not suppressed by the discovery of a hidden identity between the existential conduct of the saint and the reflective activity of the philosopher.

What does the saint do? He obeys a call that seizes hold of him at his deepest core, which calls him to receptivity, sacrifice, love. By responding to this call he progressively strips himself of everything that could inhibit him from attaining the fullness of faith, hope and charity. And what is the principle of this divesting of self, if not the attraction of the *Unum Necessarium*?

What does the philosopher do? His proper task is to elaborate a reflexive "problematic" in the light of which the saint's conduct can appear as a concrete approach to the mystery of being. In this perspective what plays the role of a metaphysical reference point is no longer, as it once was, the *idea* of sanctity, but the personal witness of the saint. Or the lived experience of the *homo viator* proceeding to holiness.

The two procedures remain distinct but they communicate at a fundamental level. Without the witness of the saint the ontological problematic would remain formal. The latter's concrete "charge" comes to it from this existential center. On the other hand, the metaphysician brings to the lived experience of the saint the reflexive element that allows one to bring to light its ontological, or rather its "ontogenetic," meaning.

At the end we have to acknowledge that we have not exhausted the riches of Marcel's religious philosophy. Perhaps, though, we have said enough to justify an answer to our initial question: If it is permissible to present Marcel as a philosopher of religious experience, it is on the condition that we underscore the word "philosopher," with all its reflexive implications.

Translated by Paul Seaton